The Freelance Photographer's
MARKET HANDBOOK

The Freelance Photographer's
MARKET
HANDBOOK

 BFP BOOKS London

EDITOR: *John Tracy*
CONTRIBUTING EDITOR: *John Wade*
ASSISTANT EDITOR (**Markets**): *Stewart Gibson*
ASSISTANT EDITOR (**Services & Supplies**): *Brian Durrant*

First Edition 1983
ISBN 0 907297 03 X

Published for the Bureau of Freelance Photographers by BFP Books (Lyndtree Ltd), Focus House, 497 Green Lanes, London N13 4BP. Printed in Great Britain by A. Wheaton & Co. Ltd., Exeter.

CONTENTS

PREFACE

The Freelance Photographer's Market Handbook represents a significant development in the market research service provided by the Bureau of Freelance Photographers. Since 1965, the Bureau has been chronicling the freelancing scene by providing vital information on markets and trends. Indeed, *Market Newsletter*, the BFP monthly that has for so long been signposting the route to successful freelancing, is considered essential reading by most serious freelance photographers and photojournalists.

There has, however, long been a need for a directory which would provide comprehensive listings of the markets available, and at the same time include the kind of detailed and accurate information that has become the hallmark of the BFP *Newsletter*. The *Handbook* has been published to fill this need. The Bureau set out to provide a publication that would be genuinely useful to the freelance photographer and have every reason to believe that they have succeeded in this task: no other directory contains the wealth of detailed market information to be found in the pages of this volume.

Putting together the *Handbook* has proved a gargantuan task, and here the publishers would like to express their thanks to the many hundreds of editors and other picture buyers who assisted by providing information on their requirements. Detailed questionnaires were sent to every periodical published in Britain as well as to picture agencies and other markets. This was augmented by the extensive market intelligence and research facilities of the Bureau of Freelance Photographers.

Right up to page-proof stage, new entries were being included, and all entries were checked and double-checked against the latest information available to ensure the highest possible degree of accuracy. All this is of course, encumbent on any directory or handbook publisher, but the fact that this was to be the official handbook of an organisation whose sole *raison d'etre* is providing accurate market information greatly facilitated the task. BFP researchers are constantly monitoring the subtle shifts and changes that occur in the freelance market, and this has resulted in important last minute changes being made to many of the entries in the *Handbook*.

It is not intended that the *Handbook* should supplant *Market Newsletter*. As subscribers to the latter publication will be aware, the Newsletter is intended to keep the freelance in touch with new markets, urgent requirements, changes in editorial needs, and so on. The purpose of the *Handbook* is to provide a comprehensive guide to all the most important markets together with the fullest possible information on their continuing requirements. *Market Newsletter* can be employed as a useful supplement to the *Handbook*, since it will pinpoint changes in the market as they occur.

Much depends upon the reception accorded this first edition, but it is hoped that the *Handbook* will become a regular publication, with new editions appearing annually or bi-annually.

Since this is the first edition of what will hopefully become an indispensable tool for the freelance photographer, photojournalist and writer, the publishers will be glad to hear from readers who have any comments to make on their use of the *Handbook*, or suggestions for future editions.

John Tracy

ABOUT THE BFP

Founded in 1965, the Bureau of Freelance Photographers is today the major body for the freelance photographer. It has a worldwide membership of some 10,000, comprising not only full-time freelances, but also amateur and semi-professional photographers. Being primarily a service organisation, membership of the Bureau is open to anyone with an interest in freelance photography.

The major service offered to members is the *Market Newsletter*, a confidential monthly report on the state of the freelance market. A well-researched and highly authoritative publication, the *Newsletter* keeps freelances in touch with the market for freelance pictures. It gives full information on the type of pictures currently being sought by a wide range of publications and other outlets. It gives details of new magazines and their editorial requirements, and generally reports on what is happening in the publishing world and how this is likely to affect the freelance photographer. The *Newsletter* is considered essential reading for the freelance and aspiring freelance photographer, and because it pinpoints changes in the marketplace as they occur, it will henceforth also act as a useful supplement to the *Handbook*.

Other services provided to members for the modest annual subscription include:

● A periodic *Market Survey Special* which takes a particular market area and examines its current needs in depth.

● Advisory service. Individual advice on all aspects of freelancing is available to members.

● Fee Recovery Service. The Bureau tries to protect its members' interests in every way it can. In particular, it has been able to assist individual members in recovering unpaid reproduction fees.

● Exclusive Items and Special Offers. The Bureau regularly offers books and other items to members, usually at discount prices. It originated Contributor's Submission Forms for use by members, and is also able to supply Model Release Forms. The Bureau also publishes a list of photographic companies willing to provide special discounts to BFP members.

HOW TO USE THIS BOOK

Anyone with the ability to use a camera correctly has the potential to make money from his pictures. Taking saleable photographs isn't difficult. The difficulty lies in finding the market. It isn't enough for the photographer in search of a sale to find what he thinks *might* be a suitable market; rather he must find *exactly* the right magazine, newspaper, agency or whatever for his particular type of work. Many a sale has been lost because a picture which is, in itself, technically perfect fails to fulfil the total requirements of the buyer.

The Freelance Photographer's Market Handbook has been designed to help resolve these difficulties. It puts you in touch with major markets for your work, telling you exactly what each is looking for, together with hints and tips on how to sell to them and, wherever possible, the rates they pay.

The *Handbook* covers three big markets for your pictures: magazines (by far the largest), agencies and greetings card and calendar companies. There are three ways of using the book, depending on the way you need or wish to work:

1. If you are out to sell to magazines and you have pictures on a theme particularly applicable to a certain type of publication (i.e. gardening, angling, sport, etc.) turn to the magazine section and look for the subject. The magazines are listed under 34 categories, each of which has a broad heading covering specific magazines. The categories are in alphabetical

order, as are the magazines within those categories. You need only read through them to discover which is best for your type of pictures.

2. If you have a set of pictures that follow a specific photographic theme (i.e. landscapes, children, glamour etc.), turn to the subject index on page 20. Look up your chosen subject and there you will find a list of all the magazines interested in that particular type of picture. You have only then to look up each one mentioned in the appropriate section for precise details of their requirements. (If in doubt as to where to find a particular magazine, consult the general index at the back of the book.) There is a separate subject index for agencies on page 233, showing you which agents specialise in what subjects.

3. If you are looking for the requirements of a specific magazine, agency, greetings card or calendar market, whose name is already known to you, refer to the general index at the back of the directory.

With this wealth of information open to you, and with those three options for finding the right market, there is no reason why you shouldn't start earning top cash from your camera. But before you rush off to put your pictures in the post, here are six points worth bearing in mind and which will help you to more successful sales:

1. The golden rule of freelancing: don't send people pictures they don't want. Read the requirements listed in the various parts of this directory and obey them. When, for instance, a Scottish magazine says they want pictures of all things Scottish with the exception of kilts and haggis, you can be sure they are over-stocked with these subjects. They are not going to make an exception just for you, however good you think your picture might be.

2. If you have an idea for a picture or feature for a particular market, don't be afraid to telephone first to discuss what you have in mind. Nearly every magazine editor approached when the *Handbook* was being compiled said they would be delighted to hear from potential freelances in advance, rather than have inappropriate words and pictures landing on their desks.

3. If you are working in colour, and unless the listing states otherwise, always supply transparencies rather than prints.

4. This book will also tell you who *not* to contact. If an entry specifically says that they have no freelance market, don't think they will make an exception for your work. Go on to the next appropriate entry and supply the market that *does* have your type of requirements.

5. If you are supplying pictures, make sure they are accompanied by

detailed captions, not only of the picture itself, but also of your own name and address.

6. Never send anything to a market on spec without a stamped addressed envelope for its return.

PRESENTATION

Speak to anyone in the business of buying from freelances and you will be told horror stories about the way pictures and manuscripts are submitted. Colour transparencies are often sent loose in ordinary envelopes, prints arrive bent and crumpled, manuscripts are scribbled unintelligibly on sheets of paper that have obviously been out to many markets before, pictures show no form of identification, others have writing from the back of one print transferred across the face of another.

This is an area where first impressions count for a lot and the way your work arrives on an editor's or an agency boss's desk could make all the difference to a potential sale. Here's how to get it right.

Pictures

The first thing to remember is that pictures must be identified with captions, together with your own name and address. If you are submitting prints only, these details are best marked on the back. Some freelances actually write on the back of the print with a pencil or lightly with a ballpoint pen. This is acceptable (as long as the writing doesn't show through or get transferred to another print), but a far better method is to type the details on a separate sheet of paper and attach this to the back of each print with adhesive tape.

If you are submitting prints as part of an illustrated article, it is better for the captions to be written on a separate sheet attached to the manuscript. In this instance, mark the back of the print with your name and address and a picture number. The captions are then written against the appropriate number on their separate sheet.

Unless otherwise requested by a particular market, prints should be no more than 10×8 inches and printed on a glossy surface. Never send mounted pictures to the sort of markets we are discussing here.

Prints, together with your written details, are best packed between two stiffeners. The ideal material is hardboard, but failing that, some kind of extra stiff cardboard is adequate. Never use thin card or corrugated cardboard.

Cut these stiffeners so that they are slightly larger than your prints and then pack them tightly into a suitably-sized envelope. Seal it and mark it in large letters, **Photographs, Please Do Not Bend**. Better still, buy some adhesive labels with the words already printed on them and stick one on each side of the envelope.

For transparencies, make sure first that they are spotted correctly. There are eight ways to view a transparency and only one of them is correct. It's the spot that points the way and it might be either a small adhesive circle of paper that can be bought in photo suppliers or nothing more than a mark with a pencil or pen. The correct place for the spot is the bottom left-hand corner when the slide is viewed the correct way. Like that, the spot falls in the top right-hand corner when the slide is being placed in a normal projector.

The only other details that should appear on a slide mount are your name and address, together with a picture number. Details can then be written on a separate sheet.

Use card or plastic mounts, never glass. The latter can get broken too easily in the post, thus ruining your slide. Also, if your work is meant for reproduction, glass mounts cause difficulties for the printer.

To submit slides, it is best to use a plastic filing sleeve, designed to hold a certain number in mounts, each in a separate pocket. It gives protection for the slides and it gives your potential customer an easy way of assessing your work at a glance.

The sleeves can then be packed in much the same way as described for prints.

Manuscripts

The presentation of the written word is every bit as important as the way you present your pictures. *Never* submit a hand-written article. Either type it yourself or pay someone to type it for you. The article should be typed double-spaced on one side of the sheet only and with a margin of no less than one inch on the left. The ideal paper size is A4.

The first sheet should bear your name and address in the top left-hand corner and the article itself should start, on the first page, around one-third of the way down the sheet to allow printer's instructions to be written above. On subsequent pages, the text can start at the top of each sheet. Pages should be numbered in the top, right-hand corner.

At the bottom of each page, type the letters 'm.f.' to indicate that 'more follows' and at the bottom of the last page, type the word 'end'. Try not to hyphenate words from one line to the next, but rather leave a short line and start the offending word in full on the next.

When the article is finished, place a cover sheet on the front. This is a plain sheet of paper that contains, neatly set-out, the minimum of information about the article. Type the title in the centre of the page, together with your name and the number of words involved. At the bottom of the page, write your name again, plus address and, if possible, a daytime telephone number.

Clip the complete manuscript together with a paper clip, not a staple and send it in the same packing as your pictures. Avoid folding it more than once.

The Covering Letter

The only other thing that should be packed with your manuscript and/or pictures, is a letter to the person to whom you are hoping to sell.

Using this directory for the relevant information, always address your letter to a specific person, rather than starting it 'Dear Sir'. Then keep it brief. Your work will stand or fall by its content, not by any descriptions or explanations that you include in the letter. It should, then, contain nothing more than something along these lines:

Dear Mr. Smith,
I enclose a set of pictures/illustrated article which
I hope you will consider using at your normal rates.

*I also enclose a stamped addressed envelope for the return
of my work should it prove unsatisfactory.
I look forward to hearing from you in due course.
Yours sincerely,*

Pay particular attention to that reference to the stamped addressed envelope. Never submit work anywhere without one. And make sure that the envelope is the right size with the correct postage on it.

Good presentation will never make bad work better. But bad presentation can often prevent the sale of otherwise good pictures or well-written words. If you are out to make money from freelancing, it pays to get it right first time.

MAGAZINES

The British magazine market is vast. Anyone who doubts that has only to look at the racks of periodicals in any major newsagent. And this is only the tip of the iceberg, the largest section of the consumer press. Beneath the surface there is the trade press, the controlled circulation magazines and many smaller publications that are never seen on general sale. At the last count, some 6,500 magazines were being published on a regular basis in Britain.

In this section you will find a list of magazines who are looking for freelances. Some pay a lot, others are less generous, but all have one thing in common—they are here because they need freelance contributions and they are willing to pay for them.

When you come to start looking at these lists in detail, you might be surprised by the number of magazines of which you have never heard. Don't let that put you off. What the newcomer to freelancing often fails to realise is that there are as many, if not more, trade magazines as there are consumer publications, and very few of these are ever seen on general sale.

Trade magazines, as their title implies, are aimed at people whose business is making money from the particular subject in hand. As such, their requirements are usually totally different to their consumer counterparts.

As an example, consider boating. A consumer magazine on that subject will be aimed at the boat owner or enthusiast and could contain features on boats and the way they are handled. A trade magazine on the same subject might be more interested in articles about the profits being made by the boating industry and pictures of shop displays of boating accessories.

Trade magazines do not necessarily have a separate section to themselves. If the subject is a common one, such as the example above in which there are trade and consumer publications, they have been listed for your convenience under a common heading. Despite that, however, there *is* a section specifically for trade. This contains trade magazines that have no consumer counterparts, as well as magazines whose subject is actually trade itself and trading in general.

As you go through this section, therefore, it is important for you to realise that there is very real difference between the two sides of the subject, but it is a difference which is explained under each publication's requirements. So don't ignore trade magazines of whose existence you were not previously aware. Very often, such a magazine will have just as big a market for your pictures and the fees will be just as much, and in some cases more, than those offered by the consumer press.

It is often a good idea for the freelance to aim himself at some of the more obscure publications listed here. Simply because they are a little obscure, they may not have been noticed by other freelances and, as such, your sales potential will be higher.

Another factor that will become apparent as you look through this section of the *Handbook* is how much more black and white illustrations are needed than colour. It's wise, then, to remember this when you are shooting pictures for publication. If possible, shoot both colour and mono; if you have no choice, you might be better off sticking purely to black and white.

When you are looking through the entries, don't stop at the section on illustrations. Read what the magazine needs in the way of text too. A publication that might appear to have a very small market for individual pictures often has a larger potential for illustrated articles, and all you need to do to make a sale is add a few words. (See the chapter on Putting Words To Your Pictures.)

You will also find that many publications talk about needing only commissioned work. Don't be misled by this. The commissions are given to freelances and, although this means they won't consider your work on spec, an editor could well be interested in giving you a commission if you can prove you are worth it. That's where previous experience comes in. When trying for commissions, you should always have examples of previously published work to show an editor.

Unless otherwise stated in these entries, every editor listed is happy to talk over ideas. So, if you are looking for a commission, or if you just have an idea for a feature or pictures that you think will appeal to a specific magazine, never be afraid to telephone first to discuss what you have in mind. Contrary to popular belief, editors of most magazines are quite easy to reach and most would prefer a telephone call to a letter. On the phone, you can get an immediate reaction. Write a letter and you could wait weeks for a reply.

The magazine market is one of the largest available to the freelance. You might not receive as large a fee per picture as you would from, say, the greetings card and calendar market or for certain sales that might be made on your behalf by an agency, but what this market does offer is a *steady* income.

There are so many magazines, covering so many different subjects that the freelance who has his wits about him would be hard put *not* to find one to which his own style and interests can be adapted. Make yourself known to a few chosen magazine editors, let them see that you can turn out good quality work on the right subject, at the right time, and there is no reason why this market shouldn't make you a good, regular income, either part time or full time.

Subject Index

Only magazines are included in this index, but it should be noted that many of these subjects are also required by Agencies (pp. 230–248) and Card & Calendar publishers (pp. 223–229). A separate Subject Index for agencies appears in the Agency section.

Aeroplanes

Flight and Safety Bulletin
Flight International
Journal of The Guild of Air Pilots and Air
   Navigators
Mayfair
Middle East Travel
Pilot Magazine
Popular Flying
Skyplane

Agricultural Scenes

Agri Trade
British Farmer and Stockbreeder
Dairy Farmer
Dairy Industries International
The Jewish Vegetarian
The Land Worker
Livestock Farming
The Milk Producer
Pig Farming

Poultry Farmer
Poultry World
Practical Self-Sufficiency
What's New in Farming

Architecture & Buildings

Builder and Merchant
Building Services and Environmental Engineer
Construction and Property News
Construction Surveyor
Energy in Buildings
Glass Age
Harlow News
House Builder
Journal of the Chartered Institution of Building Services
Local Government News
Maintenance and Equipment News
Middle East Construction
Municipal Journal
Now In Southampton
The Period Home
RIBA Journal

Army and Navy

Defence
The Legion
Maritime Defence
Navy International

Arts and Crafts

Art and Craft
Craft and Hobby Dealer
Fashion and Craft
Period Home
Popular Crafts
Woodworker

Boating & Yachting

Boating Business
Motor Boat and Yachting

Practical Boat Owner
Popular Motor Cruiser
RYA News
Waterways World
Yachting and Boating
Yachting Monthly
Yachting World
Yachts and Yachting

Business Scenes

Accountancy Age
Africa Economic Digest
Alam Attijarat
The Annual Investment File
BPMA News
British German Trade
Business Credit
Business in Beds, Bucks and Herts
Business Information Technology
Commerce International
Computer Talk
Cumbria Weekly Digest
Data Business
The Economist
Enterprise, Business News and Business Review
The Director
Executive Post
Graduate Post
Hampshire Monitor Business Magazine
In Touch
Journal of the Institute of Bankers
Management Accounting
Marketing
Milton Keynes Commerce & Industry
Modern Africa
Opinion
Personnel Executive
Procurement Weekly
Purchasing

Children

Amateur Photographer
Art and Craft

The British Journal of Religious Education
The Brownie
Camera
Camera Weekly
Guider
Junior Education
Mother
Mother & Baby
Movie Maker
Nursery World
Parents
Photography
Practical Education
Practical Photography
Safety
Scouting
SLR Camera
Special Education
Talk
Today's Guide

Cinema & Television

Huna London
Look-In
Movie Star
Radio Times
The Stage and Television Today
TV Directory
TV Times Magazine
What Video

Cycling

Bicycle Times
Cyclist Monthly

Domestic and Farm Animals

Amateur Photographer
Aquarist and Pondkeeper
British Farmer and Stockbreeder
Cage and Aviary Birds
Camera
Camera Weekly

Cat World Weekly
Cats
Dairy Farmer
Dairy Industries International
Horse and Driving
Horse and Rider
Horse and Pony
The Jewish Vegetarian
Kennel Gazette
Livestock Farming
Look-In
Milk Producer
Photography
Pig Farming
Pony
Poultry Farmer
Poultry World
Practical Fish Keeping
Practical Photography
Practical Self-Sufficiency
Riding
SLR Camera
The Vegetarian
Veterinary Drug
Weekend

Domestic Environment

Blinds and Shutters
Builders Merchant
Do It Yourself Magazine
Domestic Heating
The Food Magazine
Furnishing Retailer and Contractor
Home and Freezer Digest
Home Improvements Guides
Homecare
Interiors
Jewish Chronicle
Kitchens
The Period Home
Options
Superstore
The Townswoman
The Trustcard Magazine

Woman and Home
Woman's Journal

Fashion

Drapers Record
Fashion and Craft
Fashion Weekly
Hairflair
Jewish Chronicle
Leathergoods
Look Now
Men's Wear
Ms. London
My Guy
Vogue Patterns
Woman
Woman's Own
Women's Journal
Worldwide Knitting

Glamour

Amateur Photographer
Camera
Camera Weekly
Club International
Fiesta
Knave
Mayfair
Men Only
Movie Maker
Penthouse
Photography
Practical Photography
She
SLR Camera
Stream
Superbike Magazine
Weekend

Horticulture

Garden News
Garden Trade News
Gardening World

Greenhouse
Practical Gardening

Humour

Amateur Photographer
Autocar
British Farmer and Stock Breeder
Camera
Camera Weekly
The Christian Herald
Driving
Horse and Pony
In Dublin
Look-In
Movie Maker
Photography
Pig Farming
Practical Photography
She
SLR Camera
Stream
Weekend

Industrial Scenes

Aqua
Coil Winding International
Containerization International
Defence Material
Economist
Education in Chemistry
Enterprise
Eurofruit
Heating and Ventilating Review
Industrial Diamond Review
Industrial Executive
Ink and Print
Instruction Surveyor
Lighting Equipment News
Management Accounting
Middle East Industrial Products
Mining Magazine
Modern Africa
Post Magazine
Processing

Procurement Weekly
Production Management and Control
Professional Printer
Roustabout Magazine
Sign World
Solid Fuels
Tin International
World Sugar Journal

Landscapes

Aberdeen Leopard
Access Magazine
Amateur Photographer
Angling Times
Argo
Cambridge, Huntingdon and
   Peterborough Life
Camera
Camera Weekly
Caravan and Chalet Site
Caravan Industry and Park Operator
Caravanning Monthly
The Christian Herald
Catholic Gazette
Coarse Angler
Commerce International
Cornish Life
Country Life
Derbyshire Today
Devon Life
En Route
Gloucestershire and Avon Life
The Great Outdoors
Holiday Haunts in Great Britain
Holidays in Britain
Huna London
Inland Waterways Guide
Lakescene
Lancashire Life
Lincolnshire Life
Living in Kent
Manx Life
Motorcaravan World
Movie Maker
Northamptonshire and Bedfordshire Life

Photography
Popular Caravan
Practical Boat Owner
Practical Camper
Practical Camper's Site Guide
Practical Caravan
Practical Photography
Reality
Rucksack
RYA News
Scots Independent
The Scots Magazine
Scottish Field
The Sign
SLR Camera
Spotlight
This England
Warwickshire and Worcestershire Life
Waterways World
Where To Eat In

Motor Vehicles

Auto Accessory Retailer
Autocar
The Automobile
Auto Performance
Automobile Sport
Buses
Car Fleet Management
Car Numbers Monthly
Car Parts and Accessories
Disabled Driver
Driving
Garage and Transport Magazine
Headlight
Hot Car
Magic Carpet
Mayfair
Motor Trader
Practical Classics
Safer Motoring
Street Machine
Surrey Property Mail
Truck Magazine

Motorcycling

Classic Bike
The Classic Motorcycle
Cycle Trade News
Motorcycle Trade News
Motorcycling
Superbike Magazine

Performing Arts

Arts Review
Dance and Dancers
English Dance and Song
Huna London
Opera
Radio Times
Recorded Sound
The Recorder and Music Magazine
The Stage and Television Today
TV Times Magazine

Popular Music

Black Echoes
Black Music and Jazz Review
Blue Jeans
Blues & Soul
Country Music People
Country Music World
Flexipop
International Musician and Recording
  World
Judy
Kerrang!
Look-In
New Musical Express
Melody Maker
My Guy
Noise!
Organ Player & Keyboard Review
Record Mirror
Pop Pix
Smash Hits
Sounds
Zigzag

Railways

Model Railways
Rail News
Scale Trains

Shipping

Containerisation International
Marine Engineers Review
Marine Stores International
Port of London Magazine
Sea Breezes

Sport

Airgun World
Adventure Sports and Travel
Amateur Photographer
Anglers Mail
Angling Times
Automobile Sport
Bike
BMX Action Bike
Camera
Camera Weekly
Canoe Focus
Climber and Rambler
Coarse Angler
Coarse Fisherman
Compass Sport
Countryside Monthly
The Cricketer International
Cue World
Darts World
Fighters' Monthly
Footloose
Golf Monthly
Golf World
Gymnastics
Here's Health
Marathon and Distance Runner
Match Weekly
Photography
Practical Photography

Racing Pigeon Pictorial
Rangers News
Rugby Post
The Scottish Sporting Gazette
Shooting Magazine
SLR Camera
Snooker Scene
SOGAT Journal
Sportscope
Sports Trader
Sport and Leisure
Surrey Property Mail
Tackle and Guns
Target Gun
Watford
Wings
Wisden Cricket Monthly

Technology

A & V News
AGRI Trade
CB Radio
Change
Chartered Mechanical Engineer
Chemistry In Britain
Clean Air
Computer Market Place
Computing Today
Design Engineering
Domestic Heating
Electrical Times
The Electronics Location File
The Engineer
Gas World
Healthy Living
The IBM User
International Broadcasting Engineer
International Railway Journal
Laboratory News
Manufacturing Chemist
Natural Gas
Middle East Electronics

New Scientist
Next
Physics Bulletin
Process Engineering
Strain
T.V. Directory
Water Bulletin
Wireless World

Travel

Adventure Sports and Travel
Africa Economic Digest
Africa Health
Alam Attijarat
Amateur Photographer
Bicycle Times
Business Traveller
Camera
Camera Weekly
The Caribbean Chronicle
Coach Mart
The Diplomatist
The Director
Far East Health
Holiday Time Sharing
Holiday USA and Canada
Homes and Travel Abroad
Homes Overseas
International Tax-Free Trader
Middle East Travel
Motorcaravan World
Movie Maker
Options
Parents
Photography
Practical Photography
SLR Camera
SOGAT Journal
Superstore
The Traveller
Travelling
Woman & Home

Wildlife

Airgun World
Amateur Photographer
Camera
Camera Weekly
Countryside Monthly
Movie Maker
Natural World

Photography
The Scottish Sporting Gazette
Shooting Times and Country Magazine
SLR Camera
The Vegetarian
Veterinary Drug
Weekend
Wild Cat
Wild Fowl World

Angling

ANGLER'S MAIL
IPC Magazines Ltd., King's Reach Tower, Stamford Street, London SE1 9LS. Tel: 01-261 5883.
Editor: John Ingham.
Weekly publication with news and features for followers of coarse, sea and game fishing in the UK.
Illustrations: B&W and colour. Pictures of successful anglers with their catches, plus well-known fisheries showing anglers in action. Captions should give full details of where, when, how and who. Covers: Colour pictures of angling subjects, usually showing successful angler(s) with catch(es). 35mm acceptable.
Text: Features on coarse, sea and game fishing topics only. Up to 850 words.
Overall freelance potential: Minimal from non-angling freelances. Regular freelance sources are known specialists in the field and agencies.
Editor's tips: Most pictures and text seen from non-anglers are not acceptable because of lack of knowledge and experience on the part of the contributor.
Fees: Good; on a rising scale according to the size of reproduction or length of feature.

ANGLING TIMES
East Midland Allied Press, Bretton Court, Bretton, Peterborough PE3 8DZ. Tel: 0733 266222.
Editor: Allan Haines.
Weekly newspaper format covering all ranges of angling, i.e. coarse, sea and game. Includes news, features and general instruction.
Illustrations: General angling subjects—catches, action and scenics.
Text: Features on all aspects of the hobby. Up to 800 words.
Overall freelance potential: Very good. High percentage used each week.
Fees: By agreement.

COARSE ANGLER
NFA Publications Ltd., 281 Ecclesall Road, Sheffield S11 8NX. Tel: 0742 686132/3.
Co-editors: Colin Dyson and Colin Graham.
Monthly magazine for the British coarse angling community with special reference to members of the National Federation of Anglers.
Illustrations: B&W and colour. Pictures solely relating to coarse fishing. Covers: Colour pictures of picturesque coarse fishing scenes and locations or close-ups of anglers with spectacular catches. 35mm acceptable inside, 6 × 6 cm only for covers.
Text: Articles on any aspect of coarse fish or fishing. 1,000–1,250 words.
Overall freelance potential: Around 50 per cent of each issue is contributed by freelances.
Fees: Text, from £25; B&W pictures, from £7.50 according to size; covers, £25.

COARSE FISHERMAN
Delgarno Ltd., 32 Daventry Road, Norton, Northants NN11 5ND. Tel: 032-72 4751.
Editor: David Hall.
Monthly magazine for anglers.
Illustrations: B&W and colour. Angling pictures. Covers: Colour pictures of same. 35mm acceptable.
Text: Features on angling. 1,000 words.
Overall freelance potential: Around 60 per cent of the magazine comes from freelances.
Fees: Text, £20 per 1,000 words; covers, £22.50.

Animals

CATS
Watmoughs Ltd, High Street, Idle, Bradford, West Yorkshire BD10 8NL. Tel: 0274 612111.
Editor: Brian Doyle.
Weekly publication aimed at the serious cat breeder and exhibitor.
Illustrations: B&W only. Newsy photographs of interest to serious cat fanciers, and pictures of outstanding pedigree animals. All pictures must be accompanied by informative captions.
Text: Limited scope for knowledgeable features or show reports.
Overall freelance potential: Limited to the coverage of serious cat matters.
Editor's tips: This is not a market for gimmicky pictures or simple pretty portraits of ordinary pets.
Fees: By negotiation.

CAT WORLD
Scan Publishing Co. Scan House, Southwick Street, Brighton BN4 4TE. Tel: 0273 595969.
Editor: Angela Sayer.
Monthly magazine for cat lovers and, in particular, breeders of pedigree cats.
Illustrations: Pictures of cats in unusual situations.

Text: Short news items or features about cats. 200 words.
Overall freelance potential: Good if the material is right for the market.
Editor's tips: The magazine gets too many pictures of strays and pretty pictures of cats. Only news or striking pictures will be considered.
Fees: On a rising scale according to the size of reproduction or length of article.

EQUESTRIAN TRADE NEWS
Equestrian Management Consultants Ltd., Wothersome Grange, Bramham, Nr. Wetherby, Yorks LS23 6LY. Tel: 0532 892267.
Editor: Antony Wakeham.
Monthly publication for business people and trade in the equestrian world.
Illustrations: B&W only. Pictures covering saddlery, feedstuffs, new riding schools and business in the industry. Also people connected with the industry, e.g. people retiring, getting married, etc.
Text: Features on specialist subjects and general articles on retailing, marketing and business. 1,000 words.
Overall freelance potential: Around 50 per cent comes from freelances.
Editor's tips: Only stories with a business angle will be considered. No general horsey or racing material.
Fees: Text, £25 per 1,000 words; pictures by arrangemnt.

HORSE AND DRIVING
Watmoughs Ltd., Idle, Bradford, West Yorkshire, BD10 8NL. Tel: 0274 612111.
Editor: Jack Watmough.
Bi-monthly publication for those who enjoy the driving of horses and ponies, ridden dressage and horse trials.
Illustrations: B&W inside. Pictures of specialist interest with detailed caption. Covers: Colour pictures of subjects associated with contents with room left for logo. 35mm acceptable.
Text: Features of an equestrian nature. No hunting, show jumping or non-dressage and non-show trial riding. 750-1,000 words.
Overall freelance potential: Fair for the freelance with expertise in the subject.
Fees: B&W pictures inside, £12 for half-page, £8 for one-third page, £5 minimum; covers and text by negotiation.

HORSE AND PONY
EMAP National Publications Ltd., Bretton Court, Bretton, Peterborough PE3 8DZ. Tel: 0733 264666.
Editor: Sally Pearson.
Fortnightly magazine reflecting the dedication and enthusiasm of people who love horses.
Illustrations: B&W inside. Amusing or unusual pictures of horses at work and play. Covers: Colour pictures of horses; 35mm acceptable.

Text: Illustrated articles on the practical side of the subject. 1,000 words.
Overall freelance potential: Around 30 per cent is contributed from outside.
Editor's tips: News material should be sent in fact after the event. Good presentation definitely helps acceptance.
Fees: Negotiable.

HORSE AND RIDER

D. J. Murphy (Publishers) Ltd., 104 Ash Road, Sutton, Surrey SM3 9LD. Tel: 01-641 4911.
Editor: Julia Goodwin.
Monthly magazine aimed at adult horse-riders.
Illustrations: B&W and occasional colour inside. Off-beat personality shots and pictures for photo stories illustrating equestrian subjects, e.g. plaiting up, clipping, etc. Also general yard pictures, riding pictures, people and horses. Covers: Colour pictures of anything equestrian and a little out of the ordinary. 35mm acceptable.
Text: Illustrated features on stable management and anything on horses except polo, racing and trotting. 1,500 words.
Overall freelance potential: A good possibility for freelances who show an understanding of the market.
Editor's tips: Material must be technically accurate, i.e. riders must be shown wearing the correct clothes, especially hats; horses must be fit and correctly tackled.
Fees: Text, £30 per 1,000 words; B&W pictures, £8.50; colour, £40.

KENNEL GAZETTE

The Kennel Club, 1 Clarges Street, London W1Y 8AB. Tel: 01-493 6651.
Editor: Mrs. K. C. Harrison.
Monthly publication for pedigree dog owners and exhibitors. the official organ of the Kennel Club.
Illustrations: B&W only. Pictures of pedigree dogs, with and without people; dog shows; working dogs. covers: B&W pictures of pedigree dogs.
Text: Articles on breeding, veterinary subjects, judging, grooming, police dogs, field trials, obedience classes etc. 500–1,000 words.
Overall freelance potential: Small.
Editor's tips: The readership is specialist. Submissions should reflect this.
Fees: Covers, £7.50; inside £5. Features by agreement.

NATURAL WORLD

Royal Society for Nature Conservation, 4 Bloomsbury Square, London, WC1A 2RL. Tel: 01-404 4300.
Editor: Linda Bennett.
Natural history and wildlife conservation magazine, mainly concerned with UK wildlife. Published three times per year.
Illustrations: B&W only. Natural history subjects for stock purposes; in particular, mammals, amphibians, insects and flowers and trees. Subjects must be wild. No pets or zoo animals.

Text: Short photo-features on wildlife topics, e.g. the emergence of a butterfly from a chrysalis, hatching of a lizard etc. Around 500 words.
Overall freelance potential: Small.
Fees: £10 minimum for B&W print.

PET PRODUCT MARKETING

EMAP National Publications Ltd., Bretton Court, Bretton, Peterborough PE3 8DZ. Tel: 0733 264666.
Editor: Bob Stonebridge.
Monthly trade journal for pet product retailers, wholesalers, manufacturers and importers. Controlled circulation.
Illustrations: B&W only on subjects connected with pet products and the pet trade. Covers: B&W only.
Text: Features on pets and pet products with specific relevance to the pet trade. 1,000 words.
Fees: £20 per 1,000 words. Pictures on merit.

PET STORE TRADER

Dog World Ltd., Scan House, Southwick Street, Southwick, Brighton, BN4 4TE. Tel: 0273 595969.
Editor: Ferelith Hamilton.
Monthly publication for pet shop proprietors, wholesalers and manufacturers.
Illustrations: B&W only. Any pictures of interest concerning a pet store proprietor.
Text: News items only on pet store traders. 300–400 words.
Overall freelance potential: Good, despite the fact that the subject is specialised.
Fees: Good; on a rising scale according to the size of reproduction or length of feature.

PONY

D. J. Murphy Ltd., 104 Ash Road, Sutton, Surrey SM3 9LD. Tel: 01-641 4911.
Editor: Nancy Roberts.
Monthly children's magazine about horses, ponies and riding. Aimed at 6–18 age group.
Illustrations: B&W only inside. High quality, striking, unusual pictures of an equestrian nature. Covers: Colour pictures of anything to do with the equine world. 35mm acceptable.
Text: Features about horses and the care of them. Fiction with a strong, contemporary plot. 1,000–1,500 words.
Overall freelance potential: Good quality freelance work is always welcome.
Fees: B&W pictures, £8.50; covers, £40; text by agreement.

RIDING

IPC Magazines Ltd., Lavington House, Lavington Street, London SE1 0PF. Tel: 01-261 6821.
Editor in Chief: Michael Clayton.
Monthly magazine aimed at the 'grass roots' of the equestrian world. Age range, 17 to 35. Contains informative and instructional articles on riding and horsemanship; news and

reports on equestrian events and competitions at all levels; riding clubs; and matters of general interest to this market.

Illustrations: B&W only. Anything except major events where special arrangements are made. Particularly interested in pictures of unusual events or incidents for news pages.

Text: Instructional articles and equestrian experiences of general interest to readers in any equestrian field. 1,000–2,000 words.

Overall freelance potential: A substantial amount of freelance work is used each month.

Fees: Good; on a rising scale, according to the size of reproduction or length of feature.

VETERINARY DRUG

Animal Health Services Division of Henderson Group One, 1 Roberts Mews, Lowndes Place, London SW1X 8DA. Tel: 01-235 4086.

Editor: G. N. Henderson.

Monthly publication for vets. Contains news and features on products, veterinary activities and drug companies. Features an insert called 'Surgery Door'.

Illustrations: B&W only. Pictures to illustrate articles, especially in the insert. Pictures needed here include pets, kennels, birds, wildlife etc. Eye-catching pictures needed.

Text: Illustrated features based on veterinary activity or disease outbreaks, maltreatment, research farms, etc. for main magazine. Amusing and entertaining illustrated articles aimed more at the general public for 'Surgery Door'.

Overall freelance potential: Nearly 100 per cent comes from freelance sources.

Fees: Negotiable around £35 per 1,000 words; pictures by agreement.

VETERINARY PRACTICE

A. E. Morgan Publications Ltd., Stanley House, 9 West Street, Epsom, Surrey KT18 7RL. Tel: 037-27 41411.

Editor: David Ritchie.

Bi-monthly newspaper for veterinary surgeons in general practice.

Illustrations: Pictures of veterinary surgeons engaged in activities either connected with or outside their professional work.

Text: Features particularly concerned with veterinary practice. 800–1,500 words.

Overall freelance potential: Small.

Fees: By agreement.

WILD CAT

Cat Survival Trust, 4 Ninnings Lane, Rabley Heath, Welwyn, Herts. AL6 9TD. Tel: 0438 812439.

Editor: Peter Watkiss.

Published twice per year for members, patrons and friends of the Cat Survival Trust, as well as zoological institutions in several countries.

Illustrations: B&W only. Pictures of wild cats, especially less common species. Pictures taken in the wild or overseas zoos or private collections are particularly welcome. No domestic pets. Covers: B&W pictures of same.

Text: Articles on any aspect of wild cats, e.g. biology, management, breeding, conservation, etc. 1,000–2,000 words.
Overall freelance potential: Small but expanding.
Fees: Nominal, due to the publishers being a charity.

WILDFOWL WORLD
The Wildfowl Trust, Slimbridge, Glos. GL2 7BT. Tel: 045-389 333.
Editor: S. A. Rolfe Smith.
Published twice a year for members and supporters of the Trust, plus members of the public.
Illustrations: B&W and colour. Pictures of swans, geese, ducks and flamingoes in the wild or in captivity, plus pictures of the wetland habitat in which they live. Also aspects of conservation and breeding or their use for educational and/or research purposes. Associated subjects such as migration, navigation, pollution etc. are also required. Covers: Colour pictures of swans, geese or ducks or any group of a wildfowl species. 35mm acceptable.
Text: Features on subjects detailed above. Up to 2,000 words.
Overall freelance potential: Capable of considerable expansion.
Fees: To be negotiated.

Arts and Entertainment

ARGO
Argo Publishing Company, Old Fire Station, 40 George Street, Oxford OX1 2AQ.
Editor: Hilary Davies.
Literary review, mainly devoted to poetry. Published three times per year.
Illustrations: B&W only. Pictures of artistic interest in their own right. Covers: Normally B&W, but colour might be considered. Pictures of ships, especially those suggesting the Argo of Jason and the Argonauts. 35mm acceptable.
Text: Original poetry and short stories; reviews of current literature. Poetry can be of any length; reviews and short stories, up to 2,500 words.
Overall freelance potential: Good.
Editor's tips: Potential reviewers should always contact the reviews editor before starting work on a project.
Fees: By negotiation.

ARTS REVIEW and ARTS REVIEW YEARBOOK
Star City Ltd., 16 St. James' Gardens, London W11. Tel: 01-603 7530.
Editor: Graham Hughes.
Fortnightly magazine and annual yearbook for the arts.
Illustrations: Only by commission.
Text: As above.
Fees: By agreement.

BINGO PLUS

Eaglepress Ltd., Upwood House, 111a Tupwood Lane, Caterham, Surrey CR3 6DD. Tel: 0883 44896.

Editor: Brian Mackie.

Bi-monthly publication, circulated free to all members of Mecca Leisure Social Clubs. Bingo-based, but also includes home interest section.

Illustrations: B&W and colour. Occasional need for club pictures. No stock pictures required. 6 × 6 cm minimum.

Text: Features on subjects associated with Mecca bingo clubs. Some home-interest features also considered.

Overall freelance potential: About 20 per cent of copy is contributed.

Editor's tips: Currently compiling a national directory of freelance photographers and writers for use on Mecca-related promotional and PR activities. Freelances interested would do well to contact the editor.

Fees: By arrangement.

CLUB MIRROR

St. Martins Press, 18 Queens Road, Brighton BN1 3XA. Tel: 0273 24238.

Editor: James Dowd.

Monthly publication for officials, committee members and stewards of registered clubs through the UK; proprietary club owners and managers; and discotheque owners and managers.

Illustrations: B&W and colour. Interior pictures of new clubs, new club openings, interesting general pictures of club activities. Covers: Colour shots of girls. No nudes. 6 × 6 cm minimum.

Text: Articles on new club openings, new clubs planned, news stories on clubs, special features on successful clubs. Also features on the club trade, i.e. catering services etc. 100–2,000 words.

Overall freelance potential: Good; 40 per cent from freelance sources.

Fees: By arrangement.

DANCE AND DANCERS

Brevet Publications Ltd., 445 Brighton Road, South Croydon, Surrey CR2 6EU. Tel: 01-660 3602.

Editor: John Percival.

Monthly magazine covering dance and ballet. Includes reviews, features and information on the subject.

Illustrations: B&W only inside. Pictures of current dance performances, occasionally archive and historical material. Covers: Colour pictures of current performances or personalities to tie in with a major feature. Must be up to date. 35mm acceptable.

Text: Profiles of dancers. Reviews of current performances. General features on dance. 500–2,000 words.

PETER O'ROURKE, ARPS

Overall freelance potential: Over 50 per cent is contributed, but mostly from regular contributors.
Editor's tips: Very specialist interest, using ballet/contemporary dance only. No mime, pop dance or ballet school interest.
Fees: Text, £40 per 1,000 words; covers, £40; B&W pictures, negotiable.

ENGLISH DANCE AND SONG
English Folk Dance and Song Society, Folk House, 10 Richmond Road, Exeter, Devon. Tel: 0392 77285.
Editor: Dave Arthur.
Published three times per year for music, dance and song enthusiasts.
Illustrations: B&W only. Pictures of folk singers, musicians, dancers, instruments and traditional customs. Covers: B&W pictures of same.

Text: Features on subjects detailed above. 1,000–2,000 words.
Overall freelance potential: Most material bought from photographers who are folk enthusiasts.
Fees: Variable.

ENTERTAINMENT AND ARTS MANAGEMENT
John Offord Publications, PO Box 64, Eastbourne, East Sussex. Tel: 0323 37841.
Editor: John Offord.
Monthly publication, containing features, news items correspondence etc. on all aspects of entertainment and arts in grant-aided and local government sector.
Illustrations: B&W only on subjects mentioned above, but only by prior arrangement with the Editor. No cover potential, since it consists usually of advertising.
Text: Features on dance, bands, jazz, orchestras, outdoor attractions, summer shows, puppets and a regular coverage of theatre openings and events.
Overall freelance potential: Maybe one outside contributed article per month, plus several regular freelance contributions.
Editor's tips: It is vital to contact the editor before submitting any material.
Fees: Negotiable.

HUNA LONDON
BBC Arabic Service, PO Box 76, Bush House, Strand, London WC2B 4PH. Tel: 01-240 3456 Ext. 2996/2983.
Editor: Douglas Evans.
Monthly magazine for the BBC Arabic Service, combining the *Radio Times* and the *Listener*. Cultural, scientific, technical and literary interests are catered for.
Illustrations: B&W only inside. Pictures of British scenes (town and country) and British personalities, especially in the field of the arts. Also pictures of Arab world subjects. Covers: Colour pictures of British scenes and people; 6 × 6 cm minimum.
Text: Mostly features based on programme slots, but occasionally contributions from elsewhere are used, particularly on sport, motoring and personality interviews. Up to 1,500 words.
Overall freelance potential: Low at present.
Editor's tips: Maximum contrast needed in B&W pictures.
Fees: By negotiation.

MOVIE STAR
Moststar Ltd., 43 Beak Street, London W1R 3LE. Tel: 01-437 1032.
Editors: Willy Daly and Nick Hart.
Monthly entertainments magazine for those between the ages of 18 and 35 who are interested in film stars and gossip. Contains interviews, gossip, film reviews, video and TV news.
Illustrations: B&W and colour. Pictures of film stars. Covers: Colour pictures of film stars; 35mm acceptable.

Text: Features on films and film stars. 1,000–1,500 words.
Overall freelance potential: Good; 80 per cent comes from freelance contributors.
Fees: £60 per article (negotiable).

RADIO TIMES
BBC Publications, 35 Marylebone High Street, London W1M 4AA. Tel: 01-580 5577.
Editor: Brian Gearing.
Weekly magazine containing news and details of BBC radio and television programmes.
Illustrations: Colour and B&W. Pictures concerned with broadcasting events. Covers: Colour pictures of similar.
Text: Features on BBC personalities or programmes of current interest. 1,000 words.
Overall freelance potential: Good.
Fees: Various.

THE STAGE AND TELEVISION TODAY
Carson and Comerford Ltd., 47 Bermondsey Street, London SE1 3XT. Tel: 01-403 1818.
Editor: Peter Hepple.
Weekly newspaper for those professionals engaged in arts and entertainment.
Illustrations: B&W only. News pictures. Pictures of productions. Personality pictures for file.
Text: Features on the theatre and light entertainment. 1,000 words.
Overall freelance potential: Better for writers than for photographers.
Fees: By agreement.

TV TIMES MAGAZINE
Independent Television Publications Ltd., 247 Tottenham Court Road, London W1P 0AU. Tel: 01-636 3666.
Editor: Anthony Peagam.
Weekly magazine containing details and features of current television programmes.
Illustrations: B&W and colour. Very little from the general freelance. Most comes from four staff photographers and TV companies. Other requirements are commissioned or requested from specialist sources. Covers: Quality colour portraits or groups specific to current programme content. 35mm acceptable.
Text: Articles on personalities and programmes in the current week's news. Some specialist openings for cookery, fashion, etc.
Overall freelance potential: Between 10 and 25 per cent each week is freelance, but mostly from recognised contributors.
Editor's tips: Don't try without checking first.
Fees: To be negotiated.

WHAT VIDEO
M&V Publications Ltd., 30 Wellington Street, London WC2. Tel: 01-379 3313.
Editor: Alan Smith.

Monthly magazine for newcomers and enthusiasts in video. Contains test reports, buyers' guide, general features and news of new films on video.
Illustrations: B&W and colour. Pictures of video recorders and 'ordinary people' using them. Covers: Colour pictures of similar. 35mm acceptable.
Text: Technical subjects easily explained plus interviews and showbusiness pieces. 850–1,000 words.
Overall freelance potential: Around 70 per cent is from freelance sources.
Fees: By agreement.

WHICH VIDEO?
Argus Specialist Publications Ltd., 145 Charing Cross Road, London WC2H 0EE. Tel: 01-437 1002.
Editor: Gareth Renowden.
Monthly magazine intended as a consumer's guide to the complicated world of video. Emphasis on tests and reports on domestic equipment. In a wider sense, the magazine also covers anything that can be plugged into a television set.
Illustrations: B&W only. Specialised pictures are sometimes commissioned, although the magazine has a staff photographer. No work accepted on spec.
Text: Features on domestic video or TV applications, but only on commission. Freelances should be prepared to submit examples of their previously-published work prior to commissions. 2,500 words maximum.
Overall freelance potential: Limited at the moment, but growing.
Editor's tips: Study this magazine first. No market for video tape reviewers.
Fees: £30 per published page.

Aviation

FLIGHT SAFETY BULLETIN
General Aviation Safety Committee, Church House, 33 Church Street, Henley-on-Thames, Oxfordshire RG9 1SE. Tel: 04912 4476.
Editor: John Ward.
Quarterly publication aimed at encouraging the development of general aviation in the UK along safe lines through competence among GA pilots and operators, by publishing articles and information on flight safety matters.
Illustrations: B&W only. Anything consistent with the aims of the journal. Pictures which show photographic evidence of a particular story are particularly welcomed.
Text: Features on safety and accident investigations.
Overall freelance potential: Small.
Editor's tips: Contact the editor and discuss proposals before taking any action.
Fees: Depends on the relevance of the subject.

FLIGHT INTERNATIONAL
IPC Transport Press Ltd., Quadrant House, The Quadrant, Sutton, Surrey SM2 5AS. Tel: 01-661 3500.
Editor: David Mason.
Weekly aviation magazine with world-wide circulation, aimed at aerospace professionals in all aspects of the industry.
Illustrations: B&W and colour. Weekly requirement for news pictures of aviation-related events. Feature illustrations on all aspects of aerospace, from hang gliders to satellites. 35mm acceptable inside. Covers: Colour pictures of aircraft—civil and military, light and business. 6 × 6 cm minimum.
Text: Features by prior arrangement with the appropriate section editor on air transport, defence, general aviation and technical subjects. Over 750 words.
Overall freelance potential: Approximately 10 per cent of news and 5 per cent of features come from outside sources.
Editor's tips: News copy must be submitted on spec. Features must be cleared with the appropriate section editor, due to the technical nature of the subject. Pictures should be as new as possible or have a news relevance.
Fees: News reports, £3.70 per 100 words, £37 per 1,000; commissioned features, £43.50 per 1,000 words; B&W pictures, £10.50; colour, £26 up to 30 sq. in., £30–£40 30–60 sq. in., £49.30 for cover.

HELICOPTER INTERNATIONAL
Avia Press Associates, Delta House, Summer Lane, Worle, Weston-super-Mare, Avon BS22 0BE. Tel: 0934 412701.
Editor: Elfan ap Rees.
Bi-monthly publication for military and civil helicopter news coverage, aimed at professional and helicopter industry readership.
Illustrations: B&W and colour *prints*. Newsworthy helicopter pictures, e.g. new types, new purchases, interesting operations, etc. No 'pretty' pictures.
Text: Knowledgeable articles on helicopter operations. Extended picture captions or up to 1,000 words.
Overall freelance potential: Between 60 and 70 per cent comes from freelances.
Fees: Text, £30 per 1,000 words; pictures, £2.50 each.

JOURNAL OF THE GUILD OF AIR PILOTS AND NAVIGATORS
The Guild, 30 Ecclestone Street, London SW1. Tel: 01-730 0471.
Editor: Harry Payne.
Quarterly publication containing news and notices of activities connected with the above guild, plus aviation topics.
Illustrations: B&W only. Pictures of aviation subjects.
Text: Features on general and technical subjects of aviation interest, 1,500 words.
Overall freelance potential: Small.
Fees: £10 per 1,000 words.

PILOT

Lernhurst Publications Ltd., 88 Burlington Road, New Malden, Surrey KT3 4NT. Tel: 01-949 3462.

Editor: James Gilbert.

Monthly publication for the general aviation (i.e. business and private flying) pilot.

Illustrations: Colour and B&W pictures bought on topics associated with this field of flying. Covers: colour; 35mm acceptable.

Text: Features, preferably illustrated, on general aviation. 2,000–3,000 words.

Overall freelance potential: Excellent. One hundred per cent of the magazine is contributed by freelances.

Editor's tips: Read a copy of the magazine before submitting and study style, content, subject and coverage.

Fees: £50–£300 for features. B&W pictures, £15 each; colour pictures, £50 each; covers, £150.

POPULAR FLYING

P.F.A. (Ulair) Ltd., Terminal Building, Shoreham Airport, Shoreham-by-Sea, Sussex BN4 5FF.

Editor: M. K. Grigson.

Bi-monthly for home-builders of small (one–two seater) aircraft. Controlled circulation.

Illustrations: Pictures of vintage and home-built aircraft. Colour and B&W; 35mm acceptable inside the magazine. Covers: colour only; minimum size, 6 × 6 cm.

Text: Features of any length on anything concerning home-built aircraft in the UK.

Overall freelance potential: Very low at the moment. Inadvisable to submit anything without an enquiry.

Fees: By negotiation.

WINGS

British Hang Gliding Association, 167a Cheddon Road, Taunton, Somerset TA2 7AH.

Editor: Stan Abbott.

Monthly publication for British and overseas hang gliding and microlight aviation enthusiasts.

Illustrations: B&W mostly. Most stock and news requirements are catered for. Will consider good hang gliding pictures. Covers: Usually B&W, sometimes colour pictures of hang gliders; 35mm acceptable.

Text: No market for freelances.

Overall freelance potential: Limited market, most work commissioned for an agreed fee.

Fees: On a rising scale with the size of reproduction.

Boating and Nautical

INLAND WATERWAYS GUIDE

Haymarket Publishing Ltd., 38–42 Hampton Road, Teddington, Middlesex TW11 0JE. Tel: 01-977 8787.

RAYMOND LEA

Editor: Colin Pringle.
Annual guide to canals and rivers of Great Britain, containing details of hire companies and services on each waterway. Aimed at consumer holiday and enthusiast readership.
Illustrations: B&W inside. Pictures of canals and rivers in Great Britain. Covers: Colour pictures of British waterways. 35mm acceptable.
Text: Brief reviews of all of Britain's waterways.
Overall freelance potential: Good; 75 per cent comes from outside sources.
Fees: Subject to negotiation.

MOTOR BOAT AND YACHTING
IPC Transport Press Ltd., Quadrant House, The Quadrant, Sutton, Surrey SM2 5AS. Tel: 01-661 3500.
Editor: Alex McMullen.
Monthly magazine for owners and users of motor cruisers and motor sailers.
Illustrations: B&W and colour. Pictures of motor cruisers at sea, harbour scenes, workboats. Covers: Colour pictures, mostly of motor boats at sea. Also good harbour scenes, showing exceptional composition and/or lighting. Only vertical shots with space for magazine logo. 35mm acceptable.
Text: Features on interesting, unusual or historic motor boats; first-person motor boat cruising accounts; technical motor boating topics; inland waterways topics. 1,500–2,500 words.
Overall freelance potential: Around 60 per cent of features and 40 per cent of pictures are contributed.
Editor's tips: Particularly interested in pictures of motor boats under way.
Fees: Good; on a rising scale according to the size of reproduction or length of article. Covers, £90.

POPULAR MOTOR CRUISER
Motor Cruiser Ltd., 37/39 Church Street, Lenton, Nottingham NG7 2FH. Tel: 0602 704558/704578.
Editor: John Beadsmoore.
Monthly magazine dealing with all types of motor boat, from large motor cruisers down to motorised dinghies, and aimed at the less wealthy boat owner.
Illustrations: B&W and colour. Pictures of all types of motor vessel, especially less common craft such as old boats, MTB conversions, and so on, plus pictures of people involved in some activity obviously connected with motor cruising. Also shots of locations suitable for motor cruising—rivers, canals, estuaries and coastal waters, but not deep sea locations. Covers: Striking colour shots related to the subject.
Text: Articles and features, of around 1500 words, on any practical aspect of motor cruising.
Overall freelance potential: Plenty of scope for good material.
Fees: By negotiation.

PRACTICAL BOAT OWNER
IPC Magazines Ltd., Westover House, West Quay Road, Poole, Dorset BH15 1JG. Tel: 0202 71191.

Editor: Denny Desoutter.
Monthly magazine for yachtsmen, sail and power.
Illustrations: B&W and colour. Pictures of pleasure craft, sail and power, and their equipment. Shots relating to their use, including sea marks such as light houses, harbours, etc. No 'mood' pictures. Covers: Colour pictures of pleasure boating subjects; happy with strong colours. 35mm acceptable.
Text: Features and associated illustrations must be of real use to the people who own boats. Subjects can cover any boating facet on which the reader might take action, from raising the money to buy a boat, through insurance to navigation, seamanship, care and maintenance etc. No narrative yarns.
Overall freelance potential: About 60 per cent bought from contributors.
Fees: Good; on a rising scale according to size of reproduction or length of feature.

RYA NEWS

Royal Yachting Association, Victoria Way, Woking, Surrey GU21 1EQ. Tel: 048-62 5022.
Editor: Araminta Webb.
Publication for all personal members of the RYA, affiliated clubs and class associations. Published three times per year.
Illustrations: B&W pictures of boats, yachting events and personalities, used either in their own right or as illustrations for reports and articles.
Text: Reports and articles on yachting.
Overall freelance potential: Fair.
Fees: By arrangement.

SEA BREEZES

Jocast Ltd., 202 Cotton Exchange Building, Old Hall Street, Liverpool, L3 9LA. Tel: 051-236 3935/6.
Editor: Craig Carter.
Monthly publication concerned with merchant ships, shipping companies and seamen; docks and harbours, past and present; maritime history; warships and naval affairs. Aimed at anyone interested in ships of the world.
Illustrations: Not a lot of freelance scope inside the magazine. Covers: Good, colourful pictures of ships or shipping scenes. 35mm acceptable.
Text: Shipping company histories. Ships in the news. General maritime subjects. Up to 3,000 words.
Overall freelance potential: Small, since most contributors are regular specialists.
Fees: By arrangement.

WATERWAYS WORLD

Waterway Productions Ltd., Kottingham House, Dale Street, Burton-on-Trent DE14 3TD. Tel: 0283 64290/42721.
Editor: Hugh Potter.

Monthly magazine that covers all aspects of canal and river navigations (not lakes) in Britain and abroad. Aimed at inland waterway enthusiasts and holiday boaters.
Illustrations: B&W inside. Pictures of inland waterway subjects, e.g. interesting buildings; locks, preferably with boating activity if on a navigable waterway; canal scenes. No close-ups or artistic shots. Covers: Colour pictures of canal or river scenes with boating activity prominently in the foreground; 6 × 6 cm minimum.
Text: Features on inland waterways. Send SAE for contributors' guide. 1,000–2,000 words.
Overall freelance potential: Around 20 per cent contributed.
Fees: B&W £3.50; Cover, £15.

YACHTING AND BOATING

Trekstar Ltd., 9 Bridge Street, Loddon, Norfolk. Tel: 0508 28198.
Editor: M. de Boltz.
Monthly publication for the dinghy and cruiser owner involved in cruising and racing. Also for beginners to the sport.
Illustrations: B&W only. Racing events. Also for use with features. Covers: Active yachting pictures that are topical. B&W only.
Text: Racing reports. Features on the sport. (Annual feature list available.) 500–1,500 words.
Overall freelance potential: Approximately 20 per cent from outside sources.
Fees: By negotiation.

YACHTING MONTHLY

IPC Magazines Ltd., Room 2333, King's Reach Tower, Stamford Street, London SE1 9LS. Tel: 01-261 6040.
Editor: J. D. Sleightholme.
Monthly magazine for off-shore/cruising yachtsmen.
Illustrations: B&W and colour. Technical shots, news: mainly in B&W. Covers: Colour pictures showing active cruising; 35mm acceptable.
Text: Technical articles relevant to cruising yachtsmen and short cruising stories. 2,500–3,000 words.
Overall freelance potential: Around 25 per cent comes from outside contributors.
Editor's tips: Study the magazine before submitting.
Fees: Good; on a rising scale, according to the size of reproduction or length of feature.

YACHTING WORLD

IPC Transport Press Ltd., Quadrant House, The Quadrant, Sutton, Surrey, SM2 5AS. Tel: 01-661 3314.
Editor: Dick Johnson.
Monthly magazine for informed yachtsmen, experienced and with their own boats.
Illustrations: B&W and colour. Pictures of general yachting techniques or types of boat; pictures of events and occasions. Covers: Colour pictures of yachts, on board, at sea or

general harbour pictures. No dinghies. 35mm acceptable if vertical, otherwise 6 × 6 cm minimum.

Text: Informative or narrative yachting articles; technical yachting features; short humorous articles; and news. 1,000–1,500 words and 2,000–3,000 words.

Overall freelance potential: Around 30 per cent comes from freelances.

Editor's tips: Articles should be accompanied by colour and B/W illustrations. All material should have the name and address of the contributor clearly marked. Do not exceed noted article lengths.

Fees: Text, £41 per 1,000 words; covers, £99; inside pictures on a scale according to size.

YACHTS AND YACHTING

Yachting Press Ltd., 196 Eastern Esplanade, Southend-on-Sea, Essex. Tel: 0702 582245.

Editor: Peter Cook.

Fortnightly publication covering all aspects of racing, including dinghies, offshore racers and sailboarding.

Illustrations: B&W pictures only inside. Pictures of racing dinghies, yachts and general sailing scenes. Covers: Colour action shots; 35mm acceptable.

Text: Features on all aspects of the sailing scene. 1,500–3,000 words.

Overall freelance potential: Quite good.

Fees: Negotiable.

Building and Engineering

BUILDER AND MERCHANT

The Builder Ltd., Builder House, Mayors Road, Altrincham, Cheshire WA15 9RP. Tel: 061-928 8856.

Editor: Philip Champion.

Monthly publication for builders and builders' merchants.

Illustrations: B&W and occasional colour. Pictures of construction work.

Text: Features related to building, construction etc. 300–1,000 words.

Overall freelance potential: Small.

Fees: Text, up to £60 per 1,000 words; pictures by negotiation.

THE BUILDERS MERCHANT

The Builders Merchants Federation, 15 Soho Square, London W1V 5FB. Tel: 01-439 1753.

Editor: Tony Mullard.

Monthly publication of the Builders Merchants Federation.

Illustrations: B&W only. Pictures for use with articles.

Text: Features on building, home improvements, kitchens, bathrooms, heating, etc. 250–1,000 words.

Overall freelance potential: Around 10 per cent comes from freelance sources.

Fees: Text, £100 per 1,000 words; pictures by agreement.

BUILDERS MERCHANTS NEWS
B&M Publications Ltd., PO Box 13, Hereford House, Bridle Path, Croydon CR9 4NL. Tel: 01-680 4200.
Editor: Paul Murray.
Monthly publication for builders' and plumbers' merchants, home improvement centres, large hardware and discount stores, kitchen and bathroom specialist retailers, architects, architectural ironmongers, wholesalers and distributors.
Illustrations: No freelance market.
Text: Business articles regarding merchants and merchanting.
Overall freelance potential: Variable.
Fees: By agreement.

BUILDING SERVICES AND ENVIRONMENTAL ENGINEER
Batiste Publications Ltd., Pembroke House, Campsbourne Road, London N8 7PT. Tel: 01-340 3291.
Editor: Ken Sharpe.
Monthly publication for the building services industry, particularly heating, ventilating and air conditioning.
Illustrations: Covers only: Colour pictures on building services themes. 6 × 6 cm minimum.
Text: Features of interest to the readership detailed above. 1,000–1,500 words.
Overall freelance potential: Limited.
Fees: Text, around £50 per 1,000 words; pictures by negotiation.

THE CHARTERED MECHANICAL ENGINEER
Mechanical Engineering Publications Ltd., PO 24 Northgate Avenue, Bury St. Edmunds, Suffolk IP32 6BW. Tel: 0284 63277.
Editor: Roy Cullum.
Monthly publication for members of the Institution of Mechanical Engineers.
Illustrations: B&W inside. Pictures of general and specific mechanical engineering subjects, preferably showing action; new equipment, applications, etc. Covers: Usually sold to advertiser, but would consider colour pictures of above subjects to fill in where no space has been sold. 35mm acceptable.
Text: Features with a general engineering bias with a fairly high technical level, e.g. new equipment, processes, materials applications, etc. 2,000–2,500 words.
Overall freelance potential: A considerable amount of the magazine is freelance-contributed.
Fees: Not less than around £40 per 1,000 words published; pictures by agreement.

CONSTRUCTION AND PROPERTY NEWS
Construction and Property News Ltd., 175 North Strand Road, Dublin 1. Tel: 0001 742265.
Editor: Mary Eaton.
Weekly publication concerned with construction and engineering, aimed at builders, engineers, architects, manufacturers and suppliers.

Illustrations: B&W only. Good architectural pictures of recently completed Southern Irish buildings. Interesting site shots showing plant in action. Notable concrete pours. No arty shots of ancient monuments.
Text: Stories and articles related to the construction and engineering industries in Ireland. Must be newsworthy. 500–750 words—tightly written.
Overall freelance potential: Low, although the magazine always needs good technical content in a feature, couched in understandable terms and without superfluous verbiage.
Fees: £10–£20 according to content.

CONSTRUCTION SURVEYOR

Construction Surveyors' Institute, 111 Lynton Road, Chesham, Bucks. HP5 2BP. Tel: 0494 772127.
Editor: Jane Hinkley.
Quarterly journal for construction surveyors.
Illustrations: B&W only of general construction/building subjects. Sometimes education pictures are used, e.g. students working in the industry. Covers: Any construction/building topic in the news or of current interest. No colour.
Text: Features on anything of topical interest to those working in construction in the UK or overseas. 1,000–3,000 words.
Overall freelance potential: Small.
Fees: Negotiable.

DESIGN ENGINEERING

Morgan-Grampian Ltd., 30 Calderwood Street, Woolwich, London SE18 6QH. Tel: 01-855 7777.
Editor: C. Robbie Robinson.
Monthly publication aimed at engineering designers and design management. Contains case histories, background data, surveys, products and news stories.
Illustrations: B&W and colour. Only tied in with features and news stories. Covers: Colour pictures associated with editorial inside. 6 × 6 cm minimum.
Text: Features on subjects such as fluid power, electronics, materials etc. Only from experts in their fields. 500–4,000 words.
Overall freelance potential: Open only to specialist technologists.
Editor's tips: Send synopsis first.
Fees: Covers, approximately £90; text and pictures inside by negotiation.

ENERGY IN BUILDINGS

Energy Group Publications Ltd., 30 St Georges Place, Cheltenham, GL50 3JZ. Tel: 0242 42752.
Editor: Ted Stevens.
Monthly magazine concerned with the use and conservation of energy in large buildings. Aimed at architects, energy managers, building and service engineers, and energy consultants.

Illustrations: B&W only. Limited scope for single atmospheric shots that strongly epitomise energy, or that show striking contrasts in the energy field.
Text: Some scope for writer/photographers who have good knowledge of the energy business.
Overall freelance potential: Small, unless contributors have connections within the field.
Fees: £15–£20 per picture; £50 per 1,000 words for text.

THE ENGINEER

Morgan Grampian Ltd., 30 Calderwood Street, Woolwich, London SE18 6QH. Tel: 01-855 7777.
Editor: Rob Golding.
Weekly publication for engineering management.
Illustrations: B&W and colour. Pictures showing new technology in action. Must have a news angle. Covers: Colour pictures of news in the business. 35mm acceptable.
Text: News of manufacturing industries and personnel, plus articles on technology trends. Up to 800 words.
Overall freelance potential: Small.
Fees: Text, £60 per 1,000 words; pictures by agreement.

H&V NEWS

Maclaren Publishers Ltd., PO Box 109, Maclaren House, Scarbrook Road, Croydon CR9 1QH. Tel: 01-688 7788.
Editor: Keith Sutton.
Weekly publication to all those who purchase or specify in organisations connected with heating, ventilating and air conditioning equipment.
Illustrations: B&W only inside. Action pictures of installations and equipment in use, preferably with human interest. Covers: Colour pictures tied in with specific equipment. 35mm acceptable.
Text: News stories, installation stories regarding heating, ventilating and air conditioning equipment. 200–300 words, longer features by negotiation.
Overall freelance potential: Dependent on merit and/or newsworthiness.
Editor's tips: The more current the information supplied, the better its chance of success.
Fees: £6 per 100 words; pictures by negotiation.

HEATING AND VENTILATING REVIEW

H&V Publications Ltd., 111 St. Jame's Road, Croydon, Surrey CR9 2TH. Tel: 01-684 4082.
Editor: Monty Burton.
Monthly publication covering domestic, commercial and industrial markets for all heating and ventilating. Aimed at engineers, contractors, specifiers and purchasers.
Illustrations: B&W and colour. Pictures of installations, exhibitions, personalities etc. (Most of these come from PR companies.) Covers: Colour pictures of installations or special products within the field.
Text: Trade interest stories only, connected with heating and ventilation. No consumer, technical or commercial articles. 1,500 words.

Overall freelance potential: Very low, since most material comes from PR companies and manufacturers.
Editor's tips: Intending contributors are advised to telephone first with ideas.
Fees: By negotiation.

HOUSE BUILDER
Federated Employers Press Ltd., 82 New Cavendish Street, London W1M 8AD. Tel: 01-580 5588.
Editor: Phillip Cooke.
Monthly journal of the Housebuilders Federation. Aimed at key decision-makers, managers, technical staff, marketing executives, architects and local authorities.
Illustrations: A possible market but not without prior consultation with the Editor.
Text: Features on marketing, land and planning, government liason, finance, materials, supplies, etc. All to be discussed before submission. 1,000 words.
Overall freelance potential: Around 50 per cent comes from freelances.
Editor's tips: Authoritative articles and news stories only. No PR 'puffs'.
Fees: £70 per 1,000 words; pictures by agreement.

JOURNAL OF THE CHARTERED INSTITUTION OF BUILDING SERVICES
Building Services Publications Ltd., Builder House, 1–3 Pemberton Row, London EC4P 4HL. Tel: 01-353 2300.
Editor: Stephen Ashley.
Monthly publication for engineers and senior management involved with installing heating, air conditioning, ventilation, lighting, lifts, telephones, hot and cold water systems etc. into buildings.
Illustrations: B&W and colour. Good quality pictures of building services. Pictures used for caption stories and for stock. 35mm acceptable. Covers: Colour, but usually commissioned.
Text: Ideas for articles on the above subjects. 2,500 words maximum.
Overall freelance potential: Good, since very few pictures of this subject are offered.
Editor's tips: Telephone calls and ideas for pictures and features are very welcome.
Fees: By negotiation.

MARINE ENGINEERS' REVIEW
Marine Management Holdings, Institute of Marine Engineers, 76 Mark Lane, London EC3R 7JN. Tel: 01-481 8493.
Editor: John Butchers.
Monthly publication for marine engineers.
Illustrations: B&W only for use inside the magazine, showing ships and marine machinery. No cover potential.
Text: Articles on shipping and marine engineering, including naval topics. Up to 3,000 words.

Overall freelance potential: Very little at the moment, but could take more.
Editor's tips: Enquire before submitting.
Fees: £40 per 1,000 words. Pictures by negotiation.

MIDDLE EAST CONSTRUCTION
New World Publishers Ltd., (Subsidiary of IPC Business Press Ltd.), Surrey House, 1 Throwley Way, Sutton, Surrey, SM1 4QQ. Tel: 01-643 8040, ext. 4674.
Editor: Anthony Davis.
Monthly publication for engineers, architects, surveyors, contractors and other senior management personnel in building, civil engineering and public works design and construction, plus those in importation and distribution of plant, equipment and building materials and components.
Illustrations: B&W and colour. By arrangement only. 35mm acceptable.
Text: Features on design and construction in the Middle East and North Africa. 1,000–1,500 words.
Overall freelance potential: Approximately 50 per cent of the publication comes from freelances, but mostly regular correspondents in the Middle East.
Editor's tips: It is essential to contact the magazine before submitting anything.
Fees: By negotiation.

PROCESS ENGINEERING
Morgan-Grampian (Process Press) Ltd., 30 Calderwood Street, Woolwich, London SE18 6QH. Tel: 01-855 7777.
Editor: Clive Tayler.
Monthly publication for process engineers. Read by chemical plant contractors, senior engineers and management employed in the chemical and process industries responsible for the design, construction, operation and maintenance of process plant, control systems and equipment.
Illustrations: B&W and colour. Pictures of process engineering applications. Covers: Colour pictures of a similar subject; 6 × 6 cm minimum.
Text: Features on process engineering and management articles. Up to 2,000 words.
Overall freelance potential: Minimal at present.
Editor's tips: Telephone editor or art editor if more background is required.
Fees: By agreement.

Business and Industry

ACCOUNTANCY AGE
VNU Business Publications, 53–55 Frith Street, London W1A 2HG. Tel: 01-439 4242.
Editor: Robert Bruce.
Weekly publication for qualified accounts.

Illustrations: B&W only. Pictures always commissioned but new photographers are always welcome.
Text: Articles on accountancy and aspects thereof. Synopsis preferred in first instance. 1,200 words.
Overall freelance potential: All pictures are commissioned and about 50 per cent of the features come from freelances.
Editor's tips: To gain acceptance, articles must contribute something which cannot be provided by the in-house staff.
Fees: Pictures, £50 for one subject, six or seven pictures, of which four might be used; articles by agreement.

AFRICA ECONOMIC DIGEST
Middle East Media Ltd., 21 John Street, London WC1N 2BP. Tel: 01-404 5513 Ext. 223.
Editor: Peter Robbs.
Weekly review of African business and general economic developments. Aimed at senior executives of banks, trading and manufacturing companies etc.
Illustrations: B&W only inside. Pictures of African economic and business life, including major development projects, agriculture, transport, ports, shipping, buildings, personalities and economic 'events'. Covers: Colour pictures of similar subjects, plus more general African shots. No sunsets, lions or tribal dancers. 35mm acceptable.
Text: Commissioned feature on above subjects considered. Contact editor first. Up to 1,000 words.
Overall freelance potential: A lot of material comes from agencies, but freelance approaches are welcome.
Fees: Negotiable.

AIR CUSHION REVIEW
128 Queens Road, Portsmouth, Hampshire PO2 7NE. Tel: 0705 661211.
Editor: Alan Bliault.
Bi-monthly publication covering all aspects of air cushion technology, including industrial, technical, sport, military, news.
Illustrations: B&W and colour. Pictures welcomed for both stock and news items. Requirements include pictures of hovercraft, surface effect ships, associated equipment and personnel, hover platforms and conveyor systems. Covers: Topical events or classic pictures of hovercraft etc. 10 × 8 inch colour prints preferred.
Text: Features on any subject connected with air cushion technology.
Overall freelance potential: Between 10 and 33 per cent of the publication is provided by freelances.
Editor's tips: This is a specialist magazine, but it is always looking for ways to increase its coverage.
Fees: By negotiation.

ALAM ATTIJARAT

Johnston International, 2 Pear Tree Court, London EC1. Tel: 01-250 4114.
Editor: Joseph Mach'hour.
Monthly Arabic magazine concerned with business, economic and trade topics. Aimed at businessmen and government officials.
Illustrations: B&W and colour. Pictures of projects in the Middle East.
Text: Interviews with businessmen and government officials. Features on development and economic subjects.
Overall freelance potential: Fair.
Fees: By agreement.

THE ANNUAL INVESTMENT FILE

Urban Publishing Co., 17 The Green, Richmond, Surrey TW9 1PX. Tel: 01-948 5721.
Editor: Taum von Hove.
Annual investment publication for industry and finance.
Illustrations: B&W only. Pictures related to corporate strategy, labour, real estate, finance, energy and industry in various different countries.
Text: Features connected with worldwide industrial investment. 2,000–3,000 words.
Overall freelance potential: Around 50 per cent of the contents come from freelances.
Fees: Good; on a rising scale according to size of reproduction or length of feature.

APPAREL INTERNATIONAL

Piel-Caru Publishing Ltd., 51 Hillcrest Road, Purley, Surrey CR2 2JF. Tel: 01-660 6267.
Editor: Kenneth Clark.
Monthly publication for clothing and footwear manufacturers.
Illustrations: B&W only. News pictures and pictures of individual processes in the trade.
Text: Features on manufacturing and marketing of clothing and footwear. 1,000 words.
Overall freelance potential: Limited, owing to specialist nature of the subject matter.
Fees: News pictures, £15; industrial pictures and words by arrangement.

AQUA

International Water Supply Association, 1 Queen Anne's Gate, London. SW1H 9BT. Tel: 01-222 9675.
Editor: Russell Clark.
Bi-monthly journal to convey the latest information on technology in water services. Provides a platform for ideas and opinions of experts in the water services sector world-wide and a commentary on the activities of the IWSA.
Illustrations: B&W inside. Pictures of water installations anywhere in the world—clean and dirty water, coastal waters, sewerage etc. People engaged in water services. All equipment from the primitive to the most sophisticated. Covers: Colour close-ups, *not scenes*, which convey a story about the industry or serve to focus on special problems.
Text: Features on any water-related subjects for public use from amenity uses to cleaning of dirty water; distribution, treatment etc. Text should be in English or French with summary in the alternative language, or preferably, a complete translation.

Overall freelance potential: Always a market for authoritative technical features; 50 per cent comes from freelance sources.
Editor's tips: Interested only in facts, not verbiage. All pictures must be fully captioned.
Fees: £50 maximum.

ASSOCIATION MANAGEMENT
J. J. Watford Ltd., 21 Farley Hill, Luton, Beds. LU1 5EE. Tel: 0582 32640.
Editor: George Mills.
Monthly publication for association managers.
Illustrations: No freelance market.
Text: Features on the education of members, services to members and technological aids to associations Approximately 1,500 words.
Overall freelance potential: Good market for new contributors.
Fees: £35 per 1,000 words.

ATOM NEWS
UK Atomic Energy Authority, Room 113, 11 Charles II Street, London SW1Y 4QP. Tel: 01-930 5454 Ext 302/456.
Editor: Derek Gomer.
Monthly newspaper for employees of UK Atomic Energy Authority. Non-technical readership.
Illustrations: B&W only. Pictures of social events involving employees. News rather than feature pictures are preferred.
Text: Topical news coverage of events involving employees and family. Up to 500 words.
Overall freelance potential: Around 10 percent of the news pictures come from freelance photographers.
Fees: Pictures from £15, rising according to size of reproduction. Text by agreement.

THE AUTHOR
The Society of Authors, 84 Drayton Gardens, London SW10 95D. Tel: 01-373 6642.
Editor: Richard Findlater.
Quarterly publication dealing with the business of authorship, e.g. financial, legal, contractual, social and historical side of writing.
Illustrations: B&W only. Usually only portraits of authors.
Text: Features on the sides of authorship detailed above. Up to 1,200 words.
Overall freelance potential: About 50 per cent of the editorial is contributed.
Fees: £30 per 1,000 words.

BAKER'S REVIEW
Turret Press, 886 High Road, Finchley, London N12 9SB. Tel: 01-446 2411 Ext 62.
Editor: Brenda Ross.
Monthly journal of the National Association of Master Bakers, Confectioners and Caterers. Aimed at management of independent bakeries.

Illustrations: B&W only. Pictures of bakery equipment in use in bakeries, plus bakery products.
Text: Articles on aspects of running a small business. 1,000 words.
Overall freelance potential: Small, since this is a highly specialised subject and most articles are written in-house.
Fees: Negotiable.

BARCLAY NEWS

Barclays Banks Plc., 68 Lombard Street, London EC3P 3AH. Tel: 01-626 1567. Ext. 4263/3267.
Editor: Michael Gowers.
Monthly group newspaper for Barclays Bank.
Illustrations: B&W and occasional colour. Pictures that relate to the bank, its staff and customers. Also the bank's history, travel, cars, wine. 35mm acceptable.
Text: Features with a specific interest to Barclays bank, its customers and staff. 300–500 words.
Overall freelance potential: The newspaper has its own team of journalists, but they are always on the lookout for items of interest throughout the country that might not have come to their attention.
Editor's tips: Check first and a direct indication of interest will be given.
Fees: Negotiable.

BLINDS AND SHUTTERS

Wheatland Journals Ltd., Penn House, Penn Place, Rickmansworth, Herts. WD3 1SN. Tel: 0923 774262.
Editor: Colin Briers.
Quarterly publication for members of the British Blinds and Shutters Association, architects, specifiers, builders, or any body with an interest in the blinds and shutters industry.
Illustrations: B&W and colour. Pictures of buildings, rooms etc. showing blinds or shutters *in situ*; exhibitions featuring stands of BBSA members; new products in the field. Covers: no market at the moment, but colour pictures being considered for the future; 35mm acceptable.
Text: Features on any subject relating to the blinds and shutters industry. 200–2,500 words.
Overall freelance potential: Small.
Fees: Between £10 and £60 by agreement for text and/or pictures.

BPMA NEWS

Headline Promotions, Osborn House, 21–25 Lower Stone Street, Maidstone, Kent ME15 6YT. Tel: 0622 671081.
Editor: Leonard Baskett.
Bi-monthly newspaper for members of the British Premium Merchandise Association.
Illustrations: B&W only. Pictures connected with BPMA members. News pictures of new products.

Text: News and features of interest to BPMA members. News of products that could be used by this market.
Overall freelance potential: Small.
Fees: By agreement.

BRITISH GERMAN TRADE

German Chamber of Industry and Commerce, 12–13 Suffolk Street, London SW1Y 4HG. Tel: 01-930 7251.
Editor: Klaus Balzer, Rolf Prudent and Angelika Schwanhausser.
Commercial, industrial and political publication, circulated free to members of the German Chamber in the UK, Federal Republic, as well as to trade associations in both countries. Published monthly.
Illustrations: B&W only. Most pictures come from Germany, but there is an occasional market for freelance pictures of British politicians, trade unionists, industrialists etc.
Text: Topical issues concerning British industry, commerce, politics etc., with a German readership in mind. Around 2,500 words.
Overall freelance potential: Most articles are written in-house or by regular freelances. An occasional market for the more general freelance.
Fees: £30–40 per item.

THE BRITISH INSURANCE BROKER

British Insurance Brokers' Association, 130 Fenchurch Street, London EC3M 5DJ. Tel: 01-623 9043.
Editor: Dr. Eamonn Butler.
Monthly magazine for insurance brokers.
Illustrations: B&W only inside the magazine. Limited amount bought on subjects of interest to the market. Covers: Colour on related topics; 35mm acceptable.
Text: Features on insurance topics. 1,500–2,000 words.
Overall freelance potential: Small.
Fees: By agreement.

BUSINESS CREDIT

Quaintance and Co. (Publishers) Ltd., Cresta House, 20 Leas Road, Guildford, Surrey GU1 4HG. Tel: 0483 67965.
Editor: H. Quaintance.
Bi-monthly publication concerned with banking, finance, credit and insurance industries.
Illustrations: Only by commission.
Text: Features on the above industries. Around 1,500 words.
Overall freelance potential: Fair.
Fees: By agreement.

BUSINESS IN NORTHAMPTONSHIRE

Barwell-Gurney Advertising Company Ltd., Herald House, Church Street, Luton, Beds. LU1 3JG. Tel: 0582 415061.

Editor: Jonathon Gornell.

Monthly publication aimed at the managers of businesses throughout the region.

Illustrations: B&W only. Pictures concerned with business, e.g. computers, insurance, worker management, relationship between education and industry, etc.

Text: Features on business with a local angle. 100 words shorts, 400 word stories and 800 word features.

Overall freelance potential: The magazine is interested in hearing from photographers who might join their team of regular contributors.

Fees: Photographers are paid at the rate of £10 per picture plus expenses on the basis that they work for a full day, averaging about eight pictures in that day.

BUSINESS INFORMATION TECHNOLOGY

Business Publications Ltd., 109–119 Waterloo Road, London SE1 8UL. Tel: 01-928 3388.

Editor: Charles Newman.

Monthly guide to new technologies in business, covering data processing, office automation and communications. Aimed at senior management and non-expert business people who want to make the most of new technologies in their businesses.

Illustrations: Any suitable photographic contributions will be considered. B&W only. Covers: Colour illustrations are often commissioned from freelances. In all cases, contact the Editor first.

Text: Features are commissioned on the subject. Apply first to editor. 1,200 words.

Overall freelance potential: Variable.

Fees: By arrangement.

CABINET MAKER AND RETAIL FURNISHER

Benn Publications Ltd., Sovereign Way, Tonbridge, Kent TN9 1RW. Tel: 0732 364422.

Editor: George White.

Weekly publication for all those in the furniture and furnishing trade and industry.

Illustrations: Freelances are commissioned to cover news assignments in the trade. Pictures to illustrate features.

Text: Features about companies starting to make furniture for sale to retailers and interior designers. Length from one to twelve pages (1,000 words plus three pictures makes two pages).

Overall freelance potential: Around 10 per cent, including news coverage.

Editor's tips: It is best to approach the editor, features editor or news editor for a brief before submitting.

Fees: By agreement.

CERTIFIED ACCOUNTANT

Chapter Three Publications Ltd., 8A Hythe Street, Dartford, Kent. Tel.: 0322 28584.

Editor: Leon Hopkins.

Monthly journal of the Association of Chartered Accountants.

Illustrations: B&W only. Commissioned as required.
Text: Articles on accountancy, taxation and finance. 1,000–2,000 words.
Overall freelance potential: Around 10 per cent comes from freelances.
Fees: Text, £40 per 1,000 words; pictures by agreement.

COIL WINDING INTERNATIONAL

Henhelds Ltd., PO Box 1, Ferndown, Wimborne, Dorset BH22 9SY. Tel: 0202 891339.
Editor: J. C. McNeill.
Published three times per year for electrical/electronic original equipment manufacturers.
Illustrations: B&W only. Pictures of automatic production machines, processes, components, all relating to wound components.
Text: Features on new techniques in the production of electric motors, transformers, etc. 1,500–2,000 words.
Overall freelance potential: Small.
Fees: By agreement.

COIN LAUNDRY NEWS

John Laithwaite Associates, Belmont Trading Estate, Rochdale Road, Sowerby Bridge, West Yorkshire. Tel: 0422 32428.
Editor: John Laithwaite.
Published twice a year for anyone involved in heavy-duty 'on premise' laundry systems and launderette owners.
Illustrations: B&W only considered, dependent on price. Subjects concerned with the trade.
Text: Features on new developments and the history of laundry equipment. 500–1,000 words.
Overall freelance potential: 'Variable.'
Editor's tips: No unsolicited material is considered. All ideas should be discussed first by telephone.
Fees: Negotiable.

COMMERCE INTERNATIONAL

Guardian Communications Ltd., Queensway House, Redhill, Surrey RH1 IQ5. Tel: 0737 68611.
Editor: C. B. H. Bailey-Watson.
Monthly journal of the London Chamber of Commerce and Industry, aimed at directors, proprietors and partners of companies and firms registered with the organisation. Its interest ranges from giant corporations such as Shell and ICI, right down to the one-man business.
Illustrations: Good London scenes of serious, as opposed to populist appeal are always welcome. B&W only for both inside and cover use.
Text: Commercial, industrial, export, transport, communications and business administration features. 150–1,500 words.

Overall freelance potential: Good. The publication is always open to receive new material. If it is good enough and fits the subject requirements, it has a reasonable chance of being used.

Editor's tips: Pictures should be sharp and not too contrasty. They should show a good centre of interest, uncluttered by surroundings. Text should be short, sharp and to the point.

Fees: £50 per 1,000 words. £12.50 for a single picture. £10 per picture for multiple pictures.

COMPUTER TALK

IPC Electrical-Electronic Press, Quadrant House, The Quadrant, Sutton, Surrey SM2 5AS. Tel: 01-661 3500.

Editor: Judith Morris.

Weekly publication for computer professionals.

Illustrations: B&W only. Pictures of people, rarely machines. The people concerned are usually in the computer business.

Text: Articles of technical and non-technical interest to computer professionals.

Overall freelance potential: Approximately £800 worth bought each month.

Fees: Features, £70; stock pictures, £20, commissioned pictures, £40.

CONFERENCE BRITAIN

International Trade Publications Ltd., Queensway House, 2 Queensway, Redhill, Surrey. Tel: 0737 68611.

Editor: Robert Redman.

Quarterly publication for conference and exhibition organisers worldwide.

Illustrations: No freelance market.

Text: Specifically commissioned features only. 1,500 words.

Overall freelance potential: Small.

Fees: By agreement.

CONTAINERISATION INTERNATIONAL

National Magazine Co. Ltd., 72 Broadwick Street, London W1V 2BP. Tel: 01-439 7144.

Editor: Jane Boyes.

Monthly business-oriented magazine on issues facing the international container transport industry.

Illustrations: B&W and occasional colour. Unusual pictures of container shipping activities, especially in exotic locations overseas.

Text: Well-researched and *exclusive* articles, preferably on some aspect of the container transport business not covered by staff writers, e.g. insurance, use of computers, etc. Around 2,000 words.

Overall freelance potential: About 5 per cent comes from freelance sources.

Fees: By agreement.

LORNA MINTON

CUMBRIA WEEKLY DIGEST

Lakescene Publications, 12 Lonsdale Street. Carlisle CA1 1DD. Tel: 0228 24321.
Editor: John Barker.
Weekly business and property journal for professionals, businessmen and industrialists.
Illustrations: No freelance market.
Text: Features about business in Cumbria. 500 words.
Overall freelance potential: No market for photographers. Very good for writers, if the material is suitable.
Fees: By negotiation.

DATA BUSINESS

VNU Business Publications, 53–55 Frith Street, London W1A 2HG. Tel: 01-439 4242.
Editor: Roger Cowe.
Monthly supplement to *Accountancy Age*. Deals with computers for accountancy uses in a non-technical way.
Illustrations: B&W only. All pictures commissioned.
Text: By commission. 1,200 words.
Overall freelance potential: All pictures are commissioned from freelances. Slightly more than 50 per cent of the articles come from freelance sources.
Fees: Pictures, £50 for one subject, six or seven pictures, of which four might be used; articles by agreement.

THE DIRECTOR

Institute of Directors, 116 Pall Mall, London SW1Y 5ED. Tel: 01-839 1233.
Editor: George Bull.
Monthly magazine for boardroom directors.
Illustrations: B&W only inside the magazine. Pictures showing overseas surveys of particular areas, i.e. Far East, Singapore, Japan, New York, etc. Covers: Colour pictures, usually linked to company chairmen or personalities. 35mm acceptable, but 6 × 6 cm preferred.
Text: No freelance market.
Overall freelance potential: Small.
Fees: By negotiation.

THE ECONOMIST

The Economist Newspaper Ltd., 25 St. James's Street, London SW1A 1HG. Tel: 01-839 7000.
Editor: Andrew Knight.
Weekly publication covering world political, business and scientific affairs.
Illustrations: B&W only inside. Pictures of politicians, businessmen, social conditions (housing, health service etc.), major industries (e.g. coal, steel, oil, motor, agriculture etc.). Always prepared to keep pictures for stock. Covers: Colour pictures of a topical and political nature; 35mm acceptable.

Text: No unsolicited articles.
Overall freelance potential: Around 20 per cent of the issue comes from freelance photographers.
Editor's tips: Telephone picture editor for an appointment to view work. Contact sheets preferred.
Fees: On a rising scale according to size of reproduction inside; covers, £125.

ENERGY ECONOMICS

Butterworth Scientific Ltd., P.O. Box 63, Westbury House, Bury Street, Guildford GU2 5BH. Tel: 0483 31261.
Editor: L. H. Driscoll.
Bi-monthly publication containing articles concerned with economic theory and its application, methodology, statistics and mathematical modelling. Aimed at post graduate level of readership.
Illustrations: No freelance market.
Text: Features on any topic dealing with the economic analysis of energy. 6,000 words.
Overall freelance potential: Small.
Editor's tips: All articles are refereed.
Fees: £60 for commissioned work. No fees paid for unsolicited material.

ENERGY MANAGER

MCM Publishing Ltd., Century House, Tanner Street, London SE1 3P.J. 01-231 1481.
Editor: Patrick Coyne.
Published 11 times a year for energy managers in industry, commerce and government.
Illustrations: B&W only for use inside the magazine and concerned with the subject in hand.
Text: Articles concerning energy use and management. 1,000–2,000 words.
Fees: Good. On a rising scale according to size of reproduction or number of words.

EUROPEAN RUBBER JOURNAL

Crain Communications Inc., 20–22 Bedford Row, London WC1R 4EB. Tel: 01-831 9511.
Editor: Bob Grace.
Published 10 times per year for the rubber trade.
Illustrations: B&W only inside. Pictures of rubber and rubber applications of a technical nature, e.g. tyres, belting, etc. Also news pictures. Covers: Top class colour pictures of rubber-related subjects. Must have human interest as well as technical content. 6 × 6 cm minimum.
Text: Features on new applications of rubber products, product stories, new products, news stories. 1,500–2,000 words.
Overall freelance potential: Around 25 per cent of the publication comes from freelances.
Editor's tips: All contributions must be of a high news value or have a sound technical content.
Fees: By arrangement.

EXECUTIVE POST

Professional and Executive Recruitment, Moorfoot, The Moor, Sheffield S1 4PQ. Tel: 0742 753275.

Editor: John Baker.

Weekly jobs newspaper concerning professional and executive recruitment. Contains also news and features for job-seekers at professional and executive level.

Illustrations: B&W only. By commission only.

Text: Features on successful job-finding, self-employment, redundancy rights, self-help, etc. Up to 1,500 words.

Overall freelance potential: A big market, but mostly supplied by writers with a specialist knowledge of the field.

Fees: £40 per 1,000 words; pictures by agreement.

GAS WORLD

Benn Publications Ltd., 25 New Street Square, London EC4A 3JA. Tel: 01-353 3212.

Editor: Roger Pechey.

Monthly journal aimed at middle and senior management in the engineering and commercial disciplines of the international gas supply, transmission and distribution industries.

Illustrations: B&W inside. Pictures of pipelines, compressor stations, liquefaction plants, ocean going liquified natural gas carriers and exploration rigs. Covers: Colour pictures of same. 6 × 6 cm minimum.

Text: Features on new developments in engineering, marketing, business and political fields. Up to 2,000 words.

Overall freelance potential: Around 50 per cent is bought from freelance contributors.

Fees: By arrangement.

GRADUATE POST

The New Opportunity Press Ltd., Yeoman House, 76 St. James's Lane, London N10 3RD. Tel: 01-444 7281.

Editor: Andrew Sich.

Fortnightly newspaper aimed at graduates and recent graduates plus HND students who are seeking their first professional post.

Illustrations: B&W only. Pictures·mostly as illustrations to features. Also pictures illustrating aspects of various careers.

Text: Illustrated features on subjects such as working overseas, recruitment fairs, TOPS and other training schemes, coping with unemployment, employment law etc. 2,000–3,000 words.

Overall freelance potential: Regular freelances employed, but always happy to consider new people.

Fees: Approximately £30 per picture; text by agreement.

GRAPHICS WORLD

The Graphic Communications Centre Ltd., Bernard House, Granville Road, Maidstone, Kent ME14 2BJ. Tel: 0622 675324.

Editor: David Le Tissier.
Bi-monthly magazine aimed at Britain's packaging and advertising market. Editorial takes a 'how to' and practical slant.
Illustrations: B&W and colour. Very specialised. Photographers are advised to contact the editor with proposals. No market for cover shots.
Text: As for pictures. 1,000–5,000 words.
Overall freelance potential: Good; approximately 40 per cent contributed.
Editor's tips: Ring the magazine before submitting.
Fees: £30–50 per published page.

HAMPSHIRE MONITOR BUSINESS MAGAZINE
Monitor Publications, 27 North Street, Havant, Hants PO9 1PW. Tel: 0705 453939/453794.
Editor: Larry Dillner.
Monthly publication for directors and other decision makers and specifiers.
Illustrations: B&W only. Mainly for use with articles.
Text: Features on business-related matters. 500–2,000 words.
Overall freelance potential: Around 30 per cent comes from freelances.
Editor's tips: Obtain a copy of the publication and write to the set style.
Fees: By arrangement.

HEADLIGHT
K. Publications (London) Ltd., 8 Bloomsbury Way, London WC1A 2SH. Tel: 01-242 6605.
Editor: J. Kelson.
Monthly publication for drivers and hauliers in the commercial transport business.
Illustrations: No freelance market.
Text: Features strictly on commercial transport subjects. 1,500 words.
Overall freelance potential: Reasonably good.
Fees: By negotiation.

IN TOUCH
Brant Wright Associates, The Dutch House, 307–308 High Holborn, London WC1V 7LS.Tel: 01-405 1358.
Editor: Arthur Potter.
Monthly official magazine of the Netherlands-British Chamber of Commerce. Aimed at management level.
Illustrations: B&W only. Pictures used with text as a platform for a company anxious to reach the Dutch market.
Text: General business matters of interest to the Dutch market. 1,500–2,000 words.
Overall freelance potential: Very little from independent freelances. Most contributions come from members of the Chamber of Commerce or from public relations agencies.
Editor's tips: Deadline is first Monday of previous month.
Fees: By arrangement.

INCENTIVE MARKETING AND SALES PROMOTION

Maclaren Publishers Ltd., P.O. Box 109, Maclaren House, Scarbrook Road, Croydon CR9 1QH. Tel: 01-688 7788.

Editor: Max Cuff.

Monthly publication for brand managers, SP managers, incentive managers etc. Concerned with incentive ideas for staff motivation and sales promotion campaigns, aids and general marketing themes.

Illustrations: B&W only inside. Pictures limited to the marketing and/or promotions profession. Covers: Highly creative colour pictures, usually linked to the main feature inside; 35mm acceptable.

Text: Authoritatively written articles on technical aspects of the marketing and/or promotions profession. 2,000–3,000 words.

Overall freelance potential: Around 50 per cent bought from freelances.

Editor's tips: Contact the magazine first.

Fees: By negotiation, depending on ability and subject matter.

INDUSTRIAL DIAMOND REVIEW

De Beers Industrial Diamond Division (PTY) Ltd., Charters, Sunninghill, Ascot, Berks. SL5 9PX. Tel: 0990 23456.

Editor: Paul Daniel.

Bi-monthly publication designed to promote a wider and more efficient use of diamond tools, i.e. grinding wheels, drill bits, saw blades, etc. in all branches of engineering.

Illustrations: B&W and colour. Pictures of any type of diamond tool in action; pictures of diamond mines in Africa, USSR, etc. Covers: Colour pictures of diamond tools in use. 35mm acceptable inside, 6 × 6 cm minimum for covers.

Text: Case histories on the use of diamond tools in engineering, mining, etc. Synopsis preferred in first instance. Up to 2,000 words for finished feature.

Overall freelance potential: Excellent but highly specialised.

Editor's tips: Technical case histories are welcome.

Potential contributors are advised to win the confidence of a diamond tool supplier or a major user in industry as a source for material.

Fees: Good; by arrangement.

INDUSTRIAL EXECUTIVE

Celtic Sea Publications, Offshore House, The Royal Dockyard, Pembroke Dock, Pembrokeshire, Dyfed SA72 6YH. Tel: 0646 684382/683590.

Editor: David Allen.

Bi-monthly publication for senior and middle-management within trade and industry, with particular emphasis on business in Wales.

Illustrations: B&W only inside. Pictures that show a good artistic interpretation of industry, provided they are shots of installations within South Wales and have not been outdated by recent developments. Covers: Colour or B&W, showing South Wales industry, particularly appreciated if they have an artistic flair: 35mm acceptable.

Text: Most editorial material is specially tailored to a planned programme, involving only commissioned work, but the journal might occasionally consider a spontaneous piece, especially if well illustrated. 750 words.
Overall freelance potential: Relatively low.
Fees: According to merit and whether commissioned.

INDUSTRIAL PARTICIPATION
IPA, 78 Buckingham Gate, London SW1E 6PQ. Tel: 01-222 0351.
Editor: D. Wallace Bell.
Quarterly journal for members of the Industrial Participation Association, e.g. senior and middle managers, supervisors and shop stewards.
Illustrations: B&W only. Occasional pictures to illustrate articles.
Text: Features on employee participation and involvement. Specific, rather than general angle. Up to 3,000 words.
Overall freelance potential: Most material is commissioned.
Fees: £10–£15 per 1,000 words.

INDUSTRIAL SOCIETY
The Industrial Society, 3 Carlton House Terrace, London SW1Y 5DG. Tel: 01-839 4300.
Editor: Denise Granatt.
Quarterly publication specialising in man management and industrial relations in industry, commerce and the public service.
Illustrations: B&W only. Pictures used only with text.
Text: Short features covering aspects of man management, supervisory leadership, good industrial practice, etc. 1,000 words.
Overall freelance potential: Quite good potential, but mostly commissioned.
Editor's tips: Send outline before submission.
Fees: Negotiated before acceptance.

INDUSTRY, COMMERCE AND DEVELOPMENT
MCB (Industrial Development) Ltd., 198–200 Keighley Road, Bradford, West Yorkshire BD9 4JQ. Tel. 0274 499821.
Editor: Mike Kiddey.
Monthly publication to provide information to senior managers in industry, industrial development and commerce.
Illustrations: B&W only. Pictures to illustrate specific articles only.
Text: Features on all subjects of real interest to UK and Europe, public and private sector senior management, especially in the field of industrial development in its widest sense.
Fees: By negotiation.

INK AND PRINT
Batiste Publications Ltd., Pembroke House, Campsbourne Road, Hornsey, London N8 7PT.
Tel: 01-340 3291 Ext. 45.
Editor: Dr. Robert Leach.

Quarterly publication that provides a forum of communication between all involved in the production of printed material. Produced for printing companies, inplant printers, industry and commerce, advertising companies, government and local authorities, research establishments, manufacturers and suppliers.

Illustrations: B&W and colour. Pictures of all printing subjects, i.e. machinery, ink, paper, raw materials, personalities etc. Covers: Interesting or unusual shots of printing processes; 6 × 6 cm minimum.

Text: Technical articles on the ink and print business. 1,500–2,500 words.

Overall freelance potential: Growing.

Fees: By agreement.

INTERNATIONAL REINFORCED PLASTICS INDUSTRY

Channel Publications Ltd., 48 Wellington Street, Slough, Berks SL1 1UB. Tel: 0753 77256.

Editor: David Pamington.

Bi-monthly publication issued to all moulders of fibre reinforced plastics, i.e. fibreglass. Aimed at management level in industry.

Illustrations: B&W and colour. Examples of components or completed structures manufactured from reinforced plastic materials, i.e. boats, aircraft, vehicles, chemical plant, pipes and building applications. Covers: Colour pictures, preferably unpublished, of components or structures relating to the industry; 6 × 6 cm minimum.

Text: Features describing the use of reinforced plastics materials in boat building, aircraft manufacture, vehicle construction, tank and vessel fabrication and cladding for buildings. 1,500–2,000 words.

Overall freelance potential: Around 15 per cent bought from outside.

Fees: By negotiation; around £30–£50 per 1,000 words; pictures by agreement.

INTERNATIONAL SECURITY REVIEW

Unisaf Publications Ltd., Queensway House, 2 Queensway, Redhill, Surrey RH1 1QS. Tel: 0737 68611 Ext. 404.

Editor: Tony Slinn.

Bi-monthly publication for high-ranking security experts and consultants throughout the world.

Illustrations: No freelance market.

Text: Features on security subjects, but only after consultation with the editor. 2,000–4,000 words.

Overall freelance potential: Almost all articles are supplied by freelance writers.

Fees: On application.

IRON AND STEEL INTERNATIONAL

IPC Industrial Press Ltd., Room 901, Quadrant House, The Quadrant, Sutton, Surrey SM2 5AS. Tel: 01-661 3500.

Editor: R. Robinson.

Bi-monthly publication for all those interested in the iron and steel industry.

Illustrations: B&W only. Pictures related to the industry.
Text: Articles on new products, processes and contracts in the industry plus economic and review articles on the steel industry.
Overall freelance potential: Small.
Fees: £40 per 1,000 words; pictures by negotiation.

JOURNAL OF THE INSTITUTE OF BANKERS

Institute of Bankers, 10 Lombard Street, London EC3. Tel: 01-623 3531.
Editor: Eric Glover.
Bi-monthly publication for bank employees from junior staff taking the Institute's qualifying examinations to top management.
Illustrations: B&W only. Pictures of machinery and technology in banks.
Text: Features on practical banking subjects, legal cases with reference to banking, international banking subjects, technology in banks, new developments in banks, competition in the finance sector. 2,000–2,500 words.
Overall freelance potential: If a feature or photograph is well presented and suitable in content, the possibility of use is very high. About 20–25 per cent is contributed from outside sources.
Fees: £45 per 1,000 words; pictures by agreement.

KEYPOINTS

Department for National Savings, Press Office, Department for National Savings, 4th Floor, Charles House, 375 High Street, Kensington W14 8SD. Tel: 01-603 2000 Ext. 109.
Editor: Ian Crichton.
Bi-monthly newspaper carrying news and information about National Savings and Post Office staff.
Illustrations: B&W and colour. Pictures with a National Savings connection, particularly related to post offices. Also pictures as illustrations to articles. covers: Usually commissioned in relation to specific requirements; 35mm acceptable, but 6 × 6 cm preferred.
Text: Interesting features about post office staff, particularly in relation to National Savings matters. Picture features about interesting personalities such as sub-postmasters and post-mistresses. 500–1,000 words.
Overall freelance potential: Marginal. Most material is originated internally or specially commissioned.
Editor's tips: Telephone first to see if an idea is of interest before starting work on it.
Fees: Good; on a rising scale according to size of picture or length of feature.

LABORATORY NEWS

World Media Ltd., 40 The Boulevard, Crawley, West Sussex. Tel. 0293 510422.
Editors: D. Davy and Mrs. H. Hobbs.
Fortnightly publication for directors, principals, chief technicians, scientific officers, lecturers, senior engineers, and heads of departments in universities, hospitals, research establishments,

education departments and industrial laboratories. Aims to keep readers up to date on new products, applications and services.
Illustrations: B&W only. Pictures mainly used in conjunction with articles detailed below.
Text: Stories of a newsworthy nature, particularly original material of developments in research or laboratory technology, accompanied by suitable B&W pictures.
Overall freelance potential: Negligible at present.
Fees: By arrangement.

LIGHTING EQUIPMENT NEWS
Maclean-Hunter Ltd., 76 Oxford Street, London W1N 0HH. Tel: 01-434 2233.
Editor: R. J. Abbott.
Monthly publication for all buyers of lighting, e.g. specifiers, contractors, wholesalers, retailers, local authorities etc. Deals with lighting and lamp technology, design, new products and news.
Illustrations: B&W and colour. Pictures of new lighting installations in commercial, domestic and industrial situations, as well as street lighting. Covers: Colour pictures of similar; 6 × 6 cm minimum.
Text: No market.
Overall freelance potential: A considerable amount is bought from outside contributors, but this is very much a specialist market.
Fees: By negotiation.

MAINTENANCE AND EQUIPMENT NEWS
Dial Publications Ltd., PO Box 249, Ascot, Berks SL5 0BZ. Tel: 0990 26394.
Editor: Simon Whitney.
Bi-monthly, dealing with maintenance in schools and churches.
Illustrations: B&W only, illustrating maintenance in public buildings. e.g. roofs and roofing maintenance, heating systems, garden equipment, electronic organs, fund-raising, office equipment, cleaning and redesigning old buildings.
Text: Features which cover the subjects mentioned above and other allied topics. 1,500 words.
Overall freelance potential: Small.
Editor's tips: Telephone with ideas before submitting.
Fees: By negotiation.

MANAGEMENT ACCOUNTING
Institute of Cost and Management Accountants, 63 Portland Place, London W1N 4AB. Tel: 01-637 2311.
Editor: John Hillary.
Monthly publication for members and students of the Institute.
Illustrations: B&W inside. Small market for top quality general industrial/commercial

subjects. Covers: Colour pictures of industrial and commercial subjects, plus computers. 35mm acceptable.

Text: No freelance market.

Overall freelance potential: Limited.

Fees: Covers, up to £100; inside pictures by agreement.

MANUFACTURING CHEMIST

Morgan-Grampian (Process Press) Ltd., 30 Calderwood Street, Woolwich, London SE18 6QH. Tel: 01-855 7777.

Editor: Neil Eisberg.

Monthly journal for the chemical industry. Read by senior management involved in research, development production and marketing of general chemicals, petrochemicals, drugs, household products, cosmetics, toiletries and aerosol products.

Illustrations: B&W and colour. Pictures of any aspect of the chemical industry from petrochemicals to drugs and cosmetics. Covers: Colour pictures of same. 35mm acceptable, but 6 × 6 cm preferred.

Text: Features on any aspect of the chemical industry as detailed above. 2,000–3,000 words.

Overall freelance potential: Approximately 50 per cent is contributed by freelances.

Fees: Text, £50 per 1,000 words for features, £10 per 100 words for news stories; pictures by agreement.

MARINE STORES INTERNATIONAL

International Trade Publications Ltd., Queensway House, 2 Queensway, Redhill, Surrey RH1 1QS. Tel: 0737 68611.

Editor: Iain Macnaughtan.

Published ten times per year for the ship supply industry.

Illustrations: B&W only. Pictures of stores being delivered to ships, ship suppliers' premises—particularly if new or enlarged—and ship suppliers themselves, all to be supplied with small news items. Also pictures covering manufacture of equipment and goods supplied to ships, e.g. deck and engine equipment, cabin and galley requisites, bonded stores and provisions.

Text: News items, with and without illustrations, on ship suppliers' activities; local situation regarding port operations; regulations, new liner business, etc. Also new products with a marine application. No yacht or pleasure craft chandlery. News, around 500 words; features, 2,000–4,000 words.

Overall freelance potential: A number of regular freelances are used, but the magazine is interested in hearing from new contacts.

Editor's tips: While the editorial does contain technical articles, most of the content is non-technical.

Fees: Text, £53 per 1,000 words; original pictures, £5; hand-out pictures, £1.50.

MARKETING

Marketing Publications Ltd./Haymarket Publishing Ltd., 22 Lancaster Gate, London W2 3LY. Tel: 01-402 1231.

Editor: Brian Bell.
Weekly publication for senior marketing management.
Illustrations: B&W inside. All subjects relating to marketing. Covers: Colour pictures of similar. 35mm acceptable.
Text: Features with a marketing angle and objective case histories. 1,000 words plus.
Overall freelance potential: All pictures are freelance contributed; around 30 per cent of the text comes from freelances.
Editor's tips: A synopsis in the first instance is very important.
Fees: Variable.

MEDIA PRODUCTION

Macro Publishing Ltd., 41b High Street, Hoddesdon, Herts EN11 8TA. Tel: 09924 69556.
Editor: Paul Rowney.
Monthly trade magazine for creative services industry.
Illustrations: No freelance market.
Text: Features on anything related to the subject. Up to 2,000 words.
Overall freelance potential: Up to 50 per cent is contributed by freelances.
Fees: On a rising scale according to the length of the article.

MIDDLE EAST INDUSTRIAL PRODUCTS

IPC Middle East Publishing Company Ltd., Crown House, 14th Floor, London Road, Morden, Surrey SM4 5DX. Tel: 01-542 1736.
Editor: Lee Brown.
Bi-monthly publication for senior managers involved in setting up and running industrial units in public and private sectors in the Middle East.
Illustrations: B&W only. Pictures of light industrial plant and processes in the Middle East (not petrochemicals), e.g. factories, assembly lines, packaging processes.
Text: No freelance market.
Overall freelance potential: Small.
Fees: On a rising scale according to the size of reproduction.

MILLING FEED AND FERTILISER

Turret Press, 886 High Road, Finchley, London N12 9SB. Tel: 01-446 2411.
Editor: Christopher Warren.
Monthly international business journal for the flour milling, feed compound and agricultural industries. Covers news, sales management, products, government policies and market reports on flour, wheat, animal feeds, seeds, fertiliser, etc.
Illustrations: B&W only. Exciting pictures from the industry. Explosions/fires in milling plants, insects/mice in grain stores etc. No cover market.
Text: Market reports, opinion polls, articles discussing top personnel or products available in the market. Off-beat features which will create discussion on new ideas to run an agricultural company. 1,500 words.

Overall freelance potential: The magazine uses a lot of freelance work. Always on the lookout for features of a funny or offbeat nature.
Editor's tips: Phone before submission.
Fees: £30 per published page; £7 per B&W picture. More if the material warrants it.

MILTON KEYNES COMMERCE & INDUSTRY
Station House, Station Road, Newport Pagnell, Milton Keynes. Tel: 0908 611941.
Editor: Richard Meredith.
Monthly regional business magazine aimed at 'decision makers'. Sold mainly by direct mail and some subscription.
Illustrations: B&W mostly and occasionally colour on business and commerce subjects as well as faces, well-known nationally and locally to the area—politicians, industrial leaders etc. Covers: colour of similar subjects; 35mm acceptable.
Text: Features on business and commerce subjects. Around 1,000 words. An advanced features list is always available.
Overall freelance potential: Around 20 per cent comes from outside freelances.
Editor's tips: Always contact the magazine and talk over ideas before submission.
Fees: Negotiable.

MINING MAGAZINE
Mining Journal Ltd., 15 Wilson Street, London EC2M 2TR. Tel: 01-606 2567.
Editor: Tony Brewis.
Monthly magazine aimed at geologists, mining engineers, mineral technologists and metallurgists at senior management level in metal mining and coal mining industries worldwide.
Illustrations: B&W and colour. Up to date pictures of mining in progress, plus pictures of equipment. Single photographs with 20–30 word captions are welcome. Covers: Colour pictures of up to date mining activity. 35mm acceptable.
Text: Technical articles with illustrations on mining and mineral processing topics. 600–900 words or 2,500–3,500 words.
Overall freelance potential: Small.
Fees: Negotiable.

MODERN AFRICA
Johnston International Publishing Corp., 1st Floor, 2 Pear Tree Court, London EC1. Tel: 01-250 4114.
Editor: Ms Brooke Hyde.
Bi-monthly business magazine for black Sub-Saharan Africa. Aimed at businessmen and diplomats.
Illustrations: B&W and colour. Pictures of African ministers, agriculture, construction, development, industries, water resources, telecommunications, electrical energy, aid projects, markets, commodities, shipping, transport, major projects, street scenes. Covers: Colour pictures of similar subjects. 35mm acceptable, but larger formats preferred.

DAVID BEARE

Text: Features on the subjects detailed above, plus company profiles, African projects, government policies and attitudes towards commerce and economy. 1,500–2,000 words.
Overall freelance potential: Between 50 and 75 per cent of any issue is contributed by freelances.
Editor's tips: Material should not be too technical or political.
Fees: Text, £60 per 1,000 words; B&W pictures, from £10; covers, from £80.

NATURAL GAS

Benn Publications Ltd., 25 New Street Square, London EC4 3JA. Tel: 01-353 3212.
Editor: Victoria Thomas.
Bi-monthly publication concerned with the application of natural gas in commerce and industry with particular reference to efficient usage. Aimed at managing directors, chief engineers, architects and energy specialists, hotels, universities, schools, local authorities, hospitals, etc.
Illustrations: B&W and colour. Pictures of natural gas application in commerce and industry. Colour pictures of same. 35mm acceptable.
Text: General interest, well illustrated features with some reference to natural gas. Features on specific gas installations with particular reference to the economic use of gas. 600–1,500 words.
Overall freelance potential: Around thirty per cent bought from freelance sources.
Fees: Negotiable.

NETWORK

Broadcast Ltd., 48 Shalstone Road, East Sheen, London SW14 7HR. Tel: 01-878 0912.
Editor: Richard Thomas.
Published four times a year for anyone involved in the communications business.
Illustrations: B&W and colour. Pictures on communications subjects, e.g. video, inflight entertainment, local radio stations at work, Japanese management techniques with British work forces. 6 × 6 cm preferred.
Text: Features that concentrate on the software side of communication. Illustrated interviews with leading opinion formers.
Overall freelance potential: Very high.
Fees: Negotiable.

OPINION

Society of Civil and Public Servants, 124–130 Southwark Street, London SE1 0TU. Tel: 01-928 9671 Ext. 287.
Editor: Alan Slingsby.
Monthly publication for members of the SCPS, a middle management trade union in the Civil Service and related bodies, including the Post Office and British Telecom.

Illustrations: Trade union activity of any kind, but especially involving Civil Servants who are SCPS members. No market for covers.
Text: No requirements.
Overall freelance potential: Good: 75 per cent of pictures come from outside contributors.
Fees: Good: on a rising scale according to size of reproduction.

OVERSEAS ADVERTISING
Publishing and Distributing Co. Ltd., 177 Regent Street, London W1. Tel: 01-734 6534.
Editor: H. R. Vaughan.
Monthly publication for exporters.
Illustrations: B&W and colour. Pictures of interest to the export trade. Covers: Colour pictures of industrial subjects.
Text: Features on economics. 1,000 words.
Overall freelance potential: Around 10 per cent comes from outside contributors.
Fees: By agreement.

PACKAGING
Wheatland Journals Ltd., Penn House, Penn Place, Rickmansworth, Herts. WD3 1SN. Tel: 0923 774262.
Editor: Sue Meeson.
Monthly publication for management and executive staff responsible for the purchasing or design of packs, the buying of packaging materials and machinery, or who are involved with packaging services.
Illustrations: No freelance market.
Text: Features on virtually anything to do with packaging materials and equipment, e.g. development, case histories, stories relating to packaged goods within specified areas. 1,000 words.
Overall freelance potential: A growing need for freelance material.
Editor's tips: Articles should, if possible, have both technical and marketing details included.
Fees: Approximately £40 per 1,000 words, dependent on subject and quality.

PENSIONS
Wootten Publications, 150–152 Caledonian Road, London N1 9RD. Tel: 01-278 7951.
Managing Editor: James Wootten.
Monthly publication concerned with pensions and all those connected with them.
Illustrations: B&W only. Pictures used mainly as illustrations for features. Covers: B&W pictures that illustrate subjects detailed below.
Text: Features that relate to pension funds, investment of pension funds, anything that illustrates, illuminates or elaborates on pension funds and how they interact with unions etc. 2,000–2,500 words.
Overall freelance potential: Between 10 and 15 per cent is contributed from outside freelances.

Editor's tips: This is a specialised subject. Intending contributors should study the magazine before submitting.
Fees: Good; on a rising scale according to the size of reproduction or length of feature.

PERSONNEL EXECUTIVE
Business Publications Ltd., 109–119 Waterloo Road, London SE1 8UL. Tel: 01-928 3388.
Editor: Tim Burt.
Monthly publication for personnel managers and managers in related functions, e.g. training, health and safety, recruitment and selection.
Illustrations: B&W only inside. Pictures of people at work for stock purposes. Industrial and commercial scenes, training and seminars, health and safety at work. Covers: Colour pictures, often made up from a montage of different transparencies. 5″ × 4″ minimum.
Text: Features on subjects detailed above. 1,500–2,000 words.
Overall freelance potential: Small.
Fees: By negotiation.

PLANT AND TOOL HIRER
Giddings Business Journals Ltd., 283–289 Cricklewood Broadway, London NW2 6NZ. Tel: 01-450 0466.
Editor: George Mills.
Monthly publication for all hire companies.
Illustrations: No freelance market.
Text: Features of technical or commercial interest to owners/managers of hire shops and small plant hire companies.
Overall freelance potential: Occasional use for freelance material.
Editor's tips: Avoid plugs for commercial products.
Fees: £35 per 1,000 words.

PLASTICS AND RUBBER INTERNATIONAL
Plastics and Rubber Institute, 11 Hobart Place, London SW1W 0HL. Tel: 01-245 9555.
Managing Editor: Patricia Battams.
Bi-monthly technical publication for those working in the plastics and rubber industries.
Illustrations: Freelance photographers occasionally commissioned to cover functions. Otherwise only market is for covers: Colour pictures of a fairly abstract type, whose subjects are connected with plastics and rubber. 6 × 6 cm minimum.
Text: Freelance writers are sometimes commissioned to write in-depth reviews of the industry. 3,000–4,000 words.
Overall freelance potential: Small.
Fees: Negotiable.

PORT OF LONDON MAGAZINE
Port of London Authority, Leslie Ford House, Tilbury Docks, Tilbury, Essex RM18 7EH.
Editor: Terry Hatton.
Quarterly publication for business executives in the shipping, port and transport industries.

Illustrations: B&W and colour. Mostly in association with features and usually shot in-house or obtained from agencies. Prepared to consider pictures from other sources with articles. Covers: Colour pictures connected with shipping ports. 35mm acceptable.

Text: Illustrated features on subjects connected with shipping and ports. 2,000 words.

Overall freelance potential: Limited.

Fees: Negotiable.

POST MAGAZINE AND INSURANCE MONITOR

Buckley Press Ltd., The Butts, Half Acre, Brentford, Middlesex TW8 8BN. Tel: 01-568 8441.

Editor: Fennell Betson.

Weekly Publication. Both aimed at insurance at home and abroad.

Illustrations: B&W only. Pictures of motoring, traffic, houses, offices, building sites/ construction projects, damage (including fire and motoring accidents), shipwrecks or aviation losses, aircraft, etc.

Text: Features on insurance, including life assurance, general insurance, reinsurance, pensions, savings, offices and personnel areas.

Overall freelance potential: Around 20 per cent of the magazine is contributed from outside.

Fees: By negotiation.

PROCESSING

IPC Industrial Press Ltd., Quadrant House, The Quadrant, Sutton, Surrey SM2 5AS. Tel: 01-661 3370.

Editor: Lance Sucharov.

Controlled readership monthly for management and engineers in the chemicals and petrochemicals, food, drink, pharmaceutical and allied industries.

Illustrations: B&W only on new process plant being erected, accident (or other) damaged plant, newsworthy pictures of interest to the industry.

Text: Articles concerning the technical, financial or marketing of processing industries.

Overall freelance potential: Quite good.

Editor's tips: Contact the journal before submitting. A CV of the intending contributor is usually required.

Fees: £40 per 1,000 words. £12 per picture.

PROCUREMENT WEEKLY

Institute of Purchasing and Supply, IPS House, High Street, Ascot, Berks SL5 7HG. Tel: 0990 23711.

Editor: Bob Brooks.

Weekly publication for buyers, purchasing officers, materials managers in industry and public service. Covers news, commercial and legal developments, economic news and key indicators.

Illustrations: B&W only. Pictures of new, interesting or dramatic material to illustrate stories on the production, distribution and use of commodities, i.e. agricultural produce such as tea, coffee, rubber, etc.; as well as minerals and metals such as zinc, copper, aluminium etc. Also looking for interesting pictures on subjects like scrapyards, NHS, chemical plants, power stations, British Telecom, etc.

Text: News material, written by specialist and non-specialist freelances, that is concise, credible and supplied to tight deadlines. Almost every branch of industry, commerce and government is covered. 100–2,000 words.

Overall freelance potential: Currently around 10 per cent of the publication comes from freelances. This could be higher if the right people could be found.

Editor's tips: Read the publication or call to discuss ideas. Always tell the Editor who else might have the story.

Fees: Good, on a rising scale, according to the size of picture or length of article.

PRODUCTION MANAGEMENT AND CONTROL

Institute of Production Control, National Westminster House, Wood Street, Stratford-upon-Avon, Warwickshire CV37 6JF. Tel: 0789 5266.

Editor: K. Roberts.

Bi-monthly industrial and scientific journal concerned with production control, production and materials management and its allied fields. Aimed at all levels of senior management and personnel within industry.

Illustrations: Very limited amount within the magazine. Covers: B&W pictures of industry.

Text: Features on all subject matter related to production and computerised production control systems.

Overall freelance potential: Fairly good.

Fees: By negotiation.

PROFESSIONAL PRINTER

Institute of Printing, 8 Lonsdale Gardens, Tunbridge Wells, Kent TN1 1NU. Tel: 0892 38118.

Editor: Ian Kingsley.

Bi-monthly magazine for members of the Institute of Printing, anyone concerned with the trade, students and graduates of printing colleges, trade union officials, etc.

Illustrations: B&W only. Pictures showing all aspects of the printing industry and its personalities. Covers: B&W pictures of the same.

Text: Features on any aspect of the printing industry. 2,000–3,000 words.

Overall freelance potential: Quite good, although the magazine receives a certain amount of free material from within the industry.

Fees: By arrangement.

PROSPECT

Harrington Publications Ltd., 100 Great Portland Street, London W1. Tel: 01-636 6943.

Editor: Stewart Farr.

Monthly publication for members of the Life Assurance Association.

Illustrations: No freelance market.
Text: Features on all topics relating to effective selling of life insurance, reviews of new products, pension schemes, etc. Also, discussions on selling aids, plus articles on equipment such as computers of interest to this market. 1,000 words.
Overall freelance potential: Around 50 per cent of the content comes from freelances.
Fees: By arrangement.

PURCHASING

Morgan-Grampian Ltd., 30 Calderwood Street, Woolwich, London SE18 6QH. Tel: 01-855 7777.
Editor: Anthony Barry.
Monthly magazine covering all manufacturing industries from which purchasing executives buy supplies.
Illustrations: Only by commission.
Text: Features and news on industrial and purchasing practice. News, 200–400 words; features, 1,000–2,500 words.
Overall freelance potential: Mostly commissioned, but willing to consider work from freelances who understand the magazine's needs.
Fees: By agreement.

QUARRY MANAGEMENT AND PRODUCTS

The Quarry Managers' Journal Ltd., 7 Regent Street, Nottingham NG1 5BY. Tel: 0602 411315.
Editor: Bernard Hill.
Monthly professional and technical magazine containing news and technical articles on basic extraction and processing of quarried materials, associated processes and opencast mining. Aimed at senior management levels.
Illustrations: B&W only, mostly supplied by established contacts.
Text: Features on above topics, plus news of new products, up to 2,500 words.
Overall freelance potential: Very small.
Fees: By negotiation.

RADIO DIRECTORY

Hamilton House Publishing, Grooms Lane, Creaton, Northampton NN6 8NS. Tel: 060-124 612.
Editor: Sarah Edwards.
Published twice a year for the radio industry. Lists programmes, stations, equipment, addresses etc. of use to this trade. Aimed at PRs, publishers and the music industry.
Illustrations: B&W only. Any picture connected with the radio trade.
Text: Reviews of equipment and finance. New developments. New programmes, but *not* programme reviews. Must be by experts. Around 2,000 words.
Overall freelance potential: The publication is always interested to receive ideas.
Fees: Various.

RIBA JOURNAL
RIBA Magazines Ltd., 66 Portland Place, London W1N 4AD. Tel: 01-580 5533.
Editor: Peter Murray.
Monthly magazine of the Institute of British Architects. Covers general aspects of architectural practice as well as criticisms of particular buildings.
Illustrations: B&W inside the magazine. Pictures of buildings, old, new and refurbished. Covers: Colour pictures of similar, but usually connected with main feature inside.
Text: Features on architectural subjects and criticisms of buildings.
Overall freelance potential: Fair.
Fees: About £10 per picture published.

ROUSTABOUT MAGAZINE
Roustabout Publications, 64 Great Northern Road, Aberdeen AB2 3PT. Tel: 0224 46267.
Editor: Jan Primrose-Smith.
Monthly for oil industry personnel working on and offshore in the North Sea.
Illustrations: B&W and colour both inside and on the cover. Minimum transparency size: 6 × 6 cm. All pictures must be directly related to the North Sea oil industry.
Text: Articles related to the North Sea oil industry. 1,000–2,000 words.
Overall freelance potential: Small because of extremely specialised subject.
Fees: By arrangement.

SIGN WORLD
A.E. Morgan Publications Ltd., Stanley House, 9 West Street, Epsom, Surrey KT18 7RL. Tel: 037-27 41411.
Editor: Mrs. Judy Champneys.
Monthly publication, dealing with sign manufacturing and allied industries. Aimed at architects, town planners, surveyors, traffic and design engineers, shopfitters, sign manufacturers, trade suppliers, graphic designers, advertisement agents, exhibition organisers and specifiers in major organisations.
Illustrations: B&W only as illustrations to features.
Text: Features on new technological developments in the sign manufacturing industry. Information on relevant contracts at home and abroad. 1,000 words.
Overall freelance potential: Open to development for freelance with the right specialist knowledge.
Editor's tips: Sample copies available—phone for details.
Fees: About £80 per 1,000 words; pictures by agreement.

SOGAT JOURNAL
Society of Graphical and Allied Trades, 274–288 London Road, Hadleigh, Essex SS7 2DE. Tel: 0702 553131.
Editor: John Jennings.
Monthly publication for members of the union. Gives information on union policies and activities, plus personalities and sports news.

Illustrations: B&W only. Pictures involving the trade union and labour movement, plus some general pictures, i.e. sport, personalities, travel etc. Covers: B&W pictures of similar subjects.

Text: Features on subjects mentioned above. 750–1,000 words.

Overall freelance potential: Small.

Fees: By agreement.

SOLID FUEL

Harper Trade Journals Ltd., Harling House, 47–51 Great Suffolk Street London SE1 0BS. Tel: 01-261 1604.

Editor: Alan Cork.

Monthly publication for coal merchants, solid fuel heating installers, builders' merchants, local authorities, chimney sweeps, heating engineers and the National Coal Board.

Illustrations: B&W only. Interesting pictures of coal delivery or coal burning. Unusual chimneys. Any picture of something unusual and related to the subject.

Text: Features on all aspects of solid fuel, e.g. a report on a chimney museum, technical reports on industrial chimneys, opening of retail showrooms, etc. Around 1,000 words.

Overall freelance potential: Always a market for a few freelance articles in any issue.

Editor's tips: Space is limited, so keep to the point; no padding.

Fees: By negotiation, but a higher rate for technical articles than for general interest.

STREAM

Severn-Trent Water Authority, Abelson House, 2297 Coventry Road, Sheldon, Birmingham B26 3PU. Tel: 021-743 4222.

Editor: Michael Hughes.

Monthly tabloid newspaper for water authority and water company employees. Contains a mix of features and news, including sport, personality profiles and retirements.

Illustrations: B&W only. Photographs about water industry projects or water industry people within Severn-Trent region. News, humorous and pretty girl employee pictures always welcome.

Text: News or feature material about Severn-Trent water company employees. Also cartoons with water industry theme. 50–500 words.

Overall freelance potential: Moderate; about 5 per cent of content is currently contributed from outside, but this could be increased.

Editor's tips: Needs a good understanding of the industry for anything other than news, sport or personality material. Contact the editor first.

Fees: By prior arrangement. Up to £50 for a photographic commission.

THE SUBPOSTMASTER

National Federation of Subpostmasters, Scan House, Southwick Street, Southwick, Brighton BN4 4TE. Tel: 0273 595969.

Editor: Ron Ward.

Monthly journal of the Federation, with strong news content concerning subpostmasters.

Illustrations: B&W only. Pictures of any subpostmaster in the news for any reason, with captions.
Text: No freelance market.
Overall freelance potential: Small but possible growth.
Editor's tips: More interested in subjects with unusual hobbies, histories, etc. than in attack stories.
Fees: On a rising scale, according to the size of reproduction.

SUPERVISORY MANAGEMENT
The Institute of Supervisory Management, 22 Bore Street, Lichfield, Staffordshire WS13 6LP. Tel: 05432 51346.
Editor: J. M. Towers.
Quarterly management journal aimed at supervisors, superintendents and junior and middle management.
Illustrations: No freelance market.
Text: Any article relevant to junior management, i.e. production, education, current legislation, marketing, etc. Plus articles about management in other countries. 1,000 words.
Overall freelance potential: Very small.
Fees: Negotiable.

TAXES and ASSESSMENT
Inland Revenue Staff Federation, Douglas Houghton House, 231 Vauxhall Bridge Road, London SW1V 1EH. Tel: 01-834 8254.
Editor: J. Willman.
Two publications. *Assessment* published 11 times per year, *Taxes* published 5 times per year; each for members of the Inland Revenue Staff Federation, the trade union that represents most employees in Inland Revenue.
Illustrations: B&W only. Pictures relating to the Inland Revenue or the Staff Federation, e.g. mass meetings, demonstrations, sponsored walks, fund-raising activities and achievements of individual members.
Text: Features on topics of interest to members of the Fedration.
Overall freelance potential: Only 5 per cent comes from freelance sources.
Fees: On a rising scale according to the size of reproduction or length of article.

TELECOM TODAY
British Telecom, 85 Watling Street, London EC4M 9BN. Tel: 01-631 2331.
Editor: Ted Dutton.
Monthly publication for all BT employees, pensioners, opinion formers, MPs, Press, etc.
Illustrations: B&W and colour. Pictures of all Telecom subjects, usually by commission.
Covers: Colour pictures of same. 35mm acceptable.
Text: Features related to Telecom. About 300 words.
Overall freelance potential: Small.
Fees: By agreement.

FPMH - F

TIMBER GROWER
Timber Growers' Organisation Ltd., Agriculture House, Knightsbridge, London SW1X 7NJ. Tel: 01-235 2925.
Editor: T. A. Richardson.
Quarterly publication for forestry owners, agents and managers.
Illustrations: B&W only inside. Pictures of forestry subjects and people connected with them.
Text: Features on forestry. 600 words.
Overall freelance potential: Small.
Fees: By agreement.

TIN INTERNATIONAL
Tin Publications Ltd., 7 High Road, London W4 2NE. Tel: 01-995 9277.
Editor: Paul Newman.
Monthly publication covering all aspects of the production and consumption of tin, including can-making, canning and related subjects.
Illustrations: B&W only. Pictures illustrating any aspects of the mining of tin or the application in end uses.
Text: Features on subjects detailed above. 2,000 words.
Overall freelance potential: Small.
Fees: £2 per 100 words; pictures by agreement.

TV DIRECTORY
Hamilton House Publishing, Grooms Lane, Creaton, Northampton NN6 8NS. Tel: 060-124 612.
Editor: Susan Hesse.
Published twice per year as a complete guide to events and companies on TV. Aimed at PR, advertising agencies, the TV industry, record companies and publishers.
Illustrations: B&W only. Pictures relating the TV industry, e.g. people, equipment, transmitters, buildings.
Text: Articles on new developments on TV equipment or TV policy and development. No programme reviews. Features must be by experts in the field; no general comment pieces. Around 2,000 words.
Overall freelance potential: Always open to suggestions.
Fees: By agreement.

WATER BULLETIN
National Water Council, 1 Queen Anne's Gate, London SW1H 9BT. Tel: 01-222 8111.
Editor: Les Freeman.
Weekly publication for management within the British water industry.
Illustrations: B&W only. Pictures connected with the water industry, ranging from the cleaning of dirty rivers, reservoirs and treatment plants to sewage outfalls, sewers, etc. Covers: B&W pictures of above subjects, but connected with editorial inside.

Text: Features on any subject related to the management of the water industry. 1,500 words.
Overall freelance potential: No more than 10 per cent comes from freelances.
Fees: Good, on a rising scale according to the size of reproduction or length of article.

WORKS MANAGEMENT
Findlay Publications Ltd., Franks Hall, Horton Kirby, Kent DA4 9LL. Tel 0322 77755.
Editor: Peter Chambers.
Monthly publication for managers and engineers who directly control or perform the works
management function in selected manufacturing concerns.
Illustrations: B&W and colour. Occasional need for regional coverage of managers and
workers in realistic work situations in factories. Mostly pictures are used only to illustrate
features. 35mm acceptable.
Text: Case studies, communications topics, employment, energy.
Text: Features of interest to management, e.g. case studies, automation in factories,
communications, employment, factory law, finance, etc. Around 2,000 words.
Overall freelance potential: More than 30 per cent is contributed by freelances.
Fees: By agreement.

WORLD SUGAR JOURNAL
N. G. Osman and Associates Ltd., 1 Murdock Road, Wokingham, Berks. RG11 2DL. Tel:
0734 792336.
Editor: N. G. Osman.
Monthly publication for all sectors of the sugar industry at management level, libraries,
universities and research organisations.
Illustrations: B&W and colour. Pictures of sugarbeet and sugarcane at growing, harvesting
and processing stages; pictures of sugarmills, bulk loading factories; any artistic pictures using
sugar as a subject.
Text: Analysis of any aspect of the sugar industry; facts, figures and news, etc. Around 1,500
words, longer if justified.
Overall freelance potential: Average.
Fees: £25 per printed page.

Caravanning and Camping

CARAVAN INDUSTRY AND PARK OPERATOR
A. E. Morgan Publications Ltd., Stanley House, 9 West Street, Epsom, Surrey KT18 7RL.
Tel: 037-27 41411.
Editor: David Ritchie.
Monthly publication for manufacturers, traders, suppliers and park operators in the caravan
industry.

Illustrations: B&W only. Pictures of new caravan park developments, new models, new dealer depots, etc.
Text: Company profiles on park owners and their businesses, traders and manufacturers. 900–1,200 words.
Overall freelance potential: Up to 50 per cent of the content comes from freelance contributors.
Fees: By agreement.

CARAVANNING MONTHLY

Link House Magazines (Croydon) Ltd., Link House, Dingwall Avenue, Croydon CR9 2TA. Tel: 01-686 2599.
Editor: Barry Williams.
Monthly magazine aimed at touring caravanners using either trailer or motor caravans and concentrates on the practical aspects of caravanning holidays at home and abroad.
Illustrations: B&W inside. Pictures used mostly as illustrations to features. Covers: Colour pictures, invariably tied with editorial and mostly shot by staff photographers. 6 × 6 cm minimum.
Text: Illustrated features with a relevance to the touring caravanner. Touring features; site reports. Up to 1,500 words.
Overall freelance potential: Good.
Fees: By negotiation.

EN ROUTE

The Caravan Club, 55 St James's Street, London SW1A 1LA. Tel: 01-493 9869.
Editor: Sharon Farr.
Published seven times per year for members of the Caravan Club.
Illustrations: B&W and colour. All subjects with a caravan slant or bias. Covers: Colour pictures of caravans. 6 × 6 cm minimum.
Text: Features on anything connected with caravanning. 1,500–2,000 words.
Overall freelance potential: Around 5 per cent of each issue comes from freelances.
Fees: Approximately £40 per published page.

MOTOR CARAVAN WORLD

Stone Industrial Publications Ltd., Andrew House, 2A Granville Road, Sidcup, Kent, Tel: 01-302 6150/6069 and 01-300 2316.
Editor: Douglas Mitchell.
Monthly magazine aimed at motor caravan enthusiasts with details of travel, sites, road tests etc.
Illustrations: B&W and colour for use inside the magazine on topics related to above subjects.
Text: Features on travelling by motor caravan. 1,000–1,500 words.

Overall freelance potential: Quite good.
Editor's tips: Preference for copy that requires a minimum of subbing or re-writing.
Fees: By negotiation.

POPULAR CARAVAN
Sovereign Publications, Sovereign House, Brentwood, Essex CM14 4SE. Tel: 0277 219876.
Editor: Kate Howard.
Monthly magazine for trailer caravanners from beginners to seasoned travellers. Covers holiday ideas at home and abroad, site reviews, caravan DIY, caravan cookery, etc.
Illustrations: B&W only. Pictures used only with features.
Text: Ideas for weekends and longer breaks in the UK, to include appropriate site details where possible. Site details for UK and Europe, detailing services offered etc. Features, 2,000 words maximum; site reviews, 400 words plus one picture.
Overall freelance potential: Between 90 and 95 per cent is contributed.
Editor's tips: Schedules fairly full into early 1983, schedules for DIY and caravan testing full. 'All year' site reviews always welcomed.
Fees: £20 per 1,000 words; £4 per B&W picture.

PRACTICAL CAMPER
Haymarket Publishing Ltd., 38–42 Hampton Road, Teddington, Middlesex TW11 0JE. Tel: 01-977 8787.
Editor: John Lloyd.
Monthly magazine for family campers with some lightweight content, including special lightweight issue in October.
Illustrations: B&W only inside. Camp site and touring pictures and anything else on the subject of camping. Covers: Colour pictures of happy camping subjects; sometimes good, colourful site pictures. 35mm acceptable, but 6 × 6 cm preferred.
Text: Camp site reports, touring features, DIY. 450–500 words, 1,500–2,000 words and 1,200–1,500 words respectively.
Overall freelance potential: Between 40 and 50 per cent contributed material.

PRACTICAL CARAVAN
Haymarket Publishing, 38–42 Hampton Road, Teddington, Middlesex TW11 0JE. Tel: 01-977 8787.
Editor: Mark Neeter.
Monthly magazine for caravanners and motorcaravanners.
Illustrations: B&W inside. Pictures showing anything of interest to caravanners. Covers: Colour pictures of caravans outdoors; 6 × 6 cm minimum.
Text: Features on caravans and related subjects. 1,000–2,000 words.
Overall freelance potential: Approximately 35 per cent of the magazine comes from freelance sources.
Fees: Negotiable.

Children and Teenage

THE BROWNIE
Girl Guides Association, 17–19 Buckingham Palace Road, London, SW1W 0PT. Tel: 01-834 6242 ext 62.
Editor: Mrs. J. V. Rush.
Weekly publication for Brownies in the 6–10 age group.
Illustrations: B&W only. Action pictures with Brownie subjects.
Text: Articles with Brownie themes. 300–500 words.
Overall freelance potential: Around 10 per cent is contributed.
Fees: Text, £17.25; pictures, £3.20.

GUIDER
Girl Guides Association, 17–19 Buckingham Palace Road, London SW1W 0PT. Tel: 01-834 6242 ext. 62.
Editor: Norman Bloomfield.
Monthly publication for adult members and leaders in the Guide movement.
Illustrations: B&W inside. Action pictures on Guiding subjects. Covers: Colour pictures of Guides and Brownies in action; occasionally seasonal. 35mm acceptable.
Text: Articles allied to work with young people in various fields. 750–1,000 words.
Overall freelance potential: Around 10 per cent of the magazine comes from freelances.
Fees: Text, £17.25 per 1,000 words; B&W pictures, £3.20; covers, £6.

JUDY
D. C. Thomson and Co., Ltd., Albert Square, Dundee DD1 9QJ. Tel: 0382 23131.
Editor: Stanley Stamper.
Weekly magazine for schoolgirls in the 7–11 age group.
Illustrations: B&W only. Few pictures used of pop stars, but these come mainly from record companies. Better market in the *Judy Annual*: B&W and colour pictures of interest to schoolgirls. 35mm acceptable. Covers: Mostly line drawings on the magazine, though occassionally a colour picture. Annual uses colour pictures of subjects that will appeal to young girls and their parents.
Text: Mostly strip cartoons, but some written features on subjects of interest to this readership.
Overall freelance potential: Fairly good.
Fees: B&W pictures up to 10 square inches, £9. Other fees by agreement.

LOOK-IN
ITV Publications Ltd., 247 Tottenham Court Road, London W1P 0AU. Tel: 01-636-3666.
Editor: Colin Shelbourn.
Weekly junior *TV Times*. Concerned with children's TV, pop and general interest subjects.

Illustrations: B&W and colour. Pictures of pop, sport, celebrities, animals, humour. Covers: Colour pictures of same. 35mm acceptable.
Text: Features on subjects detailed above.
Overall freelance potential: Very good.
Editor's tips: Contact John Bickerton for pictures; Richard Tippett for features.
Fees: Various.

MY GUY

IPC Magazines Ltd., 21st Floor, King's Reach Tower, Stamford Street, London SE1 9LS. Tel: 01-261 5660.
Editor: Mary Hatchard.
Weekly magazine for teenage girls in the 12–17 age group. Uses photo stories, pop pin-ups, quizzes and fiction.
Illustrations: B&W and colour. Pop pin-ups (usually only studio shots), fashion and beauty, photo stories.
Text: Features of interest to teenage girls. 1,000 words.
Overall freelance potential: Everything in the magazine comes from freelance sources, but much of it is commissioned from known workers.
Fees: By agreement.

SCOUTING

The Scout Association, Baden-Powell House, Queen's Gate, London SW7 5JS. Tel: 01-584 7030.
Editor: Allan Gordon.
Monthly publication, containing practical programme ideas for Scout meetings, plus supplements for leaders and articles of general interest to members of the Scout movement.
Illustrations: B&W inside. Pictures of Scouting activities, preferably action shots. Covers: Colour pictures, mainly head and shoulders shots, of Scouts or Cub Scouts. 35mm acceptable.
Text: Features on expeditions, major competitions and interesting or unusual news stories. Up to three pages.
Overall freelance potential: Very high proportion of pictures and around 60 per cent of the editorial comes from freelances.
Fees: By agreement.

TODAY'S GUIDE

Girl Guides Association, 17–19 Buckingham Palace Road, London SW1W 0PT. Tel: 01-834 6242 ext. 62.
Editor: Mrs. J. V. Rush.
Monthly publication on Guiding and general topics for girls in the 10–14 age group.
Illustrations: B&W only. Action pictures on Guiding subjects. Cover: B&W pictures on Guiding activities; occasionally seasonal.

Text: Stories with Guiding themes. General articles for this age group. 750 words.
Overall freelance potential: Around 10 per cent comes from freelances.
Fees: Text, £17.25 per 1,000 words; pictures, £3.20.

County and Country

ABERDEEN LEOPARD
Leopard Publications Ltd., Rose House, 27 Rose Street, Aberdeen AB1 1TX. Tel: 0224 56652.
Editor: Diane Morgan.
Monthly magazine for North and East Scotland.
Illustrations: B&W. Occasional use for pictures from the above area. Covers: Colour pictures of the area.
Text: Outstanding features relating to Aberdeen and N.E. Scotland.
Overall freelance potential: Around 50 per cent comes from freelances.
Fees: Good; on a rising scale according to size of reproduction or length of article.

CAMBRIDGE, HUNTINGDON AND PETERBOROUGH LIFE
Cambridgeshire Life Ltd., 4–5 Free Church Passage, St. Ives, Huntingdon, Cambs. PE17 4AY. Tel: 0480 62844.
Editor: S. G. Mayes.
County magazine for the above areas.
Illustrations: B&W inside. Pictures of anything with a local interest. Covers: Colour pictures of places, properties or events within the county. Must have space at top and bottom for logo and coverlines. 6 × 6 cm minimum.
Text: Features on anything relating to the county, e.g. people, places or historical interest.
Overall freelance potential: Very high.
Fees: By agreement.

CORNISH LIFE
Smart Print Publications Ltd., Belmont House, Green Lane, Redruth, Cornwall TR15 1JZ. Tel: 0209 215273.
Editor: David Clarke.
Monthly county magazine.
Illustrations: B&W only. Pictures of towns and villages, country and coastal views, unusual subjects and news connected with Cornwall.
Text: Illustrated features on personalities, places and local events. 2,000 words.
Overall freelance potential: Most copy is obtained from regular contributors, plus perhaps one feature a month from an outside source.
Fees: Text, £7–£10; pictures, £2 each.

COUNTRY LIFE
IPC Magazines Ltd., King's Reach Tower, Stamford Street, London SE1 9LS. Tel: 01-261 5747.
Executive Editor: Geoffrey Lee.
Weekly magazine for a general readership.
Illustrations: B&W only and inside magazine. Pictures of British countryside. Covers: Colour pictures of landscapes, rural and urban. 6 × 6 cm acceptable, but 5″ × 4″ prefferred.
Text: Features of general interest, but with a bias towards rural subjects, e.g. history, estate markets etc. 950–1,800 words.
Overall freelance potential: Around 20 per cent of the magazine comes from freelance sources.
Fees: Good; on a rising scale according to size of reproduction or length of feature. Covers, £85.

COUNTRYSIDE MONTHLY
Wm Carling & Co., Market Place, Hitchin, Herts. Tel: 0462 59651.
Editor: Edward Askwith.
Monthly publication for all countryside interests and pursuits, e.g. natural history, conservation, shooting, game rearing, gundog training, game and course fishing, household dogs, mammals, birds, insects, fish flowers, plants and trees.
Illustrations: B&W only. Accurately captioned pictures on any of the subjects mentioned above. Pictures should be of specific rather than general, interest. Covers: B&W pictures of mammals and birds in the wild state, with dramatic interest and in a composition to suit the dimensions of the cover and incorporate the masthead.
Text: Features on the aforementioned subjects. Style should be of a practical, direct experience character and deadly accurate. 1,000–1,100 words.
Overall freelance potential: Excellent. Tha magazine is 100 per cent freelance contributed.
Editor's tips: Photographs and articles must be authoritative. No dubious or unchecked information.
Fees: Pictures, £10 for a cover, £8 and pro rata downwards according to size inside; articles, £10 per 1,000 words.

DERBYSHIRE TODAY
Prestige Publications Ltd., 16 St. James's Street, Derby DE1 1RL. Tel: 0332 369427.
Editor: Stephen P. Orme.
Bi-monthly glossy magazine aimed at people of all ages and with varying tastes.
Illustrations: B&W and colour. Derbyshire subjects of all types, particularly in outlying areas. Covers: Colour pictures of Derbyshire scenes; 35mm acceptable.
Text: Anything connected with Derbyshire plus features on the arts, exhibitions, auctions, general seasonal items etc. Approximately 1,000 words.

Overall freelance potential: Approximately 50 per cent comes from freelance sources.
Editor's tips: Ideas can always be discussed before material is submitted
Fees: Negotiable.

DEVON LIFE
Devon Life, 22 Southernhay West, Exeter EX1 1PR. Tel: 0392 56164.
Editor: Judy Chard.
Monthly magazine concerned with Devon people and businesses, fashion, motoring, wining
and dining, etc. Aimed at general family readership.
Illustrations: B&W and colour. Mostly used with articles, but willing to consider Devon
landscapes, seascapes, people and events. Covers: Colour pictures of subjects detailed above.
6 × 6 cm minimum.
Text: Features on anything happening in Devon or about the county generally. 700–1,000
words.
Overall freelance potential: Always happy to receive freelance material.
Fees: £10 per 1,000 words; pictures by agreement.

THE FIELD
Harmsworth Press Ltd., Carmelite House, London EC4Y 0JA. Tel: 01-353 6000.
Editor: Derek Bingham.
Weekly publication concerned with all country and sporting interests.
Illustrations: B&W and colour. Pictures of rural subjects. Covers: Colour pictures of same.
5″ × 4″ minimum.
Text: Illustrated features on country and sporting subjects. Up to 1,500 words.
Overall freelance potential: Around 30 per cent comes from outside contributors.
Fees: Text, £35 per 1,000 words; pictures by agreement.

GLOUCESTERSHIRE AND AVON LIFE
Whitehorn Press Ltd., 10 The Plain, Thornbury, Bristol BS12 2AG. Tel: 0454 413173/
412604.
Editor: W. D. Amos.
Monthly county magazine majoring on country and local history topics, arts and leisure
interests.
Illustrations: B&W only inside. No stock pictures. Pictures only to illustrate features.
Covers: Colour pictures of local views or events. 6 × 6 cm minimum.
Text: Features of local, topical or historical interest. Up to 1,500 words.
Overall freelance potential: About 60 per cent of the magazine comes from freelance
sources, but much of that is from regular contributors.
Editor's tips: Contributors should have an up-to-date view of life in the area. New slants
on old topics always welcome. No potted histories of local castles or personalities.
Fees: By negotiation.

RAYMOND LEA

THE GREAT OUTDOORS
Holmes McDougall Ltd., Ravenseft House, 302 St Vincent Street, Glasgow G2 5RG. Tel: 041-221 7000.
Editor: Roger Smith.
Monthly magazine for walkers in the UK. Covers hill and mountain walking, lowland areas, other countryside topics and environmental issues.
Illustrations: B&W pictures for stock, mostly landscapes, no towns or churches. Plus pictures to illustrate features. Covers: Colour pictures of landscapes including a figure, generally commissioned to tie in with editorial. 35mm acceptable.
Text: Features on the subjects mentioned above. 1,800–2,000 words.
Overall freelance potential: Most of the magazine comes from freelance sources.
Editor's tips: Too many freelances send material which is outside the area covered by the magazine.
Fees: Articles, £30–£50 depending on length and number of illustrations; covers, £30.

IN DUBLIN
Yahoo Ltd., 40 Lower Ormond Quay, Dublin 1. Tel: 0001 726622.
Editor: John Doyle.
Fortnightly news, reviews and what's on publication for Dublin, aimed at the 18–39 age group.
Illustrations: B&W only inside. Pictures of street scenes, local colour and oddities in the Dublin area. Covers: Colour pictures of news and entertainment events. 35mm acceptable.
Text: Articles of local or national news interest. Reviews of records, films, restaurants, art, theatre etc. Also listings of what's on in the area. 700–3,000 words.
Overall freelance potential: Around 80 per cent is contributed by freelances.
Fees: Negotiable.

LAKESCENE—WHAT'S ON IN LAKELAND
Border Press Agency Ltd., 12 Lonsdale Street, Carlisle CA1 1DD. Tel: 0228 24321.
Editor: John Barker.
Monthly publication for tourists and residents in the Lake District. Gives details of events and diary dates for the area.
Illustrations: B&W only. Pictures of the Lake District. Covers: B&W prints of Cumbria leisure scenes.
Text: Articles about leisure activities in Cumbria. 500 words.
Overall freelance potential: Very good if material is suitable.
Fees: By negotiation.

LANCASHIRE LIFE
Whitehorn Press Ltd., Thomson House, Withy Grove, Manchester M60 4BL. Tel: 061-834 1234.
Editor: William Amos.
Monthly county magazine with a county readership.

Illustrations: B&W only inside the magazine. Mainly for use with features. Covers: Colour shots of Lancashire scenes to fit into an upright format with sufficient sky area for magazine's logo; 6 × 6 cm minimum.
Text: Articles and stories specifically concerned with Lancashire. 500–2,000 words.
Overall freelance potential: Good; around 25 per cent supplied from freelance sources.
Editor's tips: Prospective contributors would save themselves, and the magazine, time if they studied the publication before submitting. They are also advised to submit ideas before executing them.
Fees: £22 for covers; other material by negotiation.

LINCOLNSHIRE LIFE
Lincolnshire Life Ltd., 10 Dudley Street, Grimsby, South Humberside DN31 2AX. Tel: 0472 56094.
Editor: David Robinson.
Monthly magazine, dealing with county life past and present from the Humber to the Wash.
Illustrations: B&W only inside. Pictures of people and places within the county of Lincolnshire. No current social events. Covers: Colour pictures of landscapes, buildings, street scenes, etc. preferably with activity. 35mm acceptable, but 6 × 6 cm preferred.
Text: Features on people and places within the appropriate area. 1,000–3,000 words.
Overall freelance potential: Virtually the whole magazine comes from freelance sources.
Fees: By agreement.

KENT LIFE
South Eastern Newspapers Ltd., Jasaba House, Sheldon Way, Larkfield, Maidstone, Kent. Tel: 0662 76947.
Editor: Alan Moultrie.
Monthly consumer magazine concerned with all aspects of Kent.
Illustrations: Mainly for cover use, colour pictures of Kentish scenes; 35mm acceptable.
Text: Articles about Kent—people or places. 800–1,000 words.
Overall freelance potential: About 40 per cent bought from freelances, but all specially commissioned. Check with magazine before submitting.
Fees: Good. On a rising scale according to size of reproduction of number of words.

MANX LIFE
Isle of Man Examiner Ltd., Hill Street, Douglas, Isle of Man. Tel: 0624 3074.
Editor: Valerie Roach.
Bi-monthly magazine exclusively interested in Manx subjects, e.g. current affairs, personalities, consumer interests and freshly researched historical and cultural material.
Illustrations: B&W only inside. Pictures used only as illustrations to features. Covers: Colour pictures of views and activities in the Isle of Man. Vertical format; 35mm acceptable.
Text: Features of strictly Manx interest. Mostly factual articles, occasionally fiction and poems. 1,000–2,500 words.

Overall freelance potential: Approximately 50 per cent of material is contributed, but only from freelances with detailed and accurate knowledge of Manx affairs.
Editor's tips: Check first to see if your chosen subject has already been covered.
Fees: Text, £10 per 1,000 words; B&W pictures, up to £5; colour, £10.

METRO NEWS
11 Inman Street, Bury, Greater Manchester. Tel: 061-764 7350.
Editor: Tony Benge.
Monthly publication concerned with local problems and issues in Greater Manchester.
Illustrations: B&W only. Pictures relevant to the area. Covers: B&W pictures of the same.
Text: Features on Greater Manchester topics with a broad left bias. 300 words.
Overall freelance potential: All material is contributed.
Editor's tips: Contributors must have an interesting knowledge of the area covered.
Fees: By negotiation.

NORTH EAST TIMES
Chris Robinson (Publishing) Ltd., 8 Lansdowne Terrace, Gosforth, Newcastle-upon-Tyne. Tel: 0632 844495.
Editor: Chris Robinson.
Monthly upmarket county magazine.
Illustrations: B&W only. Any general interest pictures connected with the north-east of England.
Text: Features on fashion, property, motoring, wining and dining, sport, etc. all with north-east connections. Around 750 words with two pictures.
Overall freelance potential: Very good.
Fees: By agreement.

NORTHAMPTONSHIRE AND BEDFORDSHIRE LIFE
Cambridgeshire Life Ltd., 4–5 Free Church Passage, St. Ives, Huntingdon, Cambs PE17 4AY. Tel: 0480 62844.
Editor: S. G. Mayes.
County magazine for the above areas.
Illustrations: B&W inside. Pictures of anything with a local interest. Covers: Colour pictures of places, properties or events within the county. Must have space at top and bottom for logo and coverlines. 6 × 6 cm minimum.
Text: Features on anything relating to the county, e.g. people, places or historical interest.
Overall freelance potential: Very high.
Fees: By agreement.

RUCKSACK
The Ramblers' Association, 1–5 Wandsworth Road, London SW8 2LJ. Tel: 01-582 6878.
Editor: Cathy Brunsden.
Journal for all members of the Ramblers' Association and also libraries. Published three times per year.

Illustrations: B&W only. Any scenic views of the countryside without people or with ramblers. Also pictures of problems encountered when walking in the countryside, e.g. damaged bridges, locked gates, obstructed footpaths, etc.
Text: Articles on the work of the Ramblers' Association. Any issues affecting the countryside or walkers' interests. Maps, news, letters, book reviews.
Overall freelance potential: Most contributors are either RA members or keen walkers, sympathetic to the association's work.
Fees: By agreement, but low.

SCOTS INDEPENDENT

Scots Independent (Newspapers) Ltd., 51 Cowane Street, Stirling. Tel: 0786 3523.
Editor: Colin Bell.
Monthly publication bringing news, features and reviews to Scottish Nationalists. Political, industrial, economic, cultural and historical interests catered for.
Illustrations: B&W only. Pictures for stock—Scottish industrial subjects and townscapes. Pictures for features—anything of interest to patriotic Scots, e.g. Scots achievements world-wide, Scottish political/economic/industrial/artistic figures abroad. Factual captions imperative.
Text: Features on Scottish history, literature, economy, politics, Scots abroad, famous Scots etc. 400–800 words.
Overall freelance potential: Small; most material comes from Scottish sources and by prior arrangement.
Editor's tips: Would welcome the names of freelances outside Scotland for potential commissions. Do not send pictures of kilts, haggis or Billy Connolly.
Fees: By negotiation.

THE SCOTS MAGAZINE

D. C. Thomson and Co. Ltd., 7 Bank Street, Dundee DD1 9HU. Tel: 0382 23131.
Editor: Maurice Fleming.
Monthly magazine for Scots at home and abroad, concerned with Scottish subjects.
Illustrations: B&W inside. Scottish scenes. Covers: Colour pictures of Scottish scenes, vertical format. No heather, tartan or highland cattle. 35mm acceptable.
Text: Features on all aspects of Scottish life past and present. 2,000–3,500 words.
Overall freelance potential: Around 80 per cent of the magazine comes from freelances.
Editor's tips: Nothing on sport, politics, household, beauty, motoring or religion.
Fees: Variable.

THE SCOTSMAN MAGAZINE

The Scotsman Publication Ltd., 20 North Bridge, Edinburgh. Tel: 031-225 2468.
Editor: Richard Wilson.
Monthly magazine, given away with *The Scotsman* newspaper.
Illustrations: Pictures inside only as illustrations to articles. Covers: Colour pictures taken from inside feature. 35mm acceptable.

Text: Features of a 'quality paper' standard. General content of foreign and UK picture features. No travelogues. Around 1,500 words.
Overall freelance potential: Around 75 per cent of the magazine is freelance, but the quality must be high.
Fees: £80 per page; £40 half page, down to £20 minimum.

SCOTTISH FIELD
Holmes McDougall Ltd., Ravenseft House, 302 St. Vincent Street, Glasgow G2 5NL. Tel: 041-221 7000.
Editor: Roderick Martine.
Monthly magazine reflecting the quality of life in Scotland, e.g. sporting, leisure, the arts, social, etc. Aimed at all Scots at home and abroad.
Illustrations: B&W and colour. Scenics of Scotland plus pictures to illustrate articles. Covers: Colour pictures of people, activities and landscapes. 35mm acceptable.
Text: Features on anything related to Scottish life, either present day or historical. 1,500–2,000 words.
Overall freelance potential: Most articles are commissioned, but the magazine is 60 per cent freelance.
Fees: Negotiable.

THE SCOTTISH REVIEW
Scottish Civic Trust, 24 George Square, Glasgow G2 1EF. Tel: 041-221 1466.
Editor: Maurice Lindsay.
Quarterly magazine aimed at those interested in the arts and environment of Scotland.
Illustrations: Pictures are always related to text.
Text: Articles, short stories and poems connected with Scotland or produced by Scotland. 2,000–2,500 words.
Overall freelance potential: Most material is by invitation and very little by house writers. A lot of unsolicited material is received and the amount used varies from issue to issue.
Fees: £5 per page.

SHOOTING TIMES AND COUNTRY MAGAZINE
Burlington Publishing Co. Ltd., 10 Sheet Street, Windsor, Berkshire SL4 1BG. Tel: 075-35 56061.
Editor: W. A. Jackson.
Weekly magazine covering all aspects of field sports, e.g. hunting, shooting (clay, game and some big game), fishing (game only), also terriers, lurchers and ferrets, plus all aspects of the countryside.
Illustrations: B&W only inside. Pictures of above subjects for file use. Covers: Colour pictures of hunting, shooting, fishing, etc. Vertical shape with space for logo. 6 × 6 cm minimum.

Text: Features on any aspect of field sports, possibly humorous, preferably with one illustration, photograph or drawing.
Overall freelance potential: Good.
Fees: Features, £30–£35; B&W pictures, £6; covers, £50.

SPOTLIGHT
Spotlight Magazine Group, 16A Marine Parade West, Lee on Solent, Hampshire PO13 9LW. Tel: 0705 550397.
Editor: Jean Harvey.
Monthly glossy consumer and community magazine.
Illustrations: B&W only. All types of pictures from general scenes to anything of interest. Hampshire-related subjects especially welcome. Covers: B&W pictures of sailing, local South Hampshire scenes, people of local interest and sporting events.
Text: General illustrated articles, plus local history, sailing and women's features other than cooking or household interest. 500–1,000 words.
Overall freelance potential: Always looking for good general material for stock.
Editor's tips: Telephone inquiries are welcomed in the first instance.
Fees: By arrangement, according to the type of material submitted.

SURREY PROPERTY MAIL
Surrey Property Mail Ltd., 1 High Street, Godalming, Surrey. Tel: 04868 28811/20573/20031.
Editor: Peter Tribe.
Twice monthly publication for local news and property-orientated subjects in a 15 mile radius of Guildford.
Illustrations: B&W only. Human interest, local news and property-related subjects. Also home improvement, motoring, sport and action pictures on a local or regional basis. Covers: B/W property-related subjects, or local news, human interest or personalities with local angle.
Text: Features on subjects detailed above. Also financial, stockmarket, insurance and money matters. 400–500 words (longer at editor's discretion).
Overall freelance potential: Over 80 per cent of the issue comes from freelances and all pictures are freelance-contributed.
Fees: Text, £35 for 500 words; pictures from £15.

THIS ENGLAND
This England Ltd., Alma House, Rodney Road, Cheltenham, Gloucestershire. Tel: 0242 35185.
Editor: Roy Faiers.
Quarterly magazine on England, mainly the past, some present. Uses nostalgia, patriotism, countryside, literary subjects. Aimed at those who love England and all things English.

Illustrations: B&W and colour. Pictures for stock or use in their own right. Pictures of places, not the over-photographed areas, but the *real* England. Covers: Colour seasonal pictures of English countryside with human interest. 6 × 6 minimum.
Text: Illustrated articles on all things English. 1,500–2,000 words.
Overall freelance potential: Around 70 per cent of the magazine comes from freelances.
Fees: Covers, £30; pictures inside, from £5 depending on size. Text by agreement.

WARWICKSHIRE AND WORCESTERSHIRE LIFE
The Whitehorn Press Ltd., 27 Waterloo Place, Leamington Spa, Warwickshire CU32 5LF.
Tel: 0926 22003/22372.
Editor: W. D. Amos.
Monthly magazine for a readership in Warwickshire, Worcestershire and the West Midlands. Emphasis on subjects relating to local history, the environment, topography and personalities of the region.
Illustrations: B&W pictures to accompany features. Covers: Colour pictures of rural or urban scenes in the relevant counties, preferably in an upright format; 6 × 6 cm minimum.
Text: Any subject relating to the life of the region, past and present. 900–1,000 words.
Overall freelance potential: Limited; most material comes from staff writers and photographers.
Editor's tips: Only work of the highest standard is considered.
Fees: By arrangement.

WHAT'S ON ACROSS SCOTLAND
What's On Publications, 25 St. Bernard's Crescent, Edinburgh EH4 1NR. Tel: 031-332 0471.
Editor: Alistair Stein.
Monthly 'what's on' magazine aimed at general readership.
Illustrations: Covers only. Colour pictures on Scottish subjects. Scottish-based photographers preferred. 35mm acceptable.
Text: No freelance market.
Overall freelance potential: Good for the right photographers. Mostly commissioned.
Fees: £100 per cover shot plus expenses.

Cycling and Motorcycling

BICYCLE TIMES
Kelthorn Ltd., 26 Commercial Buildings, Dunston, Gateshead NE11 9AA. Tel: 0632 608113.
Editor: Peter Lumley.
Monthly publication aimed at touring and general bicycle use. No racing. Read by cyclists from mid-teens onwards.

Illustrations: B&W mostly, rarely colour. Pictures on unusual subjects that would appeal to tourists, especially where cyclists are featured. No carnival events. Stock photographs should be well captioned.
Text: Technical features by arrangement only. Touring articles should be written with the bicycle rider in mind. Include route details. 850–2,500 words.
Overall freelance potential: Most contributed by established contacts.
Editor's tips: Imagination in this market could be rewarding.
Fees: By negotiation.

BIKE

East Midland Allied Press, 7–11 Lexington Street, London W1. Tel: 01-437 6216.
Editor: Dave Calderwood.
Monthly motorcycling magazine aimed at road riding enthusiasts in the 16–25 age group.
Illustrations: B&W and colour. Sporting pictures for file. Freelance photographers hired to take pictures for features. These supply action pictures, 'moody' statics and shots that are strong on creative effects. 35mm acceptable.
Text: Features on touring, long term reports on bikes, incidents of interest to the readership. 1,000–4,000 words.
Overall freelance potential: All photography comes from freelances; 20 per cent of the words are contributed.
Editor's tips: Be original.
Fees: By agreement.

BMX ACTION BIKE

UKBMX Publications Ltd., 134 Tooley Street, London SE1 2TV. Tel: 01-403 3201.
Editors: Richard Grant and Nigel Thomas.
Bi-monthly publication for motocross enthusiasts and bicycle riders from the age of eight upwards.
Illustrations: B&W and colour. Only from BMX meetings covered by the magazine. Also BMX hotshots in action. Covers: Colour pictures of BMX hot shots. 35mm acceptable.
Text: No freelance market.
Overall freelance potential: Around 90 per cent of the magazine is freelance.
Fees: Colour, £30; B&W, £20.

CLASSIC BIKE

East Midlands Allied Press, Bushfield House, Orton Centre, Peterborough PE2 0UW. Tel: 0733 237111.
Editor: Mike Nicks.
Monthly magazine dealing with thoroughbred and classic motocycles from 1900 to the early 1970s with special emphasis on 1945–70.
Illustrations: B&W and colour. Pictures of vintage classic rallies, races, restored motor-cycles. 35mm acceptable.

Text: Technical features, histories of particular motorcycles, restoration stories, profiles of famous riders, designers etc. 500–2,000 words.
Overall freelance potential: Around 50 per cent of the magazine is freelance contributed.
Fees: By agreement and on merit.

CYCLIST MONTHLY

IPC Specialist & Professional Press Ltd., Surrey House, 1 Throwley Way, Sutton, Surrey SM1 4QQ. Tel: 01-643 8040.
Editor: John Wilcockson.
Monthly magazine aimed at the committed cyclist, including strong coverage of cycle sport.
Illustrations: Some colour, but mostly B&W. Major cycle races and leading cyclists, new or revolutionary bicycles, and general off-beat material of interest to cyclists. Covers: Colour, usually a racing shot and often from a major continental race.
Text: Knowledgeable articles and features on any aspect of cycling will be considered.
Overall freelance potential: Good—plenty of room for freelance material.
Fees: By negotiation.

THE CLASSIC MOTOR CYCLE

IPC Specialist and Professional Press Ltd., Surrey house, 1 Throwley Way, Sutton, Surrey SM1 4QQ. Tel: 01-643 8040.
Editor: Bob Currie.
Bi-monthly publication that specialises in a nostalgic survey of veteran, vintage and post-war classic motor cycles and motor cycling.
Illustrations: B&W and colour. Pictures that cover interesting restoration projects, unusual machines, personalities with a background story, etc. Covers: Colour pictures, usually a close-up of a well-restored and technically interesting motor cycle. Usually tied in with editorial. 35mm acceptable inside. 35mm acceptable on covers, but 6 × 6 cm preferred.
Text: Features on subjects detailed above. 850–1,500 words.
Overall freelance potential: Around 60 per cent of the magazine comes from freelances, but much of it is commissioned.
Editor's tips: Potential contributors must have a good technical knowledge of the field.
Fees: Good; on a rising scale according to size of reproduction or length of article.

CYCLE TRADE NEWS

Spalding and Watts Publishing Company, 113 Anerley Road, London SE20 8AJ. Tel: 01-659 1827/8.
Editor: John Moore.
Monthly publication for the UK cycle trade, covering every aspect of the business.
Illustrations: B&W and colour. Pictures of cycles of special interest or with a strong trade/manufacturing/importing flavour. 6 × 6 cm minimum.
Text: Illustrated features on the cycle trade, but subject only to prior consultation with the editor.

WAYNE PAULO

Overall freelance potential: Currently low, but growth is possible.
Editor's tips: This is a specialist publication and a good understanding of the subject is needed.
Fees: By agreement.

MOTORCYCLING
Media Estates Ltd., 1 Garrick House, Carrington Street, London W1Y 7LF. Tel: 01-499 0321.
Editor: Bob Goddard.
Monthly magazine for motorcycling enthusiasts, especially those in the 16–24 age group. Covers most motorcycle related topics with special emphasis on road tests and technical features.
Illustrations: B&W and colour. Pictures of all motorcycling topics; 35mm acceptable. Covers: Colour pictures of current bikes on test, but no freelance market.
Text: Features which cannot become dated. No events and no touring articles. Approximately 2,500 words.

Overall freelance potential: Around 25 per cent of the magazine is contributed.
Editor's tips: Pictures and features should be of unusual subjects. Sharp pictures and tight copy essential.
Fees: Text, £50 per 1,000 words; B&W pictures, £23.10; colour, £54.25.

MOTORCYCLE TRADE NEWS
Spalding and Watts Publishing Ltd., 113 Anerley Road, London SE20 8AJ. Tel: 01-659 1827/8.
Editor: John Moore.
Monthly publication for the UK motorcycle trade.
Illustrations: B&W and colour. Pictures of motorcycles of special interest or with a strong trade/manufacturing/importing angle. 6 × 6 cm minimum.
Text: Illustrated features on the motorcycle trade, but subject only to prior consultation with the editor.
Overall freelance potential: Currently low, but growth is possible.
Editor's tips: This is a specialist publication and a good understanding of the subject is needed.
Fees: By agreement.

SUPERBIKE MAGAZINE
Link House Magazines (Croydon) Ltd., Dingwall Avenue, Croydon CR9 2TA. Tel: 01-686 2599.
Editor: Michael Scott.
Monthly magazine for motorcycle enthusiasts, aimed at the serious rider as well as newer motorcycle fans. Humour a speciality.
Illustrations: B&W and colour. Pictures of unusual motorcycles, road-racing, drag-racing and other sports pictures of unusual interest or impact. Crash sequences. Girls with motorcycles, rallies, protest rides, etc. 35mm acceptable inside. Covers: Colour pictures with strong motorcycle interest, 6 × 6 cm minimum.
Text: Features of general or specific motorcycle interest. 1,500–3,500 words.
Overall freelance potential: Around 15 per cent of the magazine is contributed from outside sources.
Fees: B&W pictures, £5–£20; colour, £10–£50; text, £35–£60 per 1,000 words.

Defence

DEFENCE
Whitton Press Ltd., 50 High Street, Eton, Berks. SL4 6BL. Tel: 075-35 62515.
Editor: Michael Gething.
Monthly publication covering military equipment, e.g. guns, tanks, ships, aircraft and electronics, as well as military topics of world interest.

Illustrations: B&W and colour. Pictures showing the whole system (gun, tank, ship or aircraft) clearly, or a portion of the system which is of particular interest. Also good action shots. Covers: Colour pictures in close-up of military equipment in use. 35mm acceptable inside, 6 × 6 cm minimum for covers.
Text: No freelance market.
Overall freelance potential: Around 5 per cent is contributed from outside sources.
Editor's tips: The magazine is always on the look-out for a different approach to a subject.
Fees: Pictures inside, £5 for B&W, £10 for colour; covers, £25.

DEFENCE MATERIAL
Eldon Publications Ltd., 30–32 Fleet Street, London EC4Y 1AH. Tel: 01-353 9098.
Editor: Doug Richardson.
Bi-monthly journal for the worldwide promotion of British defence equipment. Aimed at the procurement authorities in 104 countries.
Illustrations: B&W only inside. Pictures of all British manufactured items of defence equipment. Covers: Colour pictures of same. 6 × 6 cm minimum.
Text: Features about any British defence equipment. 1,000–3,000 words.
Overall freelance potential: An occasional use for outside contributors.
Fees: Negotiable.

JOURNAL OF THE ROYAL UNITED SERVICES INSTITUTE FOR DEFENCE STUDIES
RUSI, Whitehall, London SWIA 2ET. Tel: 01-930 5854.
Editor: Jennifer Shaw.
Quarterly publication for all those interested in defence in Britain and overseas. Aimed at serving forces, civil servants, politicians, journalists, industrialists and academics.
Illustrations: B&W only. Pictures used only as illustrations to features.
Text: Authoritative articles relating to problems of defence and international relations, preferably with reference to current affairs. Illustrated with pictures and maps. 4,000–5,000 words.
Overall freelance potential: On spec articles always welcome.
Fees: £12.50 per 1,000 words.

THE LEGION
South Eastern Newspapers Ltd., Jasaba House, Sheldon Way, Larkfield, Kent. Tel. 0662 76947.
Editor: David Bosley.
Bi-monthly official journal of the Royal British Legion.
Illustrations: Colour and B&W on any subject concerned with the Royal British Legion or military matters. Covers: Colour shots concerned with the Legion; 35mm acceptable.
Text: Short news stories and features concerned with the Legion or with military matters.
Overall freelance potential: Small at the moment, but increasing.
Fees: Good. On a rising scale according to size of reproduction or length of article.

MARITIME DEFENCE
Eldon Publications, 30–32 Fleet Street, London EC4Y 1AH. Tel: 01-353 9098.
Editor: Geoffrey Wood.
Monthly technical publication on naval warships and their equipment.
Illustrations: B&W only. Used as illustrations to features. Covers: Pictures related to current contents.
Text: Features on naval vessels and their equipment, weapons and associated systems.
Overall freelance potential: Small. Mostly from contributors established in the field.
Fees: Negotiable.

NAVY INTERNATIONAL
Maritime World Ltd., 'Hunters Moon', Hogspudding Lane, Newdigate, Dorking, Surrey RH5 5DS. Tel: 030-677 442.
Editor: Anthony Watts.
Monthly magazine ranging across the whole field of maritime affairs, with special reference to the importance to the Free World of maintaining the freedom of the seas, the political and strategic problems involved and the military means of doing so.
Illustrations: B&W only inside the magazine. Mainly as illustrations for features. Covers: Colour pictures of naval vessels at sea.
Text: Features on maritime affairs on an international level. 2,000–3,000 words.
Overall freelance potential: Over 60 per cent of the magazine comes from freelance sources.
Fees: £35 per 1,000 words; pictures by agreement.

Education and Youth Work

ARENA
Standing Conference of Youth Organisations in Northern Ireland, 50 University Street, Belfast BT7 1HB. Tel: 0232 224440.
Editor: Roger Hope.
Bi-monthly publication for youth workers, full time, part time and volunteers.
Illustrations: B&W only. Pictures of young people engaged in any sort of activity that might have a possible use for future articles. Covers: B&W pictures linked with feature inside. Generally showing young people in some kind of activity or reflecting a situation in which young people find themselves.
Text: Features on equipment for youth groups, activity ideas for youth workers and the situation for young people in Northern Ireland. Around 1,500 words.
Overall freelance potential: Very little offered at the moment, but a good potential for the right pictures.
Fees: Pictures, £3–£10; text by agreement.

ART AND CRAFT

Scholastic Publications Ltd., 141–143 Drury Lane, London WC2B 5TG. Tel: 01-379 7333.
Editor: Kate Pountney.
Monthly publication aimed at infant and primary school teachers. Provides creative, stimulating classroom ideas in arts and crafts.
Illustrations: B&W only. Pictures involving children, especially engaged in arts activities. The magazine is always on the look-out for specific subjects and photographers are recommended to contact the editor for a current topics list.
Text: Creative, exciting ideas for classroom use. A different topic is covered each month and the topics list will also help aspiring writers in this field.
Overall freelance potential: Mostly for B&W pictures. A good market for ex-teachers and crafts people.
Editor's tips: Make sure material is tailored to classroom ideas, rather than arts and crafts in general.
Fees: £18 per single page; £30 for double page spread. Rates under review, due to be increased.

BRISTOL NEWSLETTER

University of Bristol, 9 Woodland Road, Bristol BS8 1TB. Tel: 0272 24161 ext. 483/495.
Editor: Don Carleton.
Publication aimed at staff, students and employees of Bristol University. Covers all aspects of academic life, plus local arts coverage. Published 21 times per year.
Illustrations: B&W and colour. Pictures relating to university activities. They are used in their own right and can also show Bristol university people in a newsworthy picture elsewhere. No pictures of the university buildings are required. Covers: similar to above. B&W only.
Text: No requirements.
Overall freelance potential: Small.
Editor's tips: Send contact sheets rather than full-size pictures in the first instance. 35mm is preferred.
Fees: Not more than £15 for first use of B&W.

CRAFT, DESIGN AND TECHNOLOGY NEWS

C. F. Marcom Ltd., Western Lodge, Station Road, Andoversford, Cheltenham, Gloucestershire GL50 4LA. Tel: 0242-82 740/749.
Editor: Colin Elliott.
Quarterly publication for teachers of craft, design and technology, mainly at secondary level.
Illustrations: B&W only. Pictures relating to craft teaching subjects.
Text: Features on the teaching of crafts. 1,000–1,500 words.
Overall freelance potential: Small.
Fees: By arrangement.

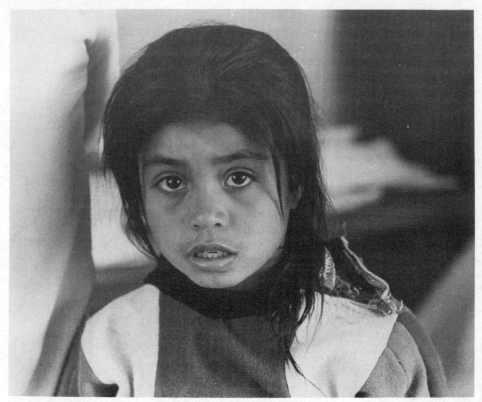

DEREK FURLONG

DEVELOPMENT EDUCATION
Lancashire Development Education Centre, 42 Fishergate, Preston PR1 2AS. Tel: 0772 52299.
Editor: Colin Scott.
Published three times per year for teachers, clergy and various adult groups.
Illustrations: B&W only. Pictures of Third World, minority interests, multiracial education, peace education, etc. Covers: B&W pictures of same.
Text: Features on subjects detailed above.
Overall freelance potential: Quite good for the contributor with the specialist knowledge.
Fees: By negotiation.

FASHION AND CRAFT
Blenheim Publications Ltd., 12 Princess Mews, Belsize Village, London NW3 5AP. Tel: 01-435 8961.
Editor: Derek Stirling.

Published five times a year for lecturers, teachers, students and craftpeople in general. Includes needlecraft, fashion, creative and rural crafts, arts and design.
Illustrations: B&W only. Pictures related to the above fields always considered.
Text: Features on the above crafts with the appropriate market well in mind. Maximum, 1,500 words.
Overall freelance potential: Quite good.
Fees: By arrangement.

ISIS NEWSLETTER

Independent Schools Information Service, 26 Caxton Street, London SW1H 0RG. Tel: 01-222 0065/7535.
Editor: Tim Devlin.
Published once per school term for staff, heads and parents. Concerns news and views on education.
Illustrations: B&W only. Pictures of children at school, activities likely to be of interest to this readership, school buildings and pupils.
Text: No freelance market.
Overall freelance potential: Low.
Fees: By agreement.

JUNIOR EDUCATION

Scholastic Publications (Magazines) Ltd., 141–3 Drury Lane, London WC2B 5TG. Tel: 01-379 7333.
Editor: Lucy Hall.
Monthly publication for junior school teachers.
Illustrations: B&W and colour. Good, unposed B&W pictures of children in the 8–12 age range in and out of school, in more or less any situation. Some portrait shots used. Pictures that can be used symbolically or where the child cannot be identified are particularly useful. Covers: Colour pictures involving natural history, shops, weather, transport, seasons or the environment. 35mm acceptable.
Text: Willing to consider good, practical ideas for work in the junior classroom. 1,000 words.
Overall freelance potential: Around 60 per cent of the pictures come from freelances or agencies.
Fees: By agreement.

PRACTICAL EDUCATION

Educational Institute of Design, Craft and Technology, 24 Elm Road, Kingswood, Bristol BS15 2ST.
Editor: Peter Dawson.
Published three times a year for teachers and others interested in craft, design and technology education.
Illustrations: Mostly as illustrations to articles. Covers: B&W pictures of historical interest, items of craftwork, schools, workshops, abstracts, etc.

Text: Illustrated features on craft education topics. Information and news of materials, tools and equipment, processes and new designs and organisational methods in education.
Overall freelance potential: Much of the material is donated gratis by members of the Institute. Occasional market for commissioned work.
Editor's tips: Do not send material without first contacting the magazine. Suitable qualifications in the subject will be expected in contributors.
Fees: Negotiable.

PRACTICAL ENGLISH TEACHING

MGP Ltd., 140 Kensington Church Street, London W8 4BN. Tel: 01-229 9531.
Editor: Philip Gallagher.
Quarterly publication featuring practical teaching ideas plus news and information for teachers of English as a foreign language in European secondary schools.
Illustrations: B&W inside. Pictures of language teaching activities being carried out in classes or teacher training sessions. Classes should be of the 9–19 age group. Covers: Colour pictures of language teachers in action, pupils participating in learning activities, teachers demonstrating a language teaching technique, etc. 35mm acceptable.
Text: Articles on language teaching techniques and issues of current interest in English language teaching. Outlines only considered in the first instance. 1,500–2,500 words.
Overall freelance potential: Fairly high.
Fees: Text, £3.50 per 100 words; B&W pictures, £15; covers, £50 plus.

SAFETY EDUCATION

The Royal Society for the Prevention of Accidents, Cannon House, The Priory, Queensway, Birmingham B4 6BS. Tel: 021-233 2461.
Editor: Jane Bishop.
Published three times per year and aimed at teachers and educationalists in local authorities.
Illustrations: B&W and colour. Pictures depicting road safety, home safety, industrial safety and water safety subjects; predominantly aimed at children. Covers: Colour pictures of similar subjects; 35mm acceptable.
Text: Features on topics detailed above. 1,000–3,000 words.
Overall freelance potential: Pictures, 10 per cent of the magazine; articles, 60–70 per cent.
Fees: Good; on a rising scale according to the size of reproduction or length of article.

SECONDARY EDUCATION JOURNAL

National Union of Teachers, Hamilton House, Mabledon Place, London WC1H 9BD. Tel: 01-387 2442.
Editor: Alan Evans.
Published three times per year for secondary school teachers and educationalists.
Illustrations: None.
Text: Articles on topical educational issues, reviews of educational books. Most subjects of interest to secondary school teachers.

Overall freelance potential: Small; most articles are commissioned on a specific theme, though unsolicited articles have been accepted occasionally.
Editor's tips: A preliminary letter, outlining the nature of the proposed article is advisable.
Fees: £30 per article.

SPECIAL EDUCATION: FORWARD TRENDS
National Council for Special Education, 12 Hollycroft Avenue, London NW3 7QL. Tel: 01-794 7109.
Editor: Margaret Peter.
Quarterly publication on the education of all types of handicapped children. Primarily for teachers, college and university lecturers, educational psychologists, administrators etc.
Illustrations: B&W only. Pictures of handicapped children in schools. Covers: Similar, B&W only.
Text: Articles are written almost exclusively by those working professionally in the field. They relate to educational innovations, research methods etc. 3,300 words.
Overall freelance potential: Very small.
Fees: Nominal.

YOUTH IN SOCIETY
National Youth Bureau, 17–23 Albion Street, Leicester LE1 6GD. Tel: 0533 554775.
Editor: Ric Rogers.
Monthly publication for youth workers, social workers, young volunteer organisers, careers officers, supervisors on youth unemployment schemes, youth counsellors and policy makers in the youth affairs field.
Illustrations: B&W only. Pictures of young people, aged between 15 and 21, involved in group activities of a formal or informal nature, e.g. street activities such as shopping, rioting, transport, relationships with police, inter-generational groups, etc.
Text: No freelance market.
Overall freelance potential: About 10 per cent of the illustrations come from general freelances and another 50 per cent from specially commissioned freelances.
Fees: From £4 per print used.

YOUTHOPIA
Catholic Youth Council, 20–23 Arran Quay, Dublin 7. Tel: 0001 725055/725407/725230.
Editor: Brian Merriman.
Published ten times per year for adults involved with youth work.
Illustrations: B&W only. Pictures of young people involved with social issues.
Text: No freelance market.
Overall freelance potential: Limited.
Fees: Negotiable.

YOUTH SERVICE SCENE
National Youth Bureau, 17/23 Albion Street, Leicester LE1 6GD. Tel: 0533 554775.
Editor: Michael Hatcliffe.

Monthly (except August) publication for full-time and part-time youth workers, paid and voluntary, in a wide range of provision for young people in the 14 to 21 age group.
Illustrations: B&W only. Pictures of young people in the 14 to 21 age group, involved in specific group activities.
Text: No freelance market.
Overall freelance potential: About 20 per cent of illustrations come from freelance sources.
Fees: From £4 per print used.

Electrical and Electronics

CB RADIO
CB Radio Magazine Ltd., British Breaker Productions, Tudor Works, Beaconsfield Road, Hayes, Middlesex UB4 0FL. Tel: 01-561 3335.
Editor: James O'Hara.
Monthly magazine for CB radio enthusiasts.
Illustrations: B&W only inside. Mostly as illustrations to features mentioned below. Covers: Colour pictures linked to leading article; 35mm acceptable.
Text: Anything CB or communications related. Technical do-it-yourself projects. Features, both technical and simplified. Up to 1,500 words.
Overall freelance potential: Potentially higher than the amount currently used—15–20 per cent.
Fees: Negotiable.

CB TRADE
CB Trade Magazine Ltd., Tudor Works, Beaconsfield Road, Hayes, Middlesex UB4 0FL. Tel: 01-561 3335.
Editor: James O'Hara.
Monthly magazine for the CB trade, covering retail, importers and manufacturers as well as in-car entertainment and radio communications specialists.
Illustrations: B&W mostly inside. Pictures linked with features mentioned below. Covers: Colour pictures linked with leading article; 35mm acceptable.
Text: Trade-orientated features, i.e. reports of shows, developments and technology; selling and presentation of CB equipment; general communications. Up to 1,500 words.
Overall freelance potential: Small.
Fees: Negotiable.

CITIZEN'S BAND
Argus Specialist Publications Ltd., 145 Charing Cross Road, London WC2H 0EE. Tel: 01-437 1002.
Editor: Chris Adam-Smith.

Monthly magazine for CB radio enthusiasts and anyone else interested in the world of two-way communications.

Illustrations: B&W only. Pictures connected with the CB world.

Text: Features on CB and two-way radio systems. News and reviews of equipment, clubs, etc. 1,000–2,000 words.

Overall freelance potential: Between 10 and 15 per cent comes from freelances. The editor prefers to commission work.

Editor's tips: The magazine is always on the look-out for features on new and novel uses for CB or short news items on how CB might have been used to report accidents, crime or traffic problems, etc.

Fees: £25 per published page.

COMPUTER MARKETPLACE

Infotec Publishing, 243 Caledonian Road, London N1 1ED. Tel: 01-278 4031.

Editor: David Crosweller.

Monthly publication for the microcomputer trade.

Illustrations: B&W only. Pictures of the microcomputer world with a strong trade angle.

Text: Features on microcomputers, but aimed at the trade. 1,000–1,500 words.

Overall freelance potential: Very small.

Fees: Negotiable.

COMPUTING TODAY

Argus Specialist Publications Ltd., 145 Charing Cross Road, London WC2H 0EE. Tel: 01-437 1002.

Editor: Henry Budgett.

Monthly magazine for the owner and user of microcomputers who wish to increase their understanding of the way they can be used for business, domestic or professional activities.

Illustrations: B&W only. Pictures to illustrate features and for stock purposes. Pictures of computer systems or their applications.

Text: Illustrated features on the subjects detailed above, submitted first in precis form. 1,500–3,000 words.

Overall freelance potential: Approximately 40 per cent of the magazine comes from freelances.

Editor's tips: Program material should be listed on plain paper and should be submitted with sufficient documentation.

Fees: By negotiation.

ELECTRICAL AND ELECTRONIC TRADER

IPC Electrical and Electronic Press Ltd., Room L202, Quadrant House, The Quadrant, Sutton, Surrey SM2 5AS. Tel: 01-661 3500.

Editor: Arthur Ord-Hume.

Fortnightly publication for retailers of electrical domestic appliances; manufacturers, distributors and wholesalers of same; repair and service departments.

Illustrations: B&W and colour. Pictures of high dealer interest; outstanding window or in-store displays. Covers: Colour pictures of same. 6 × 6 cm minimum.
Text: Dealer profiles, generally independents rather than multiples. 500–1,000 words.
Overall freelance potential: Up to 10 per cent comes from outside sources.
Editor's tips: No work is accepted without prior discussion and commission from the editor.
Fees: On a rising scale according to the size of picture or length of article.

ELECTRICAL AND RADIO TRADING

IPC Electrical and Electronic Press Ltd., Quadrant House, The Quadrant, Sutton, Surrey SM2 5AS. Tel: 01-661 3500.
Editor: Alfred Sorkin.
Weekly publication, designed to bring its readers opinion, in-depth coverage of news, trade politics, products, people, markets, marketing and statistics concerning the electrical trade. Slightly biased towards the independent retailer.
Illustrations: Very limited scope for one-off pictures.
Text: Articles mainly on marketing of domestic appliances and/or consumer electronic products. Illustrated where necessary. 1,000–3,000 words.
Overall freelance potential: Good, but highly specialised.
Editor's tips: Contact magazine before submitting, since requirements are specialised.
Fees: £45 per 1,000 words. Pictures by negotiation.

ELECTRICAL DOMESTIC APPLIANCE REVIEW

Napfield Ltd., 153 Praed Street, London W2. Tel: 01-262 0792/1470.
Editor: Roy Williams.
Monthly publication for product and trade news aimed at electrical retailers and wholesalers.
Illustrations: No freelance market.
Text: Features on anything for the electrical trade. 2,500 words.
Overall freelance potential: Small.
Fees: Around £30 per article.

ELECTRICAL TIMES

IPC Electrical and Electronic Press, Quadrant House, The Quadrant, Sutton, Surrey SM2 5AS. Tel: 01-661 3136.
Editor: Alan Jack.
Weekly publication for electrical supply industry, electrical contractors, equipment manufacturers, commercial and industrial users of electricity and area boards.
Illustrations: B&W only. Pictures of new technical products, site installation work, electrical-related exhibitions, electrical firms, new factories, personalities, power station work, new energy sources and equipment being moved by road or rail. No electronic equipment, micros, computers etc. Covers: B&W pictures of anything interesting in this field.
Text: Technical articles are usually commissioned. Opening for business related articles on the electrical industry. 750–1,500 words.
Overall freelance potential: Small but good growth potential.
Fees: Text, £40 for 1,500 words; pictures, £7.50.

THE ELECTRONICS LOCATION FILE
Urban Publishing Co., 17 The Green, Richmond, Surrey TW9 1PX. Tel: 01-948 5721.
Editor: Tonn vom Hove.
Annual management publication for the international electronics industry.
Illustrations: B&W only. Technical and personality pictures.
Text: Features on new developments in the electronics industry and multinational hi-tec companies. 1,500–2,500 words.
Overall freelance potential: Around 50 per cent of the publication comes from freelances.
Fees: Good; on a rising scale according to size of reproduction or length of feature.

THE IBM USER
EMAP National Publications Ltd., 57A Hatton Garden, London EC1N 8JD. Tel: 01-242 6552.
Editor: Roger Green.
Monthly publication for data processing and other management responsible for buying and running IBM and IBM-compatible computers.
Illustrations: B&W and colour. Only by commission. Covers: Colour pictures by commission. 35mm acceptable.
Text: Features on anything related to the use of IBM and compatible computers. 750–2,800 words.
Overall freelance potential: Around 50 per cent is obtained from freelances with strong and detailed computer backgrounds.
Fees: Negotiable.

INFORMATICS
VNU Business Publications, 53–55 Frith Street, London W1A 2HG. Tel: 01-439 4242.
Editor: Ron Condon.
Monthly magazine concerned with computers and electronics.
Illustrations: B&W inside. Pictures of politicians and heads of computer companies. Covers: Colour pictures of similar. 35mm acceptable.
Text: Features on computers and electronics.
Overall freelance potential: All pictures are taken by freelances.
Fees: £45 for half-day's work; £80 for full day.

INTERNATIONAL BROADCAST ENGINEER
Whitton Press Ltd., 50 High Street, Eton, Berks SL4 6BL. Tel: 07535 53756.
Editor: David Sparks.
Bi-monthly publication devoted to the design, manufacture and operation of professional television and radio broadcast equipment.
Illustrations: No pictures inside. Covers: Colour pictures relevant to editorial. Unusual/striking/atmospheric pictures preferred. 6 × 6 cm or 5″ × 4″ preferred.
Text: Technical articles on aspects of broadcast engineering. 2,000–4,000 words.

Overall freelance potential: Good from the right specialist contributor.
Editor's tips: Telephone with ideas.
Fees: Negotiable.

MICRO FORECAST

31–33 High Holborn, London WC1V 6BD.Tel: 01-404 0564.
Editor: Martin Whitbread.
Bi-weekly publication, containing microelectronics news, features, new products, developments, etc., extending into the area of small computers and software.
Illustrations: Very small market for pictures and only by arrangement with the publishers. B&W only.
Text: Articles and features of a reasonable technical standard, but only by arrangement with the publisher. 1,000–1,500 words.
Overall freelance potential: Very small for photographers as most pictures are supplied by photographers in the industry. Better potential for the writer, although the magazine stresses that it has numerous contacts already.
Editor's tips: Requirements are very specialised. Do nothing without first checking with publisher.
Fees: By arrangement.

MIDDLE EAST ELECTRONICS

IPC Middle East Publishing Co. Ltd., 14th Floor, Crown House, London Road, Morden, Surrey SM4 5DX. Tel: 01-543 3976.
Editor: Ray Ashmore.
Monthly publication for buyers and specifiers of electronic systems and equipment in the Arab and Farsi speaking countries.
Illustrations: B&W and colour. Pictures related to electronic subjects, in particular, those relevant to the Middle East market. 35mm acceptable.
Text: Illustrated features on subjects detailed above. 1,500–2,000 words.
Overall freelance potential: Around 25 per cent is bought from freelance contributors.
Fees: Good; on a rising scale according to the size of pictures of length of feature.

PERSONAL COMPUTING

Argus Specialist Publications Ltd., 145 Charing Cross Road, London WC2H 0EE. Tel: 01-437 1002.
Editor: Elspeth Joiner.
Monthly magazine for the newcomer to personal and home computing. Content is largely concerned with the writing and operation of programmes.
Illustrations: B&W only. Photographs to illustrate programming features. Since one of the most popular uses of personal computers is in the field of war games, there is scope for pictures of warships, tanks, military personnel, etc.

Text: Scope only for very knowledgeable features on home computing, or actual computer programmes for such use.
Overall freelance potential: Very small.
Fees: By negotiation.

PRACTICAL ELECTRONICS
IPC Magazines Ltd., Kings Reach Tower, Stamford Street, London SE1 9LS. Tel: 01-261 6676.
Editor: Mike Kenward.
Monthly magazine, publishing electronic projects for the hobbyist, student and engineer.
Illustrations: No freelance market.
Text: Constructional projects and features on any aspect of electronics and its applications. Up to 5,000 words.
Overall freelance potential: Good for writers; 80 per cent comes from outside contributors.
Editor's tips: Discuss subject matter with the editor before starting work on a feature.
Fees: Good; on a rising scale, according to the length of feature.

WIRELESS WORLD
IPC Electrical and Electronic Press Ltd., Quadrant House, The Quadrant, Sutton, Surrey. Tel: 01-661 3500.
Editor: P. R. Darrington.
Monthly technical journal covering electronics, computing, broadcasting, audio and video at a professional level.
Illustrations: B&W for use with features. Covers: Colour pictures of any subject in the area detailed above. No blatant advertising shots. 35mm acceptable.
Text: Illustrated features on subjects detailed above. 4,000 words.
Overall freelance potential: Small. Mainly from professional engineers.
Fees: £45 per printed page. Covers by agreement.

Farming

AGRI TRADE
UKASTA, 3 Whitehall Court, London SW1A 2EQ. Tel: 01-930 3611.
Editor: Amber Carroll.
Monthly publication written for, and read by, agricultural supply trade.
Illustrations: B&W only. Pictures of animal feed, seeds, fertilizer, animal health products, agrochemicals, etc.
Text: Features on above subjects. 1,000 words.
Overall freelance potential: Between 20 and 30 per cent comes from freelances, but most is commissioned.
Fees: Negotiable.

BRITISH FARMER AND STOCKBREEDER
Agricultural Press Ltd., Surrey House, 1 Throwley Way, Sutton, Surrey SM1 4QQ. Tel: 01-643 8040.
Editor: Montague Keen.
Farming news journal posted to all members of the National Farmers Union. Published 22 times per year.
Illustrations: B&W only. An occasional need for good, clear, prints of humorous agricultural subjects, suitably captioned.
Text: No freelance market.
Overall freelance potential: Limited at present.
Fees: On a rising scale, according to the size of reproduction.

DAIRY FARMER
Farming Press Ltd., Wharfedale Road, Ipswich IP1 4LG. Tel:0473 43011.
Editor: David Shead.
Monthly technical journal for dairy farmers.
Illustrations: B&W only. Captioned pictures for use as fillers. Pictures of a positive interest, technical or maybe historical. No 'pretty-pretty' pictures.
Text: Features on technical advances and other notable achievements in dairying.
Overall freelance potential: Around 50 per cent comes from outside sources, but that includes several regular contributors.
Fees: By arrangement.

DAIRY INDUSTRIES INTERNATIONAL
United Trade Press Ltd., UTP House, 33–35 Bowling Green Lane, London EC1 0DA. Tel: 01-837 1212.
Editor: Mrs. Pauline Russell.
Monthly publication for the dairy processing industry.
Illustrations: B&W only. Pictures relating to the industry.
Text: Features on the technology of dairy processing, new dairy products and overseas developments.
Overall freelance potential: Around 10 per cent comes from freelance sources.
Fees: By agreement.

THE LAND WORKER
National Union of Agricultural and Allied Workers, 308 Gray's Inn Road, London WC1. Tel: 01-278 7801.
Editor: Francis Beckett.
Monthly publication dealing with politics and agriculture. Aimed mainly at farmworkers.
Illustrations: B&W only. Pictures of all types of farm work, food processing and union activity.
Text: Features on subjects detailed above. Up to 800 words.
Overall freelance potential: Small.
Fees: On a rising scale according to size of reproduction or length of article.

RAYMOND LEA

LIVESTOCK FARMING

Morgan-Grampian Ltd., 30 Calderwood Street, Woolwich, London SE18 6QH. Tel: 01-855 7777.

Editor: Peter Hollinshead.

Published fifteen times per year and aimed at the larger UK farmer.

Illustrations: B&W only inside. Good news pictures involving agriculture, e.g. politicians in the UK and EEC, farmers demonstrating, natural disasters, etc. Pictures of significant sale animals, i.e. the animal making the highest price in an important Show and Sale. Stock shots of farmers at work, e.g. hedging, ploughing, forage harvesting, etc. Also pictures showing instances where farmers have made a success or failure in marketing their produce. Pictures from the retail end of the marketing chain. Covers: Colour pictures, usually geared to the editorial. The picture must have a message. 6 × 6 cm minimum.

Text: A small market for freelances, but recommended to contact the editor first.

Overall freelance potential: Around 50 per cent comes from freelances.

Fees: Good; on a rising scale according to the size of reproduction or length of article.

THE MILK PRODUCER

Milk Marketing Board, Thames Ditton, Surrey KT7 0EL. Tel: 01-398 4101.
Editor: Jenny Bradley.
Monthly journal of the MMB, containing information on the Board, dairy farming and the dairy industry in general.
Illustrations: B&W and colour. Pictures or dairy farming, milk and dairy products and milk tankers. 35mm acceptable inside. Covers: Colour pictures of dairying, English dairy products, bulls and cows. Minimum size, 6 × 6 cm.
Text: Only special commissions. 1,000 words.
Overall freelance potential: Very little text; 50 per cent of the photography.
Editor's tips: Always willing to consider suggestions for pictures or features. Contact first.
Fees: Negotiable.

PIG FARMING

Farming Press Ltd., Wharfedale Road, Ipswich, Suffolk IP1 4LG. Tel: 0473 43011.
Editor: Martin Looker.
Monthly publication for pig farmers.
Illustrations: B&W only. Pictures showing specific points of pig production, new ideas, systems, etc. Occasional off-beat pictures of pigs used.
Text: Technical articles on modern pig production, also some general interest features. 1,500 words.
Overall freelance potential: Small.
Fees: By arrangement.

POULTRY FARMER

Dodley Printing Co. Ltd., 69 Fleet Street, London EC4. Tel: 01-353 5787.
Editor: Charles Lloyd.
Monthly publication for poultry farmers in the UK and Europe.
Illustrations: B&W only. Any pictures concerning the poultry industry.
Text: Features on the poultry industry.
Overall freelance potential: Small at the moment, but a good potential for growth.
Fees: By agreement.

POULTRY WORLD

IPC Agricultural Press Ltd., Surrey House, 1 Throwley Way, Sutton, Surrey SM1 4QQ. Tel: 01-643 8040.
Editor: John Farrant.
Weekly publication, aimed at UK, EEC and World commercial poultry industries, with the emphasis in that order.
Illustrations: B&W only for use inside the magazine.
Text: No freelance market.
Overall freelance potential: Small.
Fees: By negotiations.

PRACTICAL SELF SUFFICIENCY

Broad Leys Publishing Company, Widdington, Saffron Walden, Essex CB11 3SP. Tel: 0799 40922.

Editor: Katie Thear.

Bi-monthly publication concerned with small scale farming, home food production, home and rural crafts and alternative energy.

Illustrations: For covers only. Colour pictures of goats, poultry, sheep, pigs, cattle, gardening, bees, with emphasis on small scale involvement and humane farming.

Text: Features on small scale farming, livestock, organic growing, homecrafts etc. Articles should be based on experience and be practically orientated. 500–1,000 words.

Overall freelance potential: Good.

Fees: £25 per colour pictures; text by negotiation.

TRACTOR AND FARM MACHINERY TRADER

Wordsworth Trade Press Ltd., 28 Hampton Road, Ilford, Essex IG1 1PS. Tel: 01-553 1409.

Editor: Richard Lee.

Bi-monthly publication for farm machinery dealers and owners.

Illustrations: B&W only. Pictures of farm machinery dealers standing, with a few of their key staff members, in front of their premises, to illustrate short reports on the people involved.

Text: Short reports (100 words) on above pictures detailing the dealer's main agencies and the situation with current trade. Illustrated short features (300 words) on dealers at county shows.

Overall freelance potential: Over 50 per cent comes from freelances.

Fees: Short reports with pictures, £20; illustrated features with five or six pictures, £40.

WHAT'S NEW IN FARMING

Morgan-Grampian (Professional Press) Ltd., 30 Calderwood Street, Woolwich, London SE18 6QH. Tel: 01-855 7777.

Editor: Stephen Mitchell.

Monthly publication concerned with new products and technical developments in farming.

Illustrations: Covers only. Colour pictures of machines at work, up-to-date farming ideas and techniques. 6 × 6 cm minimum.

Text: No freelance market.

Overall freelance potential: Low.

Fees: By agreement.

Food and Drink

AMATEUR WINEMAKER AND HOME BREWER

Amateur Winemaker Publications Ltd., 3 South Street, Andover, Hants. SP10 2BU. Tel: 0264 3177.

Editor: C. J. J. Berry.

Monthly magazine aimed at winemaking and home-brewing hobbyists.

Illustrations: B&W inside. Pictures of beer and wine, beer and wine making, also action pictures, e.g. picking blossoms, dandelions, actually making the wine or beer. Covers: Colour pictures of same, 6 × 6 cm minimum.

Text: Features on winemaking or beer brewing as a whole or in particular parts, e.g. conducting a firmentation, bottling, maturation. Also some side issues such as cooking with wine or beer, travelling in wine districts, cider, perry liquers, special wine circles outings, etc.

Overall freelance potential: Most of the magazine comes from freelances.

Editor's tips: Aim material at the *home* wine and beer maker.

Fees: Articles, £6–£10, covers, £25.

THE FOOD MAGAZINE

Perry Publications Ltd., Imprint House, 114 Highlever Road, W10 6PL. Tel: 01-960 5788/9.

Editor: Louise Steele.

Monthly magazine dealing with food, kitchens, appliances, diets, slimming, microwave cooking, wine, freezing etc.

Illustrations: Pictures planned for specific features. Usually commissioned.

Text: Commissioned text from regular freelances on subjects detailed above.

Overall freelance potential: Over 30 per cent from regular contributors.

Fees: Negotiable.

INTERNATIONAL WINE AND FOOD SOCIETY'S JOURNAL

International Wine and Food Society Ltd., 66 Wells Street, London W1P 3RB. Tel: 01-637 2895.

Editor: Conal Gregory.

Quarterly publication, specialising in gastronomic subjects; the better appreciation of wine and food. Readership is restricted to members of the International Wine and Food Society.

Illustrations: Pictures showing stages in the preparation of particular dishes or of wine. Labels advertising brands within the picture are unacceptable. No people should appear unless they form a necessary function in the preparation. B&W preferred. No market for covers.

Text: Detailed articles in a literary style on the subject of wine or food. 1,000–1,100 words.

Overall freelance potential: Under 10 per cent of the work comes from freelances.

Editor's tips: Only commissioned work is considered. Best to send a 100–150 word synopsis of any ideas in first instance. No travel articles.

Fees: By negotiation.

THE JEWISH VEGETARIAN

The Jewish Vegetarian and Natural Health Society, 855 Finchley Road, London NW11 8LX. Tel: 01-455 0692.

Editor: Philip Pick.

Quarterly publication concerned with vegetarianism, its ethics, nutritional value and health benefits.

Illustrations: B&W only. Pictures showing ecology, animal welfare and proper land use. Pictures with an emotional interest between man (especially children) and animals. Covers: B&W pictures of same.

Text: No freelance market.

Overall freelance potential: Quite good.

Fees: By agreement.

SCOTTISH LICENSED TRADE NEWS/SCOTTISH CATERING NEWS

IPC Consumer Industries Press Ltd., 3 Clairmont Gardens, Glasgow G3 7LP. Tel: 041-332 8006.

Editor: Alec Somerville.

Fortnightly publication for hoteliers, caterers, restauranteurs, drinks executives, licence holders, drinks companies. Scottish Catering News is a monthly supplement to the Licensed Trade News.

Illustrations: B&W only. Pictures connected with the above subjects.

Text: News and features of interest to the trade.

Fees: By agreement.

THE VEGETARIAN

The Vegetarian Society of the United Kingdom Ltd., Parkdale, Dunham Road, Altrincham, Cheshire WA14 4QG. Tel.: 061-928 0793.

Editor: Mrs Bronwen Humphreys.

Bi-monthly publication for vegetarians and anyone interested in the subject.

Illustrations: B&W only. Stock pictures of farm animals and poultry in free range, 'old fashioned' or modern units so that the types can be contrasted. Also, well-known vegetarian personalities.

Text: Articles on animal rights and vegetarianism. Interviews with vegetarian personalities. No cookery features.

Overall freelance potential: Between 30 and 40 per cent of the magazine is contributed by freelances.

Fees: Text, £10 per 1,000 words; pictures by negotiation.

WINE AND SPIRIT

Haymarket Publishing Ltd., 38–42 Hampton Road, Teddington, Middlesex TW11 0JE. Tel: 01-977 8787.

Editor: Kathryn McWhirter.

Monthly trade magazine for the wine and spirit industry. Aimed principally at the British wholesale trade, buyers, management, quality control, etc.

Illustrations: Covers only: Colour pictures, vertical format, of wine and spirit subjects. No bottles. 35mm acceptable.

Text: Features on marketing and production in the wine and spirits industry worldwide. 1,000–2,000 words.
Overall freelance potential: Around 40 per cent of the publication comes from freelance sources.
Editor's tips: Telephone before submitting.
Fees: Negotiable.

WINE TRADE NEWS

Spalding and Watts, 113 Anerley Road, London SE20 8AJ. Tel: 01-659 1827.
Editor: John Moore.
Monthly publication for all UK wine retailers.
Illustrations: B&W only. New products. Newsy pictures of people connected with the trade.
Text: Features on subjects detailed above. Up to 500 words.
Overall freelance potential: Small.
Fees: Variable.

WHERE TO EAT IN

Kingsclere Publications, 11 Swan Street, Kingsclere, Newbury, Berks. Tel: 0635 298839.
Editor: Glen Thimann.
Annual guide for all those interested in wining and dining and restaurants and hotels.
Illustrations: B&W only. General view of countries and cities featured in the guide. Interior and exterior shots of hotels, restaurants, inns and wine bars. Any picture featuring food or drink.
Text: No freelance market.
Overall freelance potential: Approximately 20 per cent of pictures used come from freelances.
Editor's tips: Contact the publishers first for specific instructions.
Fees: To be negotiated.

Gardening

GARDEN NEWS

EMAP National Publications Ltd., Bushfield House, Orton Centre, Peterborough PE2 0UW. Tel: 0733 237111.
Editor: Norman Wright.
Weekly consumer magazine for gardeners.
Illustrations: Pictures of general horticultural subjects.
Text: Features of interest to gardeners.
Overall freelance potential: Fair.
Fees: By agreement.

GARDEN TRADE NEWS

EMAP Business and Computer Publications Ltd., Bushfield House, Orton Centre, Peterborough PE2 0UW. Tel: 0733 237111.

Editor: Brian Gibbons.

Monthly trade publication containing news, features and advice for nurserymen, growers, garden centres, wholesalers and manufacturers of horticultural products.

Illustrations: B&W only. Pictures for illustrated features.

Text: Articles about, or of interest to nurserymen, garden centres and garden shops.

Overall freelance potential: Small.

Editor's tips: Remember, this is a trade magazine, not a consumer publication.

Fees: £20 per 1,000 words; pictures on a rising scale according to size of reproduction.

GARDENING WORLD

Sovereign Publications, Sovereign House, Brentwood, Essex CM14 4SE. Tel: 0277 219876.

Editor: Alistair Ayres.

Monthly magazine for the gardening public.

Illustrations: B&W and colour. Pictures of any gardening subject, particularly activities, step-by-step picture guides and plant portraits. Covers: Colour pictures of plants, preferably subjects with clear outlines; 35mm acceptable, but 6 × 6 cm preferred.

Text: Features on practical gardening subjects relevant to the month of publication. 1,000–1,500 words.

Overall freelance potential: Good potential for the right type of pictures. Most of the text is contributed, but usually from regular writers.

Fees: Colour, £15 per picture; B&W, £4 per picture; £25 per 1,000 words.

GREENHOUSE

Haymarket Publishing Ltd., 38–42 Hampton Road, Teddington, Middlesex TW11 0JE. Tel: 01-977 8787.

Editor: Alan Toogood.

Monthly gardening magazine specialising in growing plants in greenhouses, cold frames and cloches. Also covers appropriate tools and equipment.

Illustrations: No freelance market other than with features.

Text: Articles on ornamental greenhouse plants. Illustrated articles on amateurs' greenhouses, e.g. what they grow, how they grow it; stories of particularly interesting amateur plant collections. 1,500 words.

Overall freelance potential: Around 50 per cent comes from freelance sources.

Editor's tips: Nearly everything is commissioned. Interested freelances should contact the editor before submitting.

Fees: Text, £35 per 1,000 words: Pictures used in articles—£5 for B&W, £10–£25 for colour.

NURSERYMAN AND GARDEN CENTRE

Benn Publications Ltd., Sovereign Way, Tonbridge, Kent TN9 1RW. Tel: 0732 364422.
Editor: Jonathan Geer.
Monthly publication for nurserymen, garden centre operators, manufacturers of garden products, gardening journalists, educational establishments in the field, landscape designers and contracters, groundsmen, etc.
Illustrations: B&W only. Pictures used only as illustrations to articles.
Text: Features on most aspects of garden centre and nursery work, and the equipment used. New developments at home and abroad. 1,000–1,500 words.
Overall freelance potential: Between three and four articles per month come from freelances.
Fees: Small items, 75p per column inch; longer features, £35–£50, depending on the technical nature.

PRACTICAL GARDENING

EMAP National Publications Ltd., Bushfield House, Orton Centre, Peterborough PE2 0UW. Tel: 0733 237111.
Editor: Mike Wyatt.
Monthly guide to practical work in the garden, written by experts for enthusiastic, but not specialist, gardeners.
Illustrations: B&W and colour. Mainly for use with text. No commissions.
Text: Illustrated step-by-step sequences and practical subjects on all gardening topics, for possible future use and stock.
Overall freelance potential: Quite good.
Fees: By agreement.

General Interest

ACCESS MAGAZINE

F. R. Stewart and Associates, 3rd Floor, Silver House, 31–35 Beak Street, London W1R 3LD. Tel: 01-437 6504 and 01-734 4689.
Editor: Pamela Thomas.
Published six times a year for all Access card holders.
Illustrations: Colour only. Mostly from libraries or some by commission for specific articles.
Covers: Colour pictures of landscapes or items from magazine's contents. 35mm acceptable.
Text: Mostly upmarket features covering subjects involving the use of Access credit cards. Also articles on holidays, adult gifts, toys, do-it-yourself, gardening, fashion, conservation, microchips, diamonds, etc.
Overall freelance potential: Around 20 per cent is obtained from freelance sources.
Fees: By negotiation.

CONTEMPORARY REVIEW
Contemporary Review Co. Ltd., 61 Carey Street, London WC2A 2JG. Tel: 01-242 3215.
Editor: Rosalind Wade.
Monthly journal that goes to universities, colleges, clubs, public libraries and private subscribers worldwide. Contains a wide spectrum of interest, including home affairs, politics, literature and the arts, history, travel and religion.
Illustrations: None.
Text: Authoritative features on the above subjects. 3,000 words.
Overall freelance potential: Small. Some unsolicited material is used, but most is commissioned.
Fees: £3 per 1,000 words plus two voucher copies.

EVENT
Event Magazines Ltd., 61–63 Portobello Road, London W1 3DD. Tel: 01-221 7535.
Editor: Robert Devereux.
Weekly magazine about life in London. Aimed at 18–35 age group.
Illustrations: B&W only inside the magazine. No stock pictures. Others commissioned for specific articles. Covers: Colour or B&W portraits of personalities. 35mm acceptable.
Text: Features on subjects relating in some way to London. 1,500–2,500 words.
Overall freelance potential: The magazine uses a lot of freelance work.
Editor's tips: Study the magazine before submission.
Fees: By negotiation.

READER'S DIGEST
The Reader's Digest Association Ltd., 25 Barkeley Square, London W1X 6AB. Tel: 01-629 8144.
Editor: Michael Randolph.
Monthly magazine for a general interest readership.
Illustrations: B&W and colour. A few pictures of general interest; 35mm acceptable.
Text: High quality features on all topics.
Overall freelance potential: About 50 per cent of the magazine comes from freelances.
Fees: By agreement.

SELECT
Singles Scene Ltd., 23 Abingdon Road, London W8. Tel: 01-938 1011.
Editor: John Patterson.
Monthly publication for single people, their hobbies, interests and activities, covering as wide a variety of issues as possible. Age range is 25-plus to 50.
Illustrations: B&W only. Mostly used in conjunction with features, but freelances can contact deputy editor Sue Curtis for a list of forthcoming topics that might be in need of illustration.
Text: General interest features biased towards singles, e.g. housing, communications, love,

etc. Regular features on 'Successful Singles' (who need not be famous), and also 'Meeting Places'. 1,500–2,000 words.

Overall freelance potential: Excellent: around 75 per cent comes from freelance contributors.

Editor's tips: Read the magazine. Contributors should contact deputy editor Sue Curtis.

Fees: By arrangement.

TITBITS

IPC Magazines Ltd., King's Reach Tower, Stamford Street, London SE1 9LS. Tel: 01-261 5000.

Editor: Paul Hopkins.

Weekly general interest publication, with the emphasis on human interest stories and features.

Illustrations: B&W and Colour. A wide range of material is used, but the emphasis is on the offbeat and the unusual. Always interested in unusual animal pictures. Fairly topical human interest material used.

Text: Well-illustrated human interest features.

Overall freelance potential: Good.

Editor's tips: Study a couple of issues thoroughly before submitting anything—and then make sure you send only professional quality material.

Fees: Good; on a rising scale according to size of reproduction or length or article.

THE TRUSTCARD MAGAZINE

TSB Trustcard Ltd., 51 Eastcheap, London EC3P 3BU. Tel: 01-623 8011.

Editor: Jane Tresidder.

Quarterly magazine for current users of the TSB's Trustcard.

Illustrations: Colour only. General and family interest pictures, e.g. D-I-Y, gardening, home interests; well-known personalities. Covers: Colour pictures of families, children, holiday scenes and personalities. 6 × 6 cm minimum.

Text: Features on the subjects detailed above. Practical and noncontroversial style. 750–1,000 words.

Overall freelance potential: All material is freelance, but most is commissioned.

Fees: Text, £60 per 1,000 words; pictures by negotiation.

WEEKEND

Weekend Publications Ltd., New Carmelite House, London EC4Y 0JA. Tel: 01-353 6000.

Editor: David Hill.

Weekly family magazine that caters for all ages.

Illustrations: Colour and B&W. Amusing, unusual, interesting and dramatic photographs. Covers: Glamour material that has been taken outdoors and that has a background that will allow for coverlines and logo; 35mm acceptable.

Text: Topical, human interest and off-beat features. 1,000 words.

ROBERT HO

Overall freelance potential: Good; 50 per cent comes from freelance contributors.
Editor's tips: Avoid topical material as the magazine works eight weeks in advance.
Fees: By negotiation, depending on how and where the material is used.

YOURS

Helpage International, PO Box 30, London N1 1RF. Tel: 01-359 6318.
Editor: Mrs. Margaret Mason.
Monthly publication for the over sixties plus some young readers. Aims to entertain as well as informing the retired generation of their rights and entitlements.
Illustrations: B&W only. Pictures showing old people's achievements.
Text: Commissions only for known freelance writers. 750–1,000 words.
Overall freelance potential: Fair.
Fees: Good; on a rising scale according to the size of reproduction or length of article.

Hobbies and Crafts

THE AQUARIST AND PONDKEEPER

Buckley Press Ltd., The Butts, Half Acre, Brentford, Middlesex TW8 8BN. Tel: 01-568 8441.
Editor: Laurence Perkins.
Monthly fishkeeping magazine dealing with tropical, freshwater, marine and coldwater fish; water gardening, aquarium keeping and all allied subjects.
Illustrations: B&W and Colour. Any picture connected with indoor or outdoor keeping of pet fish. *Not* fishing or angling. Covers: Colour pictures of tropical, coldwater or marine fish; 35mm acceptable.
Text: Features on the keeping of indoor or outdoor fish. All articles should be illustrated, either by photographs or with line drawings. 1,500–4,000 words.
Overall freelance potential: Very good; over 90 per cent comes from outside contributors.
Fees: By arrangement.

CAGE AND AVIARY BIRDS

IPC Specialist and Professional Press Ltd., Room 402, Surrey House, 1 Throwley Way, Sutton, Surrey, SM1 4QQ. Tel: 01-643 8040 Ext. 4223.
Editor: Philip Read.
Weekly journal covering all aspects of birdkeeping and breeding, aimed at enthusiasts of all ages.
Illustrations: B&W only. Mostly as illustrations to features. Others should cover avicultural subjects in general. Covers: B&W, 8 × 6 in minimum of birds mentioned below.
Text: Features on all aspects of breeding birds such as canaries, British birds, budgerigars, pheasants, waterfowl and birds of prey. Any reasonable length.
Overall freelance potential: Very good. Most material comes from freelances.
Fees: Good; on a rising scale according to size of reproduction or length of feature.

CAR NUMBERS MONTHLY
PO Box 1, Bradford-on-Avon, Wilts BA15 1YQ. Tel: 0225 782550/782640.
Editor: Tony Hill.
Monthly publication for all those interested in personalised car number plates.
Illustrations: B&W only. Particularly interested in pictures of well known people with their car plus personalised number plate. Covers: B&W pictures of same.
Text: Articles concerning number plates and associated subjects. Particular interest in legal angles. 200–300 words.
Overall freelance potential: Small at the moment but growing.
Fees: Approximately £30 per picture; £10–20 per article.

CLOCKS
Model and Allied Publications Ltd., Wolsey House, Wolsey Road, Hemel Hempstead, Herts. HP2 4SS. Tel: 0442 41221.
Editor: John Hunter.
Monthly magazine for clock enthusiasts generally, i.e. people interested in building, repairing, restoring and collecting clocks as well as watches.
Illustrations: B&W and colour. Pictures of anything concerned with clocks, e.g. public clocks, clocks in private collections, clocks in museums, clock movements and parts, people involved in clock making, repairing or restoration. Covers: Colour pictures as detailed above. 35mm acceptable.
Text: Features on clockmakers, repairers or restorers; museums and collections, clock companies, etc. 1,000–2,000 words.
Overall freelance potential: Around 90 per cent of the magazine is contributed by freelances.
Fees: By arrangement.

COIN AND MEDAL NEWS
Epic Publishing Ltd., PO Box 3DE, London W1A 3DE. Tel: 01-580 4156.
Editor: Irwin Margolis.
Monthly publication for coin and medal collectors.
Illustrations: Not much scope inside. Covers: Colour pictures of coins and/or medals. 35mm acceptable.
Text: Articles on the subject, written by experts.
Overall freelance potential: Good for writers, less so for photographers.
Editor's tips: Essential to check before submitting.
Fees: £25 per 1,000 words; pictures by agreement.

CRAFT AND HOBBY DEALER
C. F. Marcom Ltd., Western Lodge, Station Road, Andoversford, Cheltenham, Gloucestershire GL54 4LA. Tel: 0242 82740/82749.
Editor: Colin Elliot.

Bi-monthly publication for retailers, wholesalers and manufacturers in the crafts and creative leisure businesses.
Illustrations: B&W only. Small market for pictures relating to crafts.
Text: Features on the craft trade. 1,000–1,500 words.
Overall freelance potential: Small.
Fees: By arrangement.

GEMS
The Randal Press Ltd., 9 Kennet Road, Crayford, Kent. Tel: 0732 622217.
Editor: Michael O'Donoghue.
Bi-monthly publication for students and collectors of gemstones and man-made crystals, jewellers and lapidaries.
Illustrations: B&W and colour pictures of minerals and gemstones. Covers: similar subjects; 35mm acceptable.
Text: Features on gemstones and minerals with a reasonable scientific content. No anecdotes or jokes; no material of a trivial nature. No set length.
Overall freelance potential: Good. Almost all material comes from freelance contributors.
Fees: 'Variable.'

THE LONDON ARCHAEOLOGIST
The London Archaeologist Association, 7 Coalecroft Road, London SW15. Tel: 01-788 2459.
Editor: Clive Orton.
Quarterly publication covering archaeology and history in the London area at a 'popular' level. Read by people with a general interest in the subject, but not necessarily any academic background.
Illustrations: B&W only. Mainly submitted with articles. Exceptions are pictures of eminent archaeologists to accompany an obituary, photographs of prize winners at the British Archaeological Awards and pictures of the openings of museums. Covers: Action pictures relating to archaeological activity, e.g. excavation, surveys, post excavation work; or pictures of events, e.g. exhibitions, open days, openings of museums. B&W only.
Text: Features relating to archaeology and local history in the London area. Excavations, artefact studies, topographical studies, place name studies, industrial archaeology, accounts of new methods and techniques. Up to 3,000 words.
Overall freelance potential: Around 25 per cent of contributions are from freelances.
Editor's tips: Contact the magazine first.
Fees: By agreement.

MODEL BOATS
Model and Allied Publications, Wolsey House, Wolsey Road, Hemel Hempstead, Herts HP2 4SS. Tel: 0442 41221.
Editor: John Cundell.
Monthly magazine that publishes any facet of model boating plus occasional articles on full-size subjects of interest to modellers.

Illustrations: B&W and very occasionally colour inside the magazine on any model boating subject, including regattas. Possible to make B&W illustrations from good, sharp colour prints, but prefer B&W originals. Covers: Model boat subjects; prefer 6 × 6 cm, but will consider 35mm if vertical format.

Text: News items, illustrated articles and plans on wide range of ship and boat modelling, e.g. scale, electric, internal combustion, steam, sail etc. Other maritime subjects considered if there is some connection with modelling. Up to 3,000 words.

Overall freelance potential: Good; 30 per cent bought from outside contributors.

Editor's tips: Send SAE with a request for a contributor's guide before submitting. Prints should be well captioned and no less than post card size.

Fees: Approximately £15 per published page.

MODEL RAILWAYS

Model and Allied Publications Ltd., Wolsey House, Wolsey Road, Hemel Hempstead, Herts., HP2 4SS. Tel: 0442 41221.

Editor: Cyril Freezer.

Monthly magazine for the model railway enthusiast.

Illustrations: B&W and colour. Pictures used only as illustrations to features. Covers: Colour pictures connected with an inside feature.

Text: Illustrated features on layouts, techniques and new innovations in the model railway world. Best supplied by a freelance with good contacts in the hobby. Very specialised field.

Overall freelance potential: Quite good for the right material. All regular contributors are well established in the hobby.

Editor's tips: No market for a contributor who is not an established model maker. Model railways, to this market, are *not* toys.

Fees: By agreement.

POPULAR CRAFTS

Model and Allied Publications, Wolsey House, Wolsey Road, Hemel Hempstead, Herts., HP2 4SS. Tel: 0442 41221.

Editor: Evelyn Barrett.

Monthly magazine for do-it-yourself crafts people.

Illustrations: B&W and colour. Pictures used only as illustrations for features. Covers: Colour pictures linked with feature inside. 35mm acceptable.

Text: All types of craft with strong emphasis on how to do it. Small market for human interest stories. 1,000–2,000 words.

Overall freelance potential: Around 75 per cent of the magazine is contributed.

Editor's tips: Articles must be written from personal experience, illustrated with step-by-step pictures.

Fees: Approximately £20 per published page.

PRACTICAL FISHKEEPING

EMAP National Publications Ltd., Bretton Court, Bretton, Peterborough PE3 8DZ. Tel: 0733 264666.

Editor: Nick Fletcher.
Monthly magazine for all freshwater, marine and coldwater fishkeepers, aimed at every level from hobbyist to expert.
Illustrations: B&W and colour. Pictures of all species of tropical, marine and coldwater fish; 35mm acceptable inside the magazine. Covers: Colour pictures of same; minimum size 6 × 6 cm.
Text: Emphasis on instructional articles on the subject. 1,000–1,500 words.
Overall freelance potential: Generally from contributors with a specific knowledge of the hobby. Freelance material is considered on its merit at all times.
Editor's tips: Telephone first to give a brief on the intended copy and/or photographs available.
Fees: Negotiable.

SCALE TRAINS
Blackfriars Press Ltd., PO Box 80, Smith Dorrien Road, Leicester LE5 4BS. Tel: 0533 760281. Editorial address: 4 Surbiton Hall Close, Kingston-upon-Thames, Surrey. Tel: 01-546 0758.
Editor: Chris Ellis.
Monthly magazine for railway modellers.
Illustrations: B&W only. Pictures showing real railway activity in the UK or overseas, or railway modelling activity.
Text: No freelance market.
Overall freelance potential: Fair.
Fees: By agreement.

SKYPLANE
Chevremont Publishing Ltd., 66 Station Road, Redhill, Surrey. Tel: 04352 2503.
Editor: Michael Woodhead.
Alternate-monthly magazine for radio-controlled model aircraft enthusiasts. Aimed at the dedicated hobbyist in particular.
Illustrations: B&W only. high-quality detailed photographs of radio-controlled model aircraft. Detailed pictures of full-scale aircraft are also required, for use as modellers reference. Covers: High quality colour shots showing an original approach. Conventional shots of modellers holding aircraft are not required, but inventive studio shots of suitable aircraft will be welcome.
Text: Illustrated articles on any aspect of radio-controlled models, showing a high degree of knowledge about the subject.
Overall freelance potential: Limited, but good for the contributor who can produce the originality required.
Editor's tips: Taking good photographs of aircraft—especially models—is not as easy as might at first be assumed. Experience in handling the subject is essential.
Fees: Up to £10 per black and white picture; up to £40 for colour covers. Text negotiable.

STAMP AND POSTAL HISTORY NEWS

Epic Publishing Ltd., PO Box 3DE, London W1A 3DE. Tel: 01-580 4156.
Editor: Guy Averill.
Fortnightly magazine for stamp collectors.
Illustrations: Not much freelance scope inside. Covers: Colour pictures of stamps and related subjects. 35mm acceptable.
Text: Features on stamps and postal history, written by experts.
Overall freelance potential: Good for writers, less so for photographers.
Editor's tips: Check before submitting.
Fees: £25 per 1,000 words.

STAMP MONTHLY

Stanley Gibbons Magazines Ltd., Drury House, Russell Street, London WC2B 5HD. Tel: 01-836 8444.
Editor: Russell Bennett.
Monthly magazine for stamp collectors.
Illustrations: Inside, only as illustrations for articles. Covers: Colour pictures of stamps; 35mm acceptable.
Text: Features on stamp collecting. 1,000 words.
Overall freelance potential: Most of the editorial comes from freelance contributors.
Fees: Negotiable.

STAMPS

Stamp Publications, Sovereign House, Brentwood, Essex CM14 4SE. Tel: 0277 219876.
Editor: Allan Daniell.
Monthly magazine for whole world stamp collecting with emphasis on Great Britain and the Commonwealth. Also, thematic collecting and postal history, 'Cinderella' stamps, postcards.
Illustrations: B&W only. Pictures used only as illustrations for features.
Text: Illustrated features on subjects detailed above, especially GB, Pacific area, Commonwealth and Canada. 1,500–2,000 words.
Overall freelance potential: Around 30 per cent comes from freelance sources.
Fees: £13.50 per 1,000 words; £2.25 per illustration.

TREASURE HUNTING

Treasure Hunting Publications, Sovereign House, Brentwood, Essex CM14 4SE. Tel: 0277 219876.
Editor: Greg Payne.
Monthly magazine for metal detecting and local history enthusiasts.
Illustrations: B&W for illustrating features detailed below. Covers: Colour pictures of models using metal detectors in a countryside or seaside setting; 35mm acceptable. Advisable to telephone the magazine before attempting a cover.

Text: Illustrated features on club treasure hunts, lost property recovery, local history etc. News stories on the subject. News, 300–1,000 words; features, 1,000–3,000 words.

Overall freelance potential: Approximately 50 per cent of the magazine comes from freelance contributions.

Fees: Covers, £55; B&W inside pictures, £4; news, £10 per 1,000 words; features, £15 per 1,000 words.

WHAT HI-FI?

Haymarket publishing Ltd., 38/42 Hampton Road, Teddington, Middlesex. Tel: 01-977 8787.

Editor: Matt Nicholson.

Monthly magazine with emphasis on equipment reviews and ideas, particularly in the lower priced areas of the market. Also contains computerised buying guide to over 2,000 units each month.

Illustrations: B&W only. Pictures from Hi-Fi shows, providing they are submitted quickly after the show. Pictures also used to illustrate articles.

Text: Features on Hi-Fi equipment. Interested in contacting freelances in the London area with access to and the ability to test equipment. Also general features on the subject 1,500–3,000 words.

Overall freelance potential: An average of 40 per cent comes from freelances, but most of these are long-standing contributors.

Editor's tips: Potential reviewers should have the ability to listen to Hi-Fi critically, plus a technical knowledge of the subject, a good product knowledge and must be able to write clearly and accurately.

Fees: Text, from £30 per piece of equipment tested, £25 per page for general articles; pictures, £10.

WOODWORKER

Model and Allied Publications Ltd., Wolsey House, Wolsey Road, Hemel Hempstead, Herts HP2 4SS. Tel: 0442 41221.

Editor: Chris Dunn.

Monthly magazine for all craftsmen in wood. Readership includes schools and woodworking businesses, as well as individual hobbyists.

Illustrations: B&W inside magazine. Pictures relative to wood and wood crafts. Mostly used as illustrations for features. Covers: Colour pictures of workshop interiors and fine furniture, particular interest in shots showing craftsmen at work. 35mm acceptable, but 6 × 6 cm preferred.

Text: Illustrated features on all facets of woodworking crafts. 1,500 words.

Overall freelance potential: Good, about 75 per cent bought from outside contributors.

Editor's tips: Clear, concise authoritative writing essential.

Fees: Negotiable, but around £15 per published page.

WORLDWIDE KNITTING
Worldwide Knitting Services, Springvale Estate, Cwmbran, Gwent NP44 5YQ. Tel: 063-33 69451.
Editor: Sandra Williams.
Monthly publication for knitters, both by hand and by domestic knitting machines.
Illustrations: B&W only. Pictures used only to illustrate articles.
Text: Features on knitting, yarns, knitwear design, fashion etc. 1,000–2,000 words.
Overall freelance potential: Variable, but willing to consider more than currently being used.
Fees: Negotiable.

Home Interests

DO-IT-YOURSELF MAGAZINE
Link House Magazines (Croydon) Ltd., Link House, Dingwall Avenue, Croydon CR9 2TA. Tel: 01-686 2599.
Editor: Tony Wilkins.
Monthly magazine for home owners of all social classes interested in maintaining and improving their property.
Illustrations: B&W and colour. Pictures only by commission. 35mm acceptable.
Text: Readers' success stories, showing work done on a property needing renovation or restoration. 1,000–1,500.
Overall freelance potential: Small, since the magazine maintains an experienced team of staff writers.
Editor's tips: Contact the magazine first with ideas or, at the most, a synopsis.
Fees: By negotiation.

DO-IT-YOURSELF RETAILING
Link House Magazines (Claydon) Ltd., Link House, Dingwall Avenue, Croydon CR2 2TA. Tel: 01-686 2599.
Editor: G. Carroll.
Monthly journal for the D-I-Y and home improvement distributive trades.
Illustrations: B&W only. Pictures used only with features.
Text: Illustrated features about D-I-Y outlets, plus exclusive news items and diary pieces on D-I-Y shops and staff. 1,000 words.
Overall freelance potential: Always happy to consider material, despite limited space.
Fees: £40 per 1,000 words.

HOME IMPROVEMENTS GUIDES
Gemini Publishing Co. Ltd., 116 Newgate Street, London EC1A 7AE. Tel: 01-726 6991.
Joint Editors: Yvonne Rees and Jan Orchard.

Variable between six and nine issues per year. Each guide covers a different aspect of the home, e.g. decoration, improvements. Ideas and information are offered to young people looking for good ideas on a budget.

Illustrations: B&W and colour. Pictures on home improvements, decoration, extensions, furniture, room sets. Case histories in colour only of real homes, tools, gardens, central heating, craftsmen, etc. Covers: Colour pictures of living rooms, kitchens, bedrooms, etc., usually taken from a case history inside. 6 × 6 cm minimum.

Text: Articles on all aspects of the home as detailed above. 1,500 words.

Overall freelance potential: Around 70 per cent of material comes from freelance sources.

Editor's tips: Most of the work is commissioned. A visit to the magazine with a portfolio is better than an unsolicited submission.

Fees: Text, £50 per 1,000 words; pictures, commissioned work: £225 for a full day.

HOMECARE

Home and Law Magazines Ltd., 2–16 Goodge Street, London W1P 1FF Tel: 01-631 4092.
Editor: Heather White.

Published three times per year and concerned with home improvement and do-it-yourself.

Illustrations: Colour only. Product pictures such as plants in different room settings. General room sets and details within the room. Covers: Colour pictures of kitchens, bathrooms, gardens, homes, bedrooms, tiling and lighting. 5″ × 4″ minimum.

Text: Features on plumbing, interior design, exterior maintenance, gardening, do-it-yourself, kitchens and bathrooms. 1,500–2,000 words.

Overall freelance potential: Most of the copy comes from freelances.

Editor's tips: The contents of the magazine are planned well in advance and all the articles are commissioned, so freelances should contact the magazine for a commission rather than sending in articles on spec. Only writers with a specialist knowledge need apply.

Fees: £65 per 1,000 words. Pictures by agreement.

HOUSE OVERSEAS

Carlton Communications Ltd., 10 East Road, London N1. Tel: 01-253 4628/01-251 1533.
Editor: Michael Furnell.

Monthly publication concerned with holiday and retirement homes for sale in Southern Europe, Caribbean, Southern States of USA and Far East.

Illustrations: B&W pictures of vacation homes with the current accent on Italy and Greece. No cover sales.

Text: Features on living costs and conditions in the lesser known countries. Information on holiday and retirement homes in Canada, Mexico, Turkey, Far East and Australasia. 1,000–1,500 words.

Overall freelance potential: About 50 per cent contributed by freelances.

Fees: £30 for 1,500 words.

INTERIORS

Pharos Publications, 228–230 Fulham Road, London SW10 9NB. Tel: 01-351 5177.
Editor: Min Hogg.

Monthly magazine showing the best interior decoration of all periods and in all countries.
Illustrations: Colour only. Extra high standard of work required. Mostly to illustrate features. 35mm acceptable.
Text: Complete coverage of interesting houses, public buildings, churches etc. 1,000–2,000 words.
Overall freelance potential: All work in the magazine comes from freelances.
Fees: Negotiable.

NURSERY WORLD

Bouverie Publishing Co. Ltd., 244–249 Temple Chambers, Temple Avenue, London EC4Y 0DT. Tel: 01-583 6486.
Editor: Mary Thompson.
Weekly publication on child care. Aimed at student nursery nurses, nursery nurses, nannies and mothers.
Illustrations: B&W only. Pictures of *young* babies involved in various activities, also photographs of babies in general. Covers: B&W pictures in close-up of a baby or child, showing the fact clearly.
Text: Features on child care, education and any aspect of bringing up children, e.g. travelling with children, holidays, days out. Also personal stories from parents living abroad with young babies or children, ideas for nursery school or playgroup projects and noteworthy people working for children's interests.
Overall freelance potential: Most of the magazine comes from freelance contributors.
Editor's tips: Style must be straightforward and informative.
Fees: Text, £2.20 per 100 words, pictures £5–£10 according to size of reproduction.

PARENTS

Gemini Publishing Co. Ltd., 116 Newgate Street, London EC1A 7AE. Tel: 01-726 6991.
Editor: Wendy Rose-Neil.
Monthly magazine for couples with children up to ten years old. Covers pregnancy, birth, babies, children, health, sex and marriage, education, travel, home ideas, food and medicine.
Illustrations: B&W and colour. Mostly used as illustration for features on above topics. Covers: Colour shots of children or children with parents. 35mm acceptable but 6 × 6 cm preferred.
Text: Features on the above subjects.
Overall freelance potential: Approximately 25 per cent of the magazine is contributed from outside.
Fees: Covers, £70–£100; inside, £70 per page, £40 per half-page.

THE PERIOD HOME

Period Home Publications Ltd., Caxton House, High Street, Tenterden, Kent TN30 6BD. Tel: 05806 4141.
Editor: Paul Norbury.

Bi-monthly magazine concerned with buildings, the craft skills used in their construction and furnishing, plus the social and cultural patterns that have shaped the fabric of our lives.
Illustrations: B&W and colour. Pictures of craftsmen at work, restoring old houses. Series of pictures of distinctive period architectural features or unusual types of historic building (particularly conversions to residential use). Pictures of genuine or reproduction room interiors, especially Victorian. Covers: Colour pictures of period homes, their interiors and details. 5″ × 4″ minimum.
Text: Features on restoration, historical developments and profiles of period houses, dating, traditional crafts, life-styles and interiors, restoration case-studies, furniture and furnishing, gardens, ownership and origins, etc. Up to 2,000 words.
Overall freelance potential: Always willing to consider new freelance contributors if they have a genuine interest in and knowledge of the subject.
Fees: By arrangement.

POPULAR DIY
Sovereign Publications, Sovereign House, Brentwood, Essex CM14 4SE. Tel: 0277 219876.
Editor: Dean Stiles.
Monthly magazine, concerning all aspects of do-it-yourself home repairs and improvements, including decorating, plumbing, carpentry, electrics, brickwork, etc.
Illustrations: B&W only inside. Pictures only as illustrations for features. Covers: Colour pictures of DIY projects detailed below, 6 × 6 cm minimum.
Text: Illustrated step by step features that illustrate DIY projects, e.g. laying a driveway, fitting door frames, glazing windows, fitting locks, laying flooring (boards and parquet), installing ventilator fans, roofing repairs, replacing tiles, insulating lofts, plumbing-in a washing machine, fitting patio doors, etc. 1,500 words.
Overall freelance potential: The majority of the magazine's material is supplied by freelance contributors.
Fees: Colour, £20; B&W, £4 per picture; text, £25 per 1,000 words.

PRACTICAL ENERGY
Switch Publications Ltd., Russell House, 40 East Street, Andover, Hampshire. Tel: 0264 59078.
Editor: Alex White.
Monthly publication on energy conservation for the general consumer market.
Illustrations: B&W and colour. Pictures showing forms of energy conservation; alternate/renewable energy sources. 35mm acceptable inside. Covers: Colour shots of similar subjects, 5″ × 4″ minimum.
Text: Features on energy conservation; alternate/renewable sources. 2,000–3,000 words.
Overall freelance potential: Between 10 and 15 per cent comes from freelance sources.
Fees: Negotiable.

Hospitals, Health and Medical

AFRICA HEALTH
IPC Middle East Publishing Co. Ltd., 14th Floor, Crown House, London Road, Morden, Surrey SM4 5DX. Tel: 01-540 0435.
Editor: Brian Pearson.
Bi-monthly publication for doctors and senior health administrators in English-speaking black African countries.
Illustrations: B&W and occasional colour. Pictures from Africa, specifically medical or general lifestyle, e.g. markets, urban deprivation, rural scenes, etc.
Text: Features on anything apertaining to health developments in Africa, plus UK-originating stories of research advances which might be of benefit to Africans.
Overall freelance potential: Good, especially for material from Africa.
Fees: £50 per 1,000 words; pictures by agreement.

CHESHIRE SMILE
The Leonard Cheshire Foundation, Le Court, Greatham, Liss, Hampshire GU33 6HL. Tel: 04207 263.
Editor: Frances Hopwood and Dennis Jarrett.
Quarterly magazine for the Leonard Cheshire Foundation, a charitable organisation that caters for the needs of severely disabled people in the UK and overseas.
Illustrations: B&W only. Pictures used only as illustrations for articles. Covers: B&W pictures of anything relating to the disabled.
Text: Features related to or concerning the disabled, e.g. fact, fiction and humour. Illustrated with pictures, drawings or cartoons. 500–1,000 words.
Overall freelance potential: Small.
Fees: Negotiable, but it should be born in mind that this is a charity organisation.

THE DENTAL LABORATORY
The Dental Laboratories Association Ltd., 17 Lambourne Drive, Wollaton, Nottingham NG8 1GR. Tel: 0602 282800.
Editor: Trevor Roadley.
Trade magazine aimed at dental laboratory owners with strong emphasis on small business legislation and new products. Circulated five times per year to all known UK dental laboratories.
Illustrations: No freelance photographs have been used so far. But small potential for illustrated features.
Text: Any items of specific interest to dental laboratories or small businesses, but *not* dental surgeries. Features with a loosely connected dental technician interest will be considered, especially if illustrated. 2,000 words maximum.
Overall freelance potential: Fair, though very little is used at present.

Editor's tips: A continuing series might be considered for inclusion in each of the year's issues.
Fees: Negotiated per item, dependent on content.

THE DENTAL TECHNICIAN
A. E. Morgan Publications Ltd., Stanley House, 9 West Street, Epsom, Surrey KT18 7RL. Tel: 037-27 41411.
Editor: David Ritchie.
Monthly newspaper for dental technicians.
Illustrations: B&W only. Pictures of dental technicians engaged in activities, either with or outside their normal work.
Text: Illustrated articles on new laboratories, new techniques, etc. 800–1,200 words.
Overall freelance potential: Small, due to lack of experienced contributors in this field.
Fees: By agreement.

FAR EAST HEALTH
IPC Asian Publishing Co. Ltd., 14th. Floor, Crown House, London Road, Morden, Surrey SM4 5DX. Tel: 01-542 9915.
Editor: Ken Edghill.
Monthly publication for doctors and health administrators in the South-East and East Asia.
Illustrations: B&W only. Pictures of new hospitals and hospital projects in the designated region.
Text: Features on medicine and medical equipment. 1,200 words.
Overall freelance potential: Small, but always interested in news stories from the region.
Fees: Good; on a rising scale according to the size of reproduction or length of article.

THE GAZETTE
Institute of Medical Sciences, 12 Queen Anne Street, London W1M 0AU. Tel: 01-636 8192.
Editor: Miss O. Dunmore.
Monthly publication of professional interest to medical laboratory scientists.
Illustrations: B&W only. Pictures of medical laboratory scientists at work. Historical photographs of famous medical laboratory scientists and of medical laboratory instruments.
Text: News items on the Institute of Medical Laboratory Sciences, safety and meetings.
Overall freelance potential: Very small.
Fees: Variable.

GENERAL PRACTITIONER
Medical Publications Ltd., 76 Dean Street, London WIA 1BU. Tel: 01-434 2266.
Editor: Jerry Cowhig.
Weekly newspaper for family doctors.
Illustrations: B&W only. Pictures of general practitioners involved in news stories.
Text: News stories, up to 400 words, preferably by prior arrangement with the news editor; features, always by prior arrangement with the features editor.

Overall freelance potential: The papers uses a lot of pictures from freelances, less news and features and only by arrangement.
Fees: By negotiation, but around £30 for 400–500 words.

HEALTHY LIVING
Turret Press Ltd., 886 High Road, London N12 9SB. Tel: 01-446 2411.
Editor: Helene Hodge.
Monthly magazine aimed at the health and fitness-conscious, and particularly concerned with up-to-date information on alternative therapies in the treatment and prevention of disease as well as findings on the use of nutrients, both for general health and in the specific treatment of sickness.
Illustrations: B&W only. Pictures concerned with subjects detailed above.
Text: Features on subjects detailed above.
Overall freelance potential: Fair.
Fees: By agreement.

HERE'S HEALTH
Newman Turner Publications Ltd., 30 Station Approach, West Byfleet, Surrey KT14 6NF. Tel: 093-23 49123.
Editor: Simon Martin.
Monthly publication, covering anything that relates to good health, from vitamin and mineral supplements to ecology and conservation. Accent is on the practical. It is aimed at people who want to help themselves to total health, physical, mental and spiritual. Looks at wholefoods, natural health, alternative medicine, etc.
Illustrations: B&W and colour. Pictures relating to above topics. 'Great outdoors' type of pictures are welcome. Also people (though not professional models), especially if 'sporty'. Prefer to hold plenty of black and white pictures for stock and order colour when necessary. Covers: Colour pictures, usually commissioned, but a good picture which fits the theme of a particular issue will always be considered. Personalities needed. Stock lists appreciated.
Text: Features on all forms of health and people who help themselves to fitness.
Overall freelance potential: Between 30 and 50 per cent is contributed from outside sources, though this includes regular contributors. Always room for good freelance articles and pictures.
Fees: On a rising scale, according to size of picture or length of article.

MEDICAL DIGEST
Maclean Hunter Ltd., 76 Oxford Street, London W1N 0HH. Tel: 01-434 2283.
Editor: J. Graeme Jackson.
Monthly publication for general practitioners in the UK.
Illustrations: B&W and colour. Usually shot to a commissioned brief, but the magazine is interested in making new contacts with freelance photographers.
Text: No freelance market.
Overall freelance potential: Small at present.
Fees: Negotiated.

MEDICINE DIGEST

Medicine Digest Ltd., York House, 37 Queen Square, London WC1N 3BL. 01-831 6806.
Editor: Dr. H. de Glanville.
Monthly review of current medical journal articles and advances. Read by overseas doctors in the Middle East, Africa and Carribbean.
Illustrations: Occasionally B&W pictures are bought. No colour inside the journal. Covers: medical and socio–medical themes related to theme of the month. Colour; 35mm acceptable.
Text: Occasional market for medical and scientific advances of interest to Third World doctors. 750–1,250 words.
Overall freelance potential: Low.
Editor's tips: It is wise to consult the editor before writing anything for this market.
Fees: £25 per 100 words.

MIDDLE EAST HEALTH

IPC Middle East Publishing Co. Ltd., Crown House, 14th Floor, London Road, Morden, Surrey SM4 5DX. Tel: 01-542 9915–7.
Editor: Mike Livesey.
Monthly publication for senior medical and health care personnel in the Middle East.
Illustrations: B&W and occasional colour. Pictures showing health care practice in the Middle East, e.g. treatment at hospitals and clinics. Also clinical photographs, e.g. disease conditions, surgery, etc.
Text: Articles of a clinical nature, written by medically qualified people or those in allied professions.
Overall freelance potential: About 25 per cent is commissioned, usually from known freelances.
Fees: On a rising scale, according to the size of reproduction or length of article.

MIDDLE EAST HOSPITAL

A. E. Morgan Publications Ltd., Stanley House, 9 West Street, Epsom, Surrey KT18 7RL. Tel: 037-27 41411.
Editor: Mrs. Judy Champneys.
Monthly for Principals of Surgery, purchasing officers, administrators, etc. of hospitals in the Middle East.
Illustrations: B&W and occasional colour. Pictures used only to illustrate features of news material.
Text: Features on developments at hospitals throughout the Middle East. News and features on equipment/services available in that area. 750–1,250 words.
Overall freelance potential: All the main feature material comes from freelances.
Fees: Up to £80 per 1,000 words.

MIMS

Medical Publications Ltd., 76 Dean Street, London W1A 1BU. Tel: 01-434 2266.
Editor: Alexandra Balsdon.
Monthly therapeutics journal for general practitioners.

Illustrations: Rare use inside. Covers: Colour pictures of excellent quality commissioned by the art director; 35mm acceptable.
Text: Features involving drug information and therapeutics. 2,000 words.
Overall freelance potential: Very low.
Fees: By agreement.

NEW MIND
National Association for Mental Health, 22 Harley Street, London W1. Tel: 01-637 0741.
Editor: Alistair Crine.
Bi-monthly for people living and working with mentally ill or mentally handicapped.
Illustrations: B&W only. Pictures of depressed, happy, shy, exuberent people, in isolation or in groups; pictures of outside and inside mental hospitals, day centres, adult training centres; people at work, in particular involved with carpentry or with semi-skilled subjects.
Text: Anything in the mental health field. 1,500 words.
Overall freelance potential: Small.
Fees: Low, since the publishers are a charity organisation.

NURSING MIRROR
IPC Building and Contracts Journals Ltd., Surrey House, 1 Throwley Way, Sutton, Surrey SM1 4OQ. Tel: 01-643 8040.
Editor: Peter Brock.
Weekly publication for nurses, midwives and health visitors.
Illustrations: B&W only. News pictures concerning hospital openings, nursing protest marches, presentations at hospitals, celebrities visiting hospitals, staff retirement parties etc. Covers always taken by staff photographers.
Text: No market for freelances.
Overall freelance potential: Occasional for photographers; hardly any for writers.
Fees: £11 per picture.

NURSING TIMES
MacMillan Journals Ltd., 4 Little Essex Street, London WC2R 3LF. Tel: 01-836 6633.
Editor: Alison Dunn.
Weekly magazine for nurses, containing clinical articles, general features and news.
Illustrations: Only with written features. No covers.
Text: News and general topical features.
Overall freelance potential: A very small proportion of the magazine comes from freelances, but freelance work is welcome, nonetheless.
Fees: By agreement.

PULSE
Morgan-Grampian (Professional Press) Ltd., 30 Calderwood Street, Woolwich, London SE18 6QH. Tel: 01-855 7777.

Editor: Howard Griffiths.
Weekly newspaper for family doctors.
Illustrations: B&W and colour. Pictures with captions, involving family doctors.
Text: News, features about family doctors.
Overall freelance potential: Good.
Fees: Negotiable.

RAD

Kingsmoor Publications Ltd., PO Box 3, Harlow, Essex CM19 4RF. Tel: 0279 29731.
Editor: D. J. Roberts.
Monthly publication for radiographers, radiologists and radiotherapists. Contains news, views and comments on NHS and hospitals with particular regard to X-Ray, radiotherapy, ultrasound and nuclear medicine departments.
Illustrations: B&W only. Pictures as illustrations to features and new product reports.
Text: Features and general news stories pertinent to this readership. Product reports. Up to 1,000 words.
Overall freelance potential: Around 70 per cent comes from outside freelances.
Fees: By agreement.

SCOTTISH OPHTHALMIC PRACTITIONERS

Scottish Committee of Ophthalmic Opticians, Crogach, Cove, Helensburgh, Dumbartonshire. Tel: 043-685 343.
Editor: Maureen Callender
Monthly publication for the ophthalmic optical profession in Scotland.
Illustrations: B&W only. News pictures of eminent people in the profession. Other pictures to illustrate articles. Covers: B&W news pictures.
Text: Articles of technical interest to the profession. 1,000–1,500 words.
Overall freelance potential: Small.
Fees: By negotiation.

TALK

National Deaf Children's Society, 45 Hereford Road, London W2 5AH. Tel: 01-229 9272.
Editor: Mrs. Freddy Bloom.
Quarterly magazine devoted to the interests of deaf children. Aimed mainly at parents, but also at teachers, doctors and social workers.
Illustrations: B&W only. Eye-catching pictures of deaf children from infancy to adolescence.
Text: Human interest, technical articles related to the development of hearing-impaired children. 1,500–3,000 words.
Overall freelance potential: Fair.
Fees: Low; the magazine is a non-commercial publication.

THERAPY
Macmillan Journals Ltd., 4 Little Essex Street, London WC2R 3LF. Tel: 01-836 6633.
Editor: Niall Dickson.
Weekly newspaper for the remedial professions and anything connected with them, e.g. physiotherapy, chiropody, occupational therapy, etc.
Illustrations: B&W only. Pictures of anything connected with the above professions.
Text: Features on the professions detailed above. 750–1,000 words.
Overall freelance potential: Small.
Fees: Good; on a rising scale according to the size of reproduction or length of feature.

Local Government

HARLOW NEWS
Harlow Council, Information Services Dept., Town Hall, Harlow, Essex CM20 1HJ. Tel: 0279 446710.
Editor: Kevin Madden.
Quarterly publication, sent free to each household in Harlow.
Illustrations: Pictures to illustrate articles detailed below. Also photographs of the town for its record centre library. This is to build up a building record of the town. Colour and B&W.
Text: Articles that deal mainly with council services in Harlow.
Overall freelance potential: Limited.
Fees: Negotiable.

LOCAL COUNCIL REVIEW
National Association of Local Councils, 2 Becketts, Hertford, Herts. SG14 2AN. Tel: 0992 552934.
Editor: Valerie Shepard.
Quarterly journal of the National Association of Local Councils, produced for members and officers of parish, town and community councils in England and Wales.
Illustrations: B&W only. No potential for covers. Photographers used on commission only. Contact magazine before submitting.
Text: Exclusive to matters related to the work or parish, town and community councils. 1,000–1,500 words.
Overall freelance potential: Small, since the magazine usually commissions their own articles.
Editor's tips: Freelances can break in, but do *nothing* without submitting a proposal first.
Fees: £20 per 1,000 words. Pictures by negotiation.

LOCAL GOVERNMENT NEWS

B&M Publications (London) ltd., PO Box 13, Hereford House, Bridle Path, Croydon CR9 4NL. Tel: 01-680 4200.

Editor: Phillip Cooper.

Monthly news magazine for professional officers, middle to higher grade, in all technical departments of local authorities, officers in water authorities and professional civil servants in relevant government departments.

Illustrations: B&W only. Pictures of architectural and building projects, road schemes, housing projects, national and local politicians and news pictures with local government angle.

Text: Features on any local government related story with exception of those dealing with education or social service policy matters. 750–1,000 words.

Overall freelance potential: More than 50 per cent of material comes from freelance sources.

Fees: By negotiation.

MUNICIPAL JOURNAL

Municipal Publications Ltd., 178–202 Great Portland Street, London W1N 6NH. Tel: 01-637 2400.

Editor: John Jackson.

Weekly publication for senior local government officers, councillors, Whitehall departments and academic and other institutions.

Illustrations: B&W only. Personalities, vehicles, buildings etc.

Text: Features on local government issues. 750–1,000 words.

Overall freelance potential: Very good.

Editor's tips: The articles and pictures must be on local government issues.

Fees: Good; on a rising scale according to the size of reproduction or length of feature.

MUNICIPAL REVIEW AND AMA NEWS

Association of Metropolitan Authorities, 37 Old Queen Street, London, SW1H 9JE. Tel: 01-222 8100.

Editor: Peter Smith.

Published 11 times per year for local authority elected members and chief officers, Universities, MPs etc. Contains news of Association's policies and activities plus articles on urban and local government.

Illustrations: B&W only. Pictures of events involving metropolitan and district county authorities, the GLC or London boroughs. No stock pictures.

Text: No freelance market.

Overall freelance potential: Publication has a strong need for appropriate pictures about local authority activities, particularly in London, Merseyside, Greater Manchester, West Midlands, West Yorkshire, South Yorkshire and Tyne and Wear.

Editor's tips: Ring before submitting.

Fees: By negotiation.

NOW IN SOUTHAMPTON
Southampton City Council, Public Relations Unit, Civic Centre, Southampton SO9 4XF.
Tel: 0703 23855 ext. 756/454.
Editor: Malcolm Grosvenor.
Quarterly civic newspaper—one of the largest and most comprehensive in Britain. Contains news on the council, features on the city and community news.
Illustrations: B&W and colour. Any pictures concerning events, activities, objects, developments or people involved in the Southampton scene. Covers: Mainly colour pictures of general subjects from the city and port of Southampton. 35mm acceptable, but larger formats preferred.
Text: No freelance market.
Overall freelance potential: Freelance photographers used on a regular, established basis. Most requirements are met by these and/or by council sources. The paper is always willing, however, to consider photographic contributions with pictorial impact, artistic or creative qualities.
Fees: Good; on a rising scale according to the size of reproduction.

PUBLIC SERVICE AND LOCAL GOVERNMENT
BWS Publishing Ltd., 3 Hammersmith Road, London W14 9BR. Tel: 01-603 4567.
Editor: Andrew Leech.
Monthly publication for all officers and personnel involved with local government and public utilities.
Illustrations: No freelance market.
Text: Features on anything of a local government nature. 900 words.
Overall freelance potential: Around 45 per cent of the copy comes from freelance contributors.
Fees: By agreement.

Male Interest

CLUB INTERNATIONAL
Paul Raymond Publications Ltd., 2 Archer Street, London W1V 7HE. Tel: 01-734 9191.
Editor: Roger Cook.
Sophisticated monthly for men.
Illustrations: Colour only, 35mm Kodachrome 25 preferred. Requires top quality glamour sets, including full frontals, of very attractive girls. Always on the look-out for sets which feature celebrities.
Overall freelance potential: Most of the published glamour material comes from freelances, but they are normally experienced glamour photographers.

Editor's tips: Study the magazine, but don't just duplicate what you see there. Go for something original and spectacular.

Fees: £500–£1000 for glamour sets of non-celebrities. For celebrity sets, 'the sky's the limit!'

ESCORT

Paul Raymond Publications Ltd., 2 Archer Street, London W1V 7HE. Tel: 01-734 9191.

Editor: Neville Player.

Monthly for men; less sophisticated than the other Paul Raymond publications, *Men Only* and *Club International*.

Illustrations: Colour only, 35mm Kodachrome preferred. Looks for glamour sets of 'normal, healthy, girl-next-door' types. Sets frequently run to fewer pages than is the case with other men's magazines. Each issue contains about eight glamour sets running to only 2 or 3 pages each. Covers: Single colour shots required for the cover, back cover and centre spread.

Text: Articles of 1,000–2,000 words on sexual or humorous topics.

Overall freelance potential: Good.

Fees: £200 for glamour sets. Articles: £50–£100.

FIESTA

Galaxy Publications Ltd., Hermit Place, 252 Belsize Road, London NW6 4BT. Tel: 01-328 5641.

Editor: Chris Lloyd.

Monthly men's magazine, actually aimed at both men and women for whom nudity and sex are not too problematic.

Illustrations: B&W and colour. The subject is sex and rarely does the magazine deviate from the topic. Picture subjects have included soho strippers, the alternative Miss World competition, girls who get wet/muddy, girls in uniform, sexy lingerie etc. plus the usual girl sets—ordinary settings in which a girl strips. Covers: Pictures of girls who are clothed, yet still obviously enticing. Space at the top and sides of the picture for logo and coverlines. 35mm acceptable.

Text: Features on all aspects of sex and what turns men and women on. 2,000–2,500 words.

Overall freelance potential: Freelances contribute a major part of the magazine. There are also a number of regular contributors.

Editor's tips: Work is rarely commissioned. Telephone for details.

Fees: Photo sets, £300; Features, £40 per 1,000 words; illustrated features, approximately £175.

KNAVE

Galaxy Publications Ltd., Hermit Place, 252 Belsize Road, London NW6 4BT. Tel: 01-328 5641.

Editor: Ian Pemble.
Monthly magazine for men.
Illustrations: B&W and colour. Humorous pictures, illustrations for articles and girl sets.
Covers: Colour glamour pictures. 35mm acceptable.
Text: Sexy, humorous, factual articles. No fiction. 3,000 words maximum.
Overall freelance potential: Most of the magazine comes from freelance sources.
Fees: Girl sets, £500; text and other pictures by agreement.

MAYFAIR
Fisk Publishing Co. Ltd., 95a Chancery Lane, London WC2A 1DZ. Tel: 01-242 1593.
Editor: Kenneth Bound.
Sophisticated monthly for men.
Illustrations: Colour only, 35mm preferred. Requires glamour sets taken in up-market
surroundings. Only top quality material can be accepted. Backgrounds should be real-life
locations, such as a nicely furnished flat, but little outdoor material is used. Also, colour sets
to form the basis of 4 or 6 page spreads on other male interests, such as custom/unusual cars,
aeroplanes and other mechanical devices. Covers: Always feature a girl, totally nude, though
nipples not shown. Potential cover pictures should be sexy, provocative, natural and
head-turning. An occasional touch of humour in a cover shot is allowable. Subject should
be shot as a square composition, but allowing a further quarter depth above the composition
for the title logo. Background should be reasonably plain and not variable so that the logo
can either be projected on top or reversed out. Thought should be given to the erotic use
of clothing and suggestion of sex appeal or sexual situation, together with a fairly simple
colour scheme.
Text: Articles on general male interests.
Overall freelance potential: Good; all the photographs and major features are the work
of freelance contributors.
Editor's tips: Get your focus and flesh tones right before you think of submitting. If these
two factors are not right, nothing will work.
Fees: £200–£600 for glamour sets. Covers: £150 and up.

MEN ONLY
Paul Raymond Publications Ltd., 2 Archer Street, London W1V 7HE. Tel: 01-734 9191.
Editor: Roger Sewell.
Sophisticated monthly for men.
Illustrations: Colour glamour sets, 35mm Kodachrome preferred. Sets should depict
beautiful girls in quality locations.
Overall freelance potential: Good; most of the published material comes from freelances.

Editor's tips: The emphasis is on very contemporary sets featuring very contemporary ladies. Photographers should therefore pay close attention to trends and fashions in clothing, make-up and settings.

Fees: £500–£1,000 for glamour sets.

PENTHOUSE

Penthouse Publications Ltd., 2 Bramber Road, London W14 9PB. Tel: 01-385 6181.

Editor: David Jones.

Sophisticated monthly aimed mainly at men between the ages of 18 and 30.

Illustrations: Colour only, 35mm Kodachrome preferred. Requires top quality glamour sets of very beautiful girls. Sets normally run to between six and ten pages.

Overall freelance potential: Good; but only those experienced in glamour photography are likely to get work accepted here.

Editor's tips: Submit a few sample shots in the first instance, so that the editor can judge whether the particular girl would be suitable for a full-scale glamour set.

Fees: Minimum rate: £75 per published page.

Miscellaneous

THE AMERICAN

British American Newspapers Ltd., 114–115 West Street, Farnham, Surrey GU9 7HL. Tel: 0252 713366.

Editor: Ray Tindle.

Fortnightly publication for American residents in the UK and short-term US visitors.

Illustrations: B&W mostly and a little colour. Pictures of Americans or American activities in the UK.

Text: Features on Americans or American activities in the UK. Human interest and 'people' stories work best, particularly if they involve business, education, arts or sports. 400–800 words.

Overall freelance potential: Several regular freelance columns plus at least one general freelance piece in each issue.

Editor's tips: Currently increasing the number of stories on Americans in the UK. Phone queries are OK, but should be followed by a query letter and manuscript within two weeks. Seasonal material should be submitted three months in advance.

Fees: 50p per column centimetre printed; £5 per picture.

ASIAN POST

Asian Publishing Ltd., Unit 4, Heston Industrial Mall, Church Road, Heston, Middlesex TW5 0LD. Tel: 01-570 1100.

Editor: Chhotu Karadia.

Weekly up-market news magazine for the Asian community in Britain. Written entirely in English, and aimed mainly at the established and second-generation Asian population.

Illustrations: Mainly B&W; some colour. Topical pictures accompanied by a story or detailed caption. Must be of genuine interest to the Asian community, but can be on any topic ranging from poor housing to the opulent lifestyles of successful businessmen. Also of interest are newsy or unusual pictures of well-known people in the Asian community, which can be filed for use with future stories. Covers: Colour shots usually relating to a major article inside the magazine.

Text: News items or topical features concerning the Asian community.

Overall freelance potential: Plenty of scope for those in touch with the Asian community. The editor will also be interested in hearing from freelances who are in a position to cover specific events of Asian interest.

Fees: On a rising scale according to size of reproduction and length of text.

THE CARIBBEAN CHRONICLE

48 Albemarle Street, London W1X 4AR. Tel: 01-629 6353/4.

Editor: David Jessop.

Published bi-monthly, and distributed internationally to those interested in political and economic developments through the Caribbean area. Readership aimed at highest levels of government and business.

Illustrations: B&W and colour. Any pictures of a Caribbean nature. Covers: Colour pictures of same; 35mm acceptable.

Text: Features on Caribbean topics aimed at the readership mentioned above. 600 words.

Overall freelance potential: Around 20 per cent bought from outside sources.

Fees: By negotiation.

CONSERVATIVE NEWSLINE

The Conservative and Union Party, Conservative Central Office, 32 Smith Square, London SW1P 3HH. Tel: 01-222 9000.

Editor: Piers Merchant.

Monthly newspaper of the Conservative Party, aimed at ordinary Party members throughout the country.

Illustrations: B&W only. Photographs with any political content will be considered, including demonstrations, strikes, picketing, and events at which politicians of all parties are present. Also local constituency activities, local Party news, fund-raising drives, etc.

Text: Short articles and news items concerning any Party activities. A small amount of scope for brief personality pieces about political figures may be found in the diary column.

Overall freelance potential: Plenty of room for freelance contributions, on a wide range of political matters.

Fees: According to size of reproduction or length of text.

NEDRA WESTWATER

THE DIPLOMATIST and **LADY DIPLOMAT**
Diplomatist Associates Ltd., 58 Theobalds Road, London WC1X 8SF. Tel: 01-405 4874.
Editor: Vanessa Peet.
Controlled circulation house journals for the foreign diplomatic community in London. *The Diplomatist* is a monthly and goes to husbands and wives; *Lady Diplomat* is published twice a year and goes to wives only.
Illustrations: Pictures are bought for illustrating forthcoming articles. *The Diplomatist* uses travel, social and diplomatic life in general subjects; *Lady Diplomat* needs pictures of shops, cookery, fashion and anything that might interest the wife of a foreign diplomat in London. Pictures are mostly B&W, but there is some colour in *Lady Diplomat*. Covers: colour pictures of diplomats' wives for *Lady Diplomat*; 35mm acceptable.
Text: Commissions are possible, but not often. They are always to a specific brief. 1,000–2,000 words.
Overall freelance potential: Small.
Fees: Variable.

FIRE PREVENTION
Fire Protection Association, Aldermary House, Queen Street, London EC4N 1TJ. Tel: 01-248 5222.
Editor: D. R. Kershaw.
A technical publication on fire safety. Aimed at fire brigades, fire equipment manufacturers, architects, insurance companies, public sector bodies, industry and commerce. Published ten times a year.
Illustrations: B&W only. Pictures of large and small fires to illustrate reports. Covers: B&W repeats of pictures used inside.
Text: Technical articles on fire prevention and protection. 2,000–3,000 words.
Overall freelance potential: Good pictures of fires are always welcome.
Fees: Text, £18 per 1,000 words; pictures £5–£10.

FORUM
Forum Press Ltd., 2 Bramber Road, London W14 9PB. Tel: 01-385 6181.
Editor: Roger Baker.
Monthly magazine dealing with all aspects of sex, i.e. social, medical, problematical, political, relationships, etc. Aimed at intelligent, aware, educated men and women.
Illustrations: B&W only. Pictures are taken only to illustrate articles. All pictures must be tasteful despite the subject matter which can be anything from fetishes to problems with love and marriage.
Text: Factual, social and medical features with a keen sex relevance. No porn. No fiction.
Overall freelance potential: All material comes from freelance sources.
Editor's tips: Study recent issues of the magazine and then submit only a synopsis or outline in the first instance.
Fees: By arrangement, but good.

GAY NEWS

Gay News Ltd., 1A Normand Gardens, Greyhound Road, London W14 9SB. Tel: 01-381 2815/0433.

Editor: Andrew Lumsden.

Fortnightly publication aimed at a male and female readership that is almost entirely homosexual. Contains news and feature material, both national and international.

Illustrations: B&W only. News, entertainment, etc. of direct interest to the readerships. No 'model' pictures.

Text: Features on any subject of interest to homosexuals. 1,000–2,000 words.

Overall freelance potential: Very good. Not much material currently offered.

Fees: £12 for three-column picture, negotiable above.

HANDICAPPED LIVING

Living Publications Ltd., 9 West Street, Epsom, Surrey KT18 7RL. Tel: 037-27 41411.

Editor: Tony Ellis.

Monthly magazine for handicapped people, taking a positive approach to coping with disability. Includes good coverage of leisure topics.

Illustrations: Black and white photographs showing the positive achievements of handicapped people. Disabled people at work, taking part in sport, on holiday, and so on. Covers: colour pictures usually related to a major feature inside the magazine.

Text: Illustrated articles and features, from 250 words upwards, concentrating on self-help and the positive approach. General leisure topics from the disabled point of view.

Overall freelance potential: An intelligent and sensitive approach to the subject will pay off.

Editor's tips: Avoid a patronising or negative approach.

Fees: £5 to £20 for black and white pictures; up to £85 for suitable cover shots. £30 per published page for articles.

HEALTH & EFFICIENCY

Peenhill Ltd., Payne House, 23–24 Smithfield Street, London EC1. Tel: 01-236 4511.

Editor: Kate Sturdy.

Monthly naturist/nudist magazine.

Illustrations: B&W and colour. Outdoor shots of people in the nude, epitomising the naturist way of life. Pretty young women are the preferred subject, but men and groups are also required. 35mm acceptable.

Text: Short illustrated articles about naturists.

Overall freelance potential: Fair.

Editor's tips: This is not a market for 'girlie' pictures of the type used by men's magazines. Study the magazine.

Fees: £20 per page and pro rata for colour; £10 per page and pro rata for black and white.

LAG BULLETIN

The Legal Action Group, 28A Highgate Road, London NW5. Tel: 01-267 0048.

Editors: Jennifer Levin and Ole Hansen.

Monthly publication for lawyers, experienced advice workers, law students and academics.
Illustrations: B&W only. Pictures of lawyers and judges, especially other than the standard head and shoulders shot. Courtroom and negotiating scenes. Plus pictures to illustrate features.
Text: Features on legal services and professional issues, including the courts. High technical detail required. Also information for news and feature material that can be written in-house.
Overall freelance potential: High, providing contributors understand the highly specialised interests.
Fees: By negotiation.

THE MIDDLE EAST

PO Box 261, 63 Long Acre, London WC2E 9LR. Tel: 01-404 4333.
Editor: Ms Nadia Hijab.
Monthly publication directed at senior management, governmental personnel and universities. Covers current affairs of a political, cultural and economic nature.
Illustrations: B&W only inside. Pictures of all Middle Eastern subjects. Covers: Colour pictures of Middle Eastern personalities and scenes.
Text: Features on Middle Eastern subjects or world subjects that relate to the area. 1,000–3,000 words.
Overall freelance potential: Most of the pictures come from freelances and around 50 per cent of the overall editorial.
Fees: Text, £70 per 1,000 words; B&W pictures, £12–£15; covers by agreement.

MILAP WEEKLY

Ramesh Kumar Soni, 307A North End Road, London W14 9NS. Tel: 01-385 8966.
Editor: R. Soni.
Weekly publication for Indian, Pakistani and Urdu-speaking people.
Illustrations: B&W only for inside and cover use, concerning immigrant matters.
Text: All matters of interest to immigrant Asian communities.
Fees: By negotiation.

NAVIN WEEKLY

Ramesh Kumar Soni, 307A North End Road, London W14 9NS. Tel: 01-385 8966.
Editor: Ramesh Kumar.
Weekly publication for Indian and Hindi-speaking people.
Illustrations: B&W only for inside and cover use, concerning immigrant matters.
Text: All matters of interest to immigrant Asian communities.
Fees: By negotiation.

PEOPLE

IPFF, 18–20 Lower Regent Street, London SW1Y 4PW. Tel: 01-839 2911.
Editor: John Rowley.
Quarterly publication concerned with population and development topics.

Illustrations: B&W only inside. Pictures showing family planning projects, family life, rural and urban living conditions, mothers and children. Covers: Colour pictures related to features.

Text: No freelance market.

Overall freelance potential: Nearly all the magazine comes from freelances.

Fees: Full page pictures, £60; half page, £30.

PREDICTION

Link House Magazines (Croydon) PLC, Link House, Dingwall Avenue, Croydon CR9 2TA. Tel: 01-686 2599.

Editor: Jo Logan.

Monthly magazine covering astrology and all aspects of the occult. Regular features on Tarot, palmistry, graphology etc.

Illustrations: Colour only for cover use. Must be pertinent to general contents of the magazine. 6 × 6 cm minimum.

Text: Articles with an occult slant, i.e. mythology, magic, alternative therapies, ESP, telepathy, UFOs, earth mysteries, dowsing, etc. 1,500–2,000 words.

Overall freelance potential: Very good; 95 per cent of content is contributed.

Fees: Variable.

THE SOCIAL DEMOCRAT

The Social Democratic Party, 4 Cowley Street, London SW1P 3NB. Tel: 01-222 4141/1200.

Editor: Roger Carroll.

Fortnightly official journal of the SDP.

Illustrations: B&W only. Picture of SDP activities around the country and general political news pictures.

Text: News items about local party activities and personalities.

Overall freelance potential: Limited to local SDP news; coverage of major national stories will be obtained largely from Fleet Street sources.

Fees: By negotiation, but may be on the low side.

SOUTH

South Publications Ltd., 13th Floor, New Zealand House, Haymarket, London SW1. Tel: 01-839 6167.

Editor: Denzil Peiris.

Monthly Third World magazine with an economic slant, aimed at the politically aware of the Third World and decision makers in the West.

Illustrations: B&W and colour. Pictures of commodities and economics in the Third World. Covers: Colour pictures of cultural subjects related to this area. 35mm acceptable.

Text: Third World and political stories and art stories.

Overall freelance potential: Fairly good.

Fees: By negotiation.

TEMPO
Department of Employment, Caxton House, Tothill Street, London SW1H 9NF. Tel: 01-213
5596/3000.
Editor: Keith Charteris.
Monthly staff newspaper of the Department of Employment.
Illustrations: B&W only. News and feature pictures connected with or about staff of the
Department.
Text: Features about staff of the Department. Human interest material is most likely to be
successful. Up to 1,000 words.
Overall freelance potential: Small, but if something interesting can be found about one
of the staff members, it is likely to be accepted.
Fees: On a rising scale according to length of article or size of published picture.

Motoring

AUTO ACCESSORY RETAILER
PO Box 46, Burke House, 21 High Street, High Wycombe, Bucks HP11 2BZ. Tel: 0494
41548/9.
Editor: Ian Wagstaff.
Monthly publication for retailers, wholesalers and manufacturers involved in automotive
parts and accessories.
Illustrations: No freelance market.
Text: Specialist articles on retailing.
Overall freelance potential: Small.
Fees: Negotiable.

AUTOCAR
IPC Transport Press Ltd., Quadrant House, The Quadrant, Sutton, Surrey SM2 5AS. Tel:
01-661 3500.
Editor: Ray Hutton.
Weekly magazine on general motoring topics. Includes road tests, historical features,
information on new cars, coverage of motor shows, etc.
Illustrations: B&W and colour. Pictures of unusual incidents, road signs etc., with captions.
General pictures of roads and motorways, traffic jams, accidents, parking, etc. considered
for stock. Unusual or special cars. 35mm acceptable inside. Covers: Colour pictures, usually
shot by staff photographer. 6 × 6 cm. minimum.
Text: Illustrated features on unusual or special cars. Veteran or vintage car features with
contemporary pictures. 1,000–2,000 words.
Overall freelance potential: Around 20 per cent of features and pictures come from
freelance sources.

Editor's tips: Technical accuracy is essential. Full information on the cars featured must be detailed. Colour features stand a better chance if accompanied by B&W pictures as well. No touring articles.
Fees: Features, £48 per 1,000 words; news items, £41 per 1,000 words; B&W pictures, £11.55 minimum; colour, £28.60 per picture.

AUTO PERFORMANCE
Link House Magazines Ltd., Link House, Dingwall Avenue, Croydon CR9 2TA. Tel: 01-686 2599.
Editor: Peter Chrisp.
Monthly magazine for those interested in high performance road cars and low-budget motor sport. Practical content concerns car modification for those wishing to achieve high performance at low cost.
Illustrations: Colour and B&W. Pictures of interesting high performance cars accompanied by detailed captions. Major photo-features will be devoted to individual cars of special interest, and will most likely concern standard road cars that have been modified and tuned-up. Also, coverage of all forms of low-budget motor sport, including grass track racing, short oval racing, and karting. Does not deal with the upper end of the motor sport scene, such as Formula One.
Text: Well illustrated articles and features on car modification, and on motor sport topics.
Overall freelance potential: A lot of the contributed photography comes from regulars, but there is a need for original material from the North and Scotland.
Fees: By negotiation.

THE AUTOMOBILE
PPG Publishing Ltd., 5 Rectory Road, Beckenham, Kent. Tel: 01-658 3533.
Editor: Michael Brisby.
Quarterly publication featuring veteran, vintage, and pre-1940's motor vehicles.
Illustrations: B&W and colour. Not much scope for single pictures unless of particular interest. The main requirement is for well-illustrated articles concerning any pre-1940's motor vehicle; not only cars but also commercial vehicles, buses, and tractors. Of particular interest are good restoration features, with both a 'before' and an 'after' picture showing what can be achieved. Also some room for coverage of race meetings, exhibitions or other events at which old motor vehicles are present.
Text: Informative illustrated articles as above, with the emphasis on entertainment.
Overall freelance potential: Although limited by the quarterly frequency, quite good for quality illustrated articles.
Editor's tips: There is absolutely no point in submitting material concerning any post-1940 vehicles.
Fees: By negotiation.

AUTOMOBILE SPORT
Automobile Sport Ltd., Ivel House, Ilchester, Somerset BA22 8JJ. Tel: 0935 840873.
Editor: Ian Bamsey.

Monthly magazine devoted to all forms of motor-racing and rallying. Also features high performance and exotic road cars.

Illustrations: Colour and B&W. Anything that reflects the current motor-racing scene, with a strong bias towards the top end of the sport. Covers: Striking colour shots that lend themselves to upright reproduction.

Text: Articles and features on motor-racing matters.

Overall freelance potential: Excellent; the magazine relies heavily on freelance contributors. Experienced motor-racing photographers and correspondents may be able to obtain commissions to cover specific events.

Editor's tips: Contributors with ideas for features should contact the editor first.

Fees: £10 per B&W picture; £20 per colour. Higher rates are payable for Grand Prix coverage. £70 per 1000 words for articles.

CAR FLEET MANAGEMENT

IPC Transport Press Ltd., Quadrant House, The Quadrant, Sutton, Surrey SM2 5AS. Tel: 01-661 3500.

Editor: John Blauth.

Bi-monthly publication for fleet managers, finance directors and fleet owners who operate 25 cars or more.

Illustrations: B&W only inside. Exclusive and newsworthy pictures relating to fleet sales or fleet cars. Covers: Colour pictures of people in the trade and new car launches. 6 × 6 cm minimum.

Text: Features on car management or cost. Exclusive material only. 1,000–1,500 words plus two to three pictures.

Overall freelance potential: Between 40 and 60 per cent comes from freelance sources.

Fees: Text, £48 per 1,000 words; B&W pictures £13.40; colour, £33.45.

CAR PARTS AND ACCESSORIES

Automedia Ltd., Faversham House, 111 St. James's Road, Croydon, Surrey CR9 2TH. Tel: 01-684 2660.

Editor: Malcolm Wood.

Monthly controlled circulation publication aimed at the parts and accessories market for both cars and motor cycles. Wholesale and retail sectors of the trade are covered.

Illustrations: Mostly come from sources within the industry, but as magazine grows there will be a need for more freelance pictures to illustrate features. Covers: colour; 35mm acceptable.

Text: Features on all types of accessories such as CB radio, in-car entertainment and telephones, computer/business machines for the trade etc. Also features of interest to the retailer, e.g. business advice, legal matters, shopfitting etc. 500–1,500 words.

Overall freelance potential: This is a new magazine that, at the moment, has a minimal use for freelance work. But the situation is likely to change as the magazine grows.

Editor's tips: Intending contributors should contact the editor before submitting material.

Fees: By negotiations.

CARE ON THE ROAD

Royal Society for the Prevention of Accidents, Cannon House, The Priory, Queensway, Birmingham B4 6BS. Tel: 021-233 2461.

Editor: Ken Rogers.

Monthly publication on road safety, aimed at professional drivers, legal authorities, police etc.

Illustrations: No market for freelances.

Text: Features on road safety, products, training etc. 1,000 words.

Overall freelance potential: Around 10 per cent comes from freelance sources.

Fees: Good; on a rising scale according to the length of the article.

THE DISABLED DRIVER

The Disabled Drivers' Motor Club, 45 Castleton Avenue, Bexleyheath, Kent DA7 6QT. 03224 47651.

Editor: Ben Tinton.

Bi-monthly journal of the Disabled Drivers Motor Club. Covers motoring, services and tourism with special reference to disabled drivers.

Illustrations: B&W only. Pictures of motoring and related subjects with special reference to the disabled.

Text: Features on motoring with the disabled driver in mind.

Overall freelance potential: Small but potential growth.

Fees: Low.

DRIVING MAGAZINE

Driving Instructor's Association, Lion Green Road, Coulsdon, Surrey CR3 2NL. Tel: 01-660 3333.

Editor: Graham Fryer.

Bi-monthly publication for driving instructors and road safety educationalists.

Illustrations: B&W and colour pictures of home or overseas motorists/driving school vehicles in unusual surroundings or circumstances. Humorous incidents, i.e. traffic accidents of an unusual nature, unusual road signs, humorous signs or those in extraordinary positions. Covers: Colour, but generally from advertising agencies.

Text: Features on road safety, driver training and general driving articles. 500–2,000 words.

Overall freelance potential: Substantial amount bought.

Fees: £5–£15, variable, according to subject and quality.

GARAGE AND TRANSPORT

Hulton Technical Press, Warwick House, Azalea Drive, Swanley, Kent BR8 8JF. Tel: 0322 68431.

Editor: Richard Gadeselli.

A monthly publication, aimed at Britain's motor dealers and traders, car fleet managers, motor factors, garages, accessory shops, wholesalers and the general motor industry.

Illustrations: None.

TONY BOXALL

Text: Any subject, technical or otherwise, that concerns the motor trade or industry in the UK and overseas. 1,000–2,000 words.
Overall freelance potential: Around five per cent from freelances each month.
Fees: £60 per 1,000 words.

HOT CAR

Business Publications Ltd., 109–119 Waterloo Road, London SE1 8UL. Tel: 01-928 3388.
Editor: Clive Househam.
Monthly magazine, dealing with performance tuning for road cars, as well as fringe areas such as kit cars and 4 × 4's.
Illustrations: Photographs are used generally as illustrations to features. Colour and B&W is used; 35mm acceptable. No freelance material bought for covers.
Text: 'How-to' features on specific popular cars such as engine uprating or transplants etc.
Overall freelance potential: A little over 10 per cent of the editorial comes from freelances.
Fees: £35 per 1,000 words. B&W pictures, approximately £4 each; colour, approximately £8 each.

FPMH – K

MAGIC CARPET
Disabled Drivers' Association, Ashwellthorpe Hall, Ashwellthorpe, Norwich NR16 1EX.
Tel: 050-841 449.
Editor: F. Nailer.
Quarterly publication for members of the Disabled Drivers' Association and kindred organisations.
Illustrations: B&W only for use inside the magazine and showing methods of mobility for disabled people or similar transport subjects. Covers: similar and B&W only.
Overall freelance potential: Very small.
Fees: 'Modest for charitable organisation'.

MOTOR TRADER
IPC Transport Press Ltd., Quadrant House, the Quadrant, Sutton, Surrey SM2 5AS. Tel: 01-661 3288.
Editor: Iain Sherriff.
Weekly trade newspaper on subscription only, read by manufacturers in the car and component industries, people in the accessory trade, garage owners, body shop workmen, etc.
Illustrations: B&W only inside the publication. Pictures on anything connected with the motor trade industry. Covers: Colour pictures of similar; 35mm acceptable.
Text: News and features relevant to the motor trade and industry. 300–1,000 words.
Overall freelance potential: Anything sent will be considered as long as it fits the market.
Editor's tips: This is the trade's only weekly newspaper; it is particularly interested in hard news.
Fees: Colour—up to 30 sq. in., £28.60; between 30 and 60 sq. in., £33.45. B&W—Up to 4 sq. in., (head shots only), £7.15; up to 12 sq. in., £11.55; between 12 and 30 sq. in., £13.40.

PRACTICAL CLASSICS
P.P.G. Publishing Ltd., 5 Rectory Road, Beckenham, Kent. Tel: 01-658 3533.
Editor: Michael Brisby.
Monthly magazine for owners/enthusiasts of older cars, pre-war to 1970, with emphasis on the practical aspects of buying, restoring, repairing and running the vehicles.
Illustrations: B&W only. Pictures for use with features. Covers shot by staff photographers only.
Text: Features of interest to older cars enthusiasts.
Overall freelance potential: Very small.
Fees: By arrangement.

SAFER MOTORING
RFWW Publications Ltd., Lloyds Bank Chambers, Cirencester, Glos. Tel: 0285 2185.
Editor: Robin Wager.
Published ten times a year for owners and enthusiasts of Volkswagen and Audi vehicles.

Illustrations: B&W only inside. Self-contained picture stories or picture as illustrations to features. Covers: Colour pictures of VW, Audi, Porsche, NSU vehicles or derivatives, either interesting vehicles in their own right or more commonplace vehicles in interesting or picturesque settings. 35mm acceptable.
Text: Features on VW and Audi interest, especially do-it-yourself, historical and technical subjects. No set length.
Overall freelance potential: Most of the material comes from freelances, but almost exclusively from regular contributors.
Editor's tips: An in-depth knowledge of the subject is needed. No articles unless illustrated with photographs and/or drawings.
Fees: By agreement.

STREET MACHINE
Business Publications Ltd., 109–119 Waterloo Road, London SE1 8UL. Tel: 01-928 3388.
Editor: George Hinton.
Monthly magazine for men in their late teens/early twenties with an interest in personalised cars which they can identify with and aspire to.
Illustrations: B&W and colour. Only as part of a story/picture package on subjects detailed below. Prefers British-source material but, since the magazine has its own staff photographer, this tends to be 'scoop' material or from outlying parts of the country.
Text: Features on completed cars, step-by-step illustrated material on how to do it subjects, track tests of modified cars and coverage of allied subjects.
Overall freelance potential: One or two stories per month used.
Editor's tips: Totally unsolicited material is a waste of time. Freelances with something to offer should telephone first to discuss the idea.
Fees: By negotiation.

Music

BLACK ECHOES
Black Echoes Ltd., 113 High Holborn, London WC1V 6JJ. Tel: 01-405 0461/0268.
Editor: Chris Gill.
Weekly tabloid publication devoted to all aspects of black popular music, with a strong emphasis on reggae.
Illustrations: B&W only. Outstanding photographs of black popular music performers, for immediate publication or for file.
Text: No scope—all produced in-house.
Overall freelance potential: Limited—many photographs are obtained free from record companies.
Fees: By negotiation.

BLACK MUSIC AND JAZZ REVIEW

Napfield Ltd., 153 Praed Street, London W2. Tel: 01-402 5051/6869.
Editor: Chris May.
Monthly magazine covering most aspects of black popular music, including jazz and reggae.
Illustrations: Mostly B&W; colour is featured on front and back covers, and centre pages.
Original and striking photographs of black music performers.
Text: Limited scope for features on black music subjects, preferably exclusive.
Overall freelance potential: Limited.
Fees: By negotiation.

BLUES AND SOUL

Napfield Ltd., 153 Praed Street, London W2. Tel: 01-402 5051/6869.
Editor: Bob Kilbourn.
Fortnightly publication devoted to blues and soul music.
Illustrations: Mostly B&W; colour used on front and back covers and centre spread.
Original and exclusive pictures of blues or soul music performers.
Text: Small amount of scope for exclusive articles or interviews.
Overall freelance potential: Limited.
Editor's tips: Think of the readership, and the format, in order to produce something really striking and eye-catching.
Fees: By negotiation.

COUNTRY MUSIC PEOPLE

Country Music Press Ltd., 128a Lowfield Street, Dartford, Kent. Tel: 0322 73591.
Editor: Tony Byworth.
Glossy monthly magazine for country and western music fans. Covers top name country music artists, as well as regional and club news.
Illustrations: B&W and colour. Oustanding photographs of country music performers.
Covers: 6 × 6 cm colour transparencies, composed to fit the upright format of the magazine.
Text: Articles on all aspects of country music, but not superficial in approach.
Overall freelance potential: Good.
Editor's tips: Contributors should contact the editor before covering an event or preparing an article.
Fees: By negotiation.

COUNTRY MUSIC WORLD

Multi-Language Publications Ltd., Payne House, 23/24 Smithfield Street, London EC1. Tel: 01-236 4511.
Editor: John Shotton.
Fortnightly newspaper covering the country music scene.
Illustrations: B&W only. All aspects of country music, especially anything different or unusual.

Text: Articles and features with an original approach, perhaps only loosely related to the subject. News items also welcomed.
Overall freelance potential: Good.
Editor's tips: Photographs in this field tend to be too obviously posed, and a different approach is desirable.
Fees: £3 per picture; £20 per thousand words for features.

FLEXIPOP
Colour Gold Ltd., 80 Bell Street, London NW1. Tel: 01-402 7535.
Editors: Barry Cain and Tim Lott.
Monthly magazine for younger pop music fans. Mainly devoted to current 'Top Twenty' performers.
Illustrations: Some B&W, but mainly colour. Photographs of any currently popular bands and singers.
Text: Interviews with, or profiles of, popular music performers.
Overall freelance potential: Very good for the right subject matter.
Editor's tips: Bear in mind that the magazine is aimed at a young readership.
Fees: £45 per full page colour picture; £35 per full page B&W.

INTERNATIONAL MUSICIAN AND RECORDING WORLD
Cover Publications Ltd., Grosvenor House, 141/143 Drury Lane, London WC2. Tel: 01-379 6342.
Editor: Tony Horkins.
Monthly magazine for musicians and recording personnel in the popular music fields. Devotes most space to instruments and allied equipment and recording studio techniques.
Illustrations: Mostly B&W; some colour. Pictures of pop/rock musicians with instruments, either in performance or in the recording studio. Covers: colour transparencies are used as reference by graphic artists.
Text: Interviews, technical features, equipment and studio reviews. Contributors should have good technical knowledge of the subject.
Editor's tips: Remember that the magazine is aimed at practising musicians, not music fans.
Fees: By negotiation.

KERRANG!
Spotlight Publications Ltd., 40 Long Acre, Covent Garden, London WC2E 9JT. Tel: 01-836 1522.
Editor: Alf Martin.
Fortnightly magazine for 'heavy metal' rock music fans.
Illustrations: B&W and colour pictures of 'heavy metal' performers. On-stage performance shots preferred, with the emphasis on action. Some posed shots and portraits of popular performers also used.
Text: Little freelance market.

Overall freelance potential: Very good. The magazine is heavily illustrated and uses a lot of colour.

Fees: According to size of reproduction.

MELODY MAKER

IPC Magazines Ltd., Berkshire House, 168–173 High Holborn, London WC1V 7AV. Tel: 01-379 3581.

Editor: Mike Oldfield.

Weekly music paper for the 15 to 18 age group.

Illustrations: B&W and occasional colour of pop music subjects.

Text: Features, news and reviews relevant to pop music. 300 words.

Overall freelance potential: Occasional use of outside contributors.

Fees: Text, £50 per 1,000 words. pictures, from £11.55, according to size of reproduction.

NEW MUSICAL EXPRESS

IPC Magazines Ltd., 5/7 Carnaby Street, London W1V 1PG. Tel: 01-439 8761.

Editor: Neil Spencer.

Weekly tabloid covering all aspects of popular music and allied youth culture.

Illustrations: B&W only of all aspects of contemporary popular music.

Text: Scope for exclusive interview with rock musicians, film stars, or other personalities of interest to a young and aware readership.

Overall freelance potential: Good, but very dependent on subject matter.

Editor's tips: NME only covers those parts of the music scene considered worthwhile by the editorial team.

Fees: On a rising scale according to size of reproduction.

NOISE!

Spotlight Publications Ltd., 40 Long Acre, Covent Garden, London WC2E 9JT. Tel: 01-836 1522.

Editor: Alan Lewis.

Fortnightly pop music magazine for the younger audience. Devotes much coverage to 'Top Twenty' performers, but does also feature lesser known artists.

Illustrations: Some B&W, but mostly colour. Live performance and portrait shots of current rock/pop musicians. Most speculative submissions are likely to be filed for use in future issues rather than used immediately.

Text: Short news items, reviews and features written for a young readership will always be considered.

Overall freelance potential: Excellent scope for pop music photographers.

Fees: Photographs according to size of reproduction. £52 per 1,000 words for text.

OPERA

Seymour Press Ltd., 6 Woodland Rise, London N10 3UH. Tel: 01-883 4415.

Editor: Harold Rosenthal.

Monthly publication for operagoers, opera performers and all those involved in the production of opera.
Illustrations: No freelance market.
Text: Articles relating to opera, opera composers and any related subjects. 1,000–2,000 words.
Overall freelance potential: Good.
Fees: By arrangement.

ORGAN PLAYER & KEYBOARD REVIEW

Bookrose Ltd., Penn House, Penn Place, Rickmansworth, Herts WD3 1SN. Tel: 09237 79815.
Editors: Steve Miller and Dave Rushton.
Monthly magazine for players of all types of keyboard instrument. Covers pianos, electric organs, theatre organs, synthesisers; and all forms of music, from pop to classical.
Illustrations: Mainly B&W; some colour. Photographs of keyboard instruments and their players, preferably accompanied by a newsy caption. Covers: Colour pictures usually featuring a well-known keyboard playing personality.
Text: Well written articles of around 1,000 words on any topic of interest to keyboard players.
Overall freelance potential: Fairly limited, but scope is there for the right type of material.
Editor's tips: Run-of-the-mill pictures of organists seated at their instruments will not be met with much enthusiasm. A strikingly different approach is required.
Fees: By negotiation.

ORGANISTS' REVIEW

Incorporated Association of Organists, 604 Rayleigh Road, Eastwood, Leigh-on-Sea, Essex SS9 5HU. Tel: 0702 524305.
Editor: Basil Ramsey.
Quarterly publication aimed generally at Church musicians. Concerned with aspects of their work, reviews of new music, relevant books and records.
Illustrations: B&W only. Pictures of organ cases, old and new. Covers: B&W pictures of similar.
Text: No market since it all comes from specialist contributors.
Overall freelance potential: Very small; only about eight to twelve pictures per year.
Editor's tips: Organ cases are the only subject the magazine is interested in from freelances and these should be photographed in a creative and visually striking way.
Fees: £10 £20 per picture.

POP PIX

81 Rothschild Road, Acton Green, London W4 5NT. Tel: 01-546 4472/3/4.
Editor: Richard Borthwick.
Highly pictorial monthly magazine for the younger pop music fan, concentrating on current 'Top Twenty' performers.

Illustrations: Some B&W, but mostly colour, depicting the most popular pop performers. Covers: 6 × 6 cm transparencies preferred, composed so as to be suitable for upright reproduction.
Text: No scope.
Overall freelance potential: Very good for photographers who can gain access to current pop favourites.
Editor's tips: The editor will always be pleased to hear from specialist pop music photographers who can cover specific artists.
Fees: By negotiation.

RECORD BUSINESS

Record Business Publications Ltd., Hyde House, 13 Langley Street, London WC2H 9JG. Tel: 01-836 9311.
Editor: Brian Mulligan.
Weekly newspaper aimed at the record industry and its associated retail trades.
Illustrations: Only by prior consultation with the editor.
Text: No freelance market.
Overall freelance potential: Small.
Fees: By arrangement.

RECORD MIRROR

Spotlight Publications Ltd., 40 Long Acre, Covent Garden, London WC2E 9JT. Tel: 01-836 1522.
Editor: Eric Fuller.
Weekly popular music magazine aimed at younger fans, covering all areas of the current music scene.
Illustrations: B&W and colour. Stage action or posed shots of popular music performers. Pictures may be used immediately or may be filed for possible future use. Coverage of major concerts always of interest.
Text: Some scope for performance reviews. Commissions may be obtained by those who can show ability. Potential reviewers should always contact the editor before the event.
Overall freelance potential: Excellent—all published material is from freelance sources.
Fees: On a rising scale according to size of reproduction.

RECORDED SOUND

The British Institute of Recorded Sound, 29 Exhibition Road, London SW7. Tel: 01-589 6603.
Editor: Dr. Anthony King.
Published twice per year, dealing with all sound recordings, with an emphasis on classical music and contemporary British music.
Illustrations: B&W only. Pictures always needed, but they tend to be specific subjects, such as African music. Covers linked with editorial.

Text: Illustrated articles on recorded sound. 10–12 finished pages.
Overall freelance potential: Very small.
Fees: By agreement.

THE RECORDER AND MUSIC MAGAZINE

Anthony Merson Ltd., 16 Little Common Road, Bexhill-on-Sea, East Sussex TN39 4JB. Tel: 0424 216900.
Editor: Edgar Hunt.
Quarterly publication for members of the Society of Recorder Players and others interested in the instrument.
Illustrations: B&W only. Pictures as illustrations to features. Covers: B&W pictures of recorders and/or recorder players in paintings, tapestries, sculpture etc. Also composers of recorder music.
Text: Articles related to the recorder, its use today and in the field of early music.
Overall freelance potential: Limited; most articles are by experts in the field.
Fees: By agreement.

SMASH HITS

EMAP National Publications Ltd., Lisa House, 52/55 Carnaby Street, London W1V 1PF. Tel: 01-439 8801.
Editor: David Hepworth.
Fortnightly popular music magazine aimed at younger fans. Features complete song lyrics of current hits accompanied by pin-up style photographs of the performers.
Illustrations: Some B&W; mostly colour. Posed, pin-up style photographs of performers who currently have a record in the charts. Usually studio shots with a fairly plain background. Faces should be clearly shown. Covers: Usually commissioned, but shots submitted on spec have been used.
Text: No scope.
Overall freelance potential: Very good for photographers in touch with the current pop music scene and its performers.
Fees: £15 to £45 for black and white pictures; £65 for full-page colour. Covers: £165.

SOUNDS

Spotlight Publications Ltd., 40 Long Acre, Covent Garden, London WC2E 9JT. Tel: 01-836 1522.
Editor: Geoff Barton.
Weekly rock and pop music tabloid, covering all areas of the current music scene.
Illustrations: B&W only, depicting up-and-coming bands as well as established performers. Both on-stage and posed shots are required. Most photographs submitted on spec are held on file for possible future use. Covers: Striking shots with a single dramatic focus. Colour is occasionally used.
Text: News items, reviews, gossip and features concerning current performers, running up to a maximum of 3,000 words.

Overall freelance potential: Very good.
Editor's tips: The paper likes to encourage new and unknown bands, and to be first in publicising new trends in the music.
Fees: £15 to £45 for pictures inside the paper; £66 for cover shots. £52 per 1,000 words for features.

THE SOUTHERN RAG

2 Eastdale, East Street, Farnham, Surrey GU9 7TB. Tel: 0252 724638.
Editor: Ian Anderson.
Quarterly publication concerned with folk music.
Illustrations: B&W only. Pictures to be used in conjunction with interviews, reviews of records or reports on events. Mostly commissioned. Covers: B&W pictures of artistes covered editorially.
Text: Interviews and reviews concerned with folk music.
Overall freelance potential: Very small for the contributor unknown in this field. The magazine favours its regular contributors.
Fees: By agreement.

ZIGZAG

Mentorbridge Ltd., 118 Talbot Road, London W11 1JR. Tel: 01-221 7422.
Editor: Mick Mercer.
Monthly publication for 18–35 age group interested in music.
Illustrations: B&W and colour. Action pictures concerned with music. Covers: Colour and B&W pictures of pop stars, recording artists, singers, musicians. 35mm acceptable.
Text: Features on music and general interest subjects; documentaries. 500–2,000 words.
Overall freelance potential: Good. The magazine needs a lot more than it is currently getting.
Editor's tips: Good picture support to features will help to sell.
Fees: £20 per 1,000 words; pictures by agreement.

Photography

AMATEUR PHOTOGRAPHER

IPC Specialist and Professional Press Ltd., Surrey House, 1 Throwley Way, Sutton, Surrey SM1 4QQ. Tel: 01-643 8040.
Editor: Roy Green.
Weekly magazine for all photographers, from beginners to experienced enthusiasts.
Illustrations: B&W and colour. Stock pictures on all subjects for files, mostly B&W. Pictures that are used to illustrate features. General portfolios in B&W and colour: Send no more than 20 pictures, prints unmounted, slides in a plastic slide wallet. No glass mounts.

Covers: Colour pictures, mostly glamour, but occasionally other strong subjects. Sometimes linked with portfolio inside. Always leave space for logo and coverlines. 35mm acceptable.
Text: Technique articles on all types of photography. Picture captions on a separate sheet. 1,000–1,500 words.
Overall freelance potential: Very good. Around 75 per cent comes from freelance sources.
Fees: Negotiable.

THE BRITISH JOURNAL OF PHOTOGRAPHY

Henry Greenwood & Co. Ltd., 28 Great James Street, London WC1N 3HL.Tel: 01-404 4202.
Editor: Geoffrey Crawley.
Weekly publication for professional photographers, technicians, etc., and all those engaged in professional photography.
Illustrations: B&W creative portfolios are published along with some biographical notes about the photographer concerned. Covers: Striking colour pictures 'which show an awareness of design'. 35mm acceptable.
Text: Interested in anything related to professional photography, particularly the more unusual aspects.
Overall freelance potential: Fair.
Editor's tips: Remember the magazine is aimed at those engaged in professional photography, and of course does not use the type of how-to-do-it material used in photo magazines aimed at amateur photographers.
Fees: Negotiable.

AUDIO VISUAL

Maclaren Publishers Ltd., PO Box 109, Scarbrook Road, Croydon, Surrey CR9 1QH. Tel: 01-688 7788.
Editor: Peter Lloyd.
Monthly magazine for managers in industry and commerce, public services, government etc. who use audio-visual communication techniques, e.g. slides, film, video, overhead projection and filmstrips, plus the new technologies of computer graphics and telecommunication.
Illustrations: B&W and colour. Pictures of programmes being shown to audiences, preferably supported by case history details; relevant news, new products or location shooting pictures. All must be backed with solid information. Covers: Colour pictures of same, but check before submission. 35mm acceptable.
Text: Case histories of either shows, conferences or studies of particular companies' use of AV techniques. Good location/conference disaster stories always welcome. 1,000–2,500 words.
Overall freelance potential: Up to 25 per cent comes from freelance sources.
Editor's tips: This is a market where it is essential to check before submitting anything. Don't be afraid to telephone.
Fees: Text, £55–£65 per 1,000 words. Pictures by agreement.

JEREMY BURGESS

CAMERA (incorporating CREATIVE PHOTOGRAPHY)

EMAP National Publications Ltd., Bushfield House, Orton Centre, Peterborough, Cambs. PE2 0UW. Tel: 0733 237111.
Editor: Malc Birkitt.

Monthly magazine, which aims at enthusiastic photographers.
Illustrations: Top-notch portfolios with a technique bias. Also single, fascinating pictures. Colour or mono. Covers: Colour, usually tied in with a feature inside 35mm acceptable.
Text: Illustrated features for enthusiastic photographers. 2,000–2,500 words.
Overall freelance potential: Between 20 and 80 per cent is contributed from outside each month.
Fees: Low, but publication is considered prestigious in this market.

CAMERA CHOICE

IPC Business Press Ltd., Surrey House, 1 Throwley Way, Sutton, Surrey, SM1 4QQ. Tel: 01-643 8040.
Editor: Stephen Bayley.
Monthly photographic magazine aimed essentially at those who want to read about or buy new equipment.
Illustrations: B&W and colour. Mostly used as illustrations to articles. Covers: Colour pictures of new photographic equipment, usually shot in-house. 35mm acceptable.
Text: Tests and reviews of new equipment. How equipment works. Very limited scope for technique features. Up to 2,000 words.
Overall freelance potential: Good for the freelance with the right specialist knowledge.
Editor's tips: This is basically an equipment-orientated market. No picture portfolios. Contact the magazine with ideas before submitting.
Fees: Good; on a rising scale according to the size of reproduction or length of article.

CAMERA WEEKLY

Haymarket Publishing Ltd., 38–42 Hampton Road, Teddington, Middlesex TW11 0JE. Tel: 01-977 8787.
Editor: George Hughes.
Weekly photographic magazine which aims to help readers choose the right equipment and then to teach them how to use it.
Illustrations: B&W and colour. Pictures of all types of subject, but quality must be high and ideally each picture should have an obvious photographic context, e.g. the use of specific lenses, filters, spectacular lighting, action, etc. Covers: Colour pictures of girls, action, natural history, but with a large space needed at the top for the magazine's particularly deep logo. 35mm acceptable.
Text: Features on all aspects of taking pictures of different subjects. 500–1,000 words.
Overall freelance potential: Around 25 per cent of the magazine comes from freelances.
Editor's tips: Try the magazine with *anything* connected with the subject; always on the look-out for new ideas.
Fees: By agreement.

CENTANEWS

The Widescreen Centre, 48 Dorset Street, London W1H 3FH. Tel: 01-935 2580.
Editor: Tony Shapps.

Quarterly publication for audio-visual and cine photography with a bias towards all forms of panoramic presentation and three-dimensional photography.
Illustrations: B&W only. Pictures that relate to audio-visual, panoramic and three-dimensional photography.
Text: Features on audio-visual subjects, CinemaScope, widescreen filming and prints, plus other sound subjects.
Overall freelance potential: Most of the contents come from freelances.
Fees: By agreement.

HOT SHOE

Grosvenor Publications Ltd., 17 South Molton Street, London W1Y 1DE. Tel: 01-408 1790.
Editor: Robert Prior.
Monthly specialist magazine for people involved in the top end of the photographic market. Aimed at professional photographers, advertising agencies, picture editors, etc.
Illustrations: B&W and colour. Pictures from every branch of professional photography. Portfolios from professionals. Pictures for news and gossip pages. Covers: Colour examples of top quality photography; 35mm acceptable.
Text: Features that concern the various aspects of the photographic image, from stills to tape to film. No ideas considered without cuttings. 1,000–1,200 words.
Overall freelance potential: Around 50 per cent bought from freelances.
Fees: £45–£50 per 1,000 words; pictures by agreement.

MOVIE MAKER

Model and Allied Publications Ltd., Wolsey House, Wolsey Road, Hemel Hempstead, Herts HP2 4SS.
Tel: 0442 41221.
Editor: Alan Cleave.
Monthly magazine offering information, advice and entertainment to makers of amateur movies on film and video.
Illustrations: B&W and colour. Pictures of amateur film makers at work or those that make technical points about camerawork, lighting etc. Pictures of seasonal action subjects that are likely to appeal to movie makers, e.g. winter sports, athletics, surfing, fireworks, etc. Covers: Colour pictures that tie in with a feature in the magazine. Usually shot in-house. 35mm acceptable.
Text: Features about the techniques of movie making, based on personal experience. 1,000–3,000 words.
Overall freelance potential: Around 75 per cent of the magazine comes from freelance sources, but mostly from regular contributors.
Editor's tips: Most contributors have achieved some success as movie makers.
Fees: Inside, £15 per published page for text and pictures; covers, £30.

THE PHOTOGRAPHER

Penblade Publishers Ltd., 15–23 Porteus Road, London W2 1UT. Tel: 01-262 1184.
Editor: Christopher Wordsworth.

Monthly magazine, published on behalf of the Institute of Incorporated Photographers and aimed at full-time professionals. Emphasis is on commercial, industrial, social and in-plant professional photography.

Illustrations: Rarely use pictures from outside contributors.

Text: Most commissioned.

Overall freelance potential: This is completely different to a consumer photographic magazine and therefore has hardly any scope for the average freelance.

Fees: By agreement.

PHOTOGRAPHY

Model and Allied Publications Ltd., Wolsey House, Wolsey Road, Hemel Hempstead, Herts. HP2 4SS.

Tel: 0442 41221.

Editor: John Wade.

Monthly magazine aimed at amateur photographers who know the basics but who want to learn more. Tells readers how to take better pictures.

Illustrations: B&W and colour. On literally any subject, but should show a definite photographic technique. B&W pictures only kept for stock. B&W and colour used for illustrating features. Covers: Colour, mainly girl shots, but pictures that show a technique, rather than a straight glamour shot are preferred. 35mm acceptable, 6 × 6 cm preferred for cover use. No picture portfolios.

Text: Illustrated features that tell readers how to take better pictures or how to use certain pieces of photographic equipment. 2,000–3,000 words.

Overall freelance potential: Very good; 75 per cent of the magazine comes from outside sources.

Editor's tips: Read the magazine first. Don't send pictures for their own sakes. Don't send features on the obvious. Make sure your technique is up to scratch. Send B&W rather than colour with features.

Fees: Around £25–£30 per published page for words and pictures; covers, £100. All fees negotiable.

PRACTICAL PHOTOGRAPHY

EMAP National Publications, Bushfield House, Orton Centre, Peterborough PE2 0UW. Tel 0733 237111.

Editor: Richard Hopkins.

Monthly magazine offering practical information to amateur photographers, plus news, reviews and general interest items on related topics.

Illustrations: Good B&W pictures on any subject considered for the magazine's files. Colour photographs are preferred as sets, preferably showing an interesting technique. Colour portfolios are used occasionally. Single colour shots rarely used inside the magazine. Covers: Glamour or portraits in colour. 35mm acceptable, but 6 × 6 cm preferred.

Text: Any feature on a practical aspect of photography will be considered, although most basic techniques are covered by staff writers. Unusual or original material stands the best chance of success.

DAVID BEARE

Overall freelance potential: Over 20 per cent of the magazine each month comes from freelances.

Editor's tips: 'Notes for Contributors' available on request.

Fees: Minimum of £20 per 1,000 words and £10 per picture. Negotiable for outstanding material.

PROFESSIONAL PHOTOGRAPHER

Maclaren Publishers Ltd., PO Box 109, Maclaren House, Scarbrook Road, Croydon CR9 1QH. Tel: 01-688 7788.

Editor: J. Charles Hall.

Monthly magazine for professional photographers.

Illustrations: Mostly with features.

Text: Features on new ideas in the photographic business. Interviews with professional photographers. News and comment.

Overall freelance potential: Quite good, but a specialist market.

Editor's tips: Do not confuse this market with the amateur photographic market. They are very different.

Fees: By agreement.

SLR CAMERA

Haymarket Publishing Ltd., 38–42 Hampton Road, Teddington, Middlesex TW11 0JE Tel: 01-977 8787.

Editor: Peter Lester.

Monthly photographic magazine aimed at advanced amateur photographers.

Illustrations: B&W and colour. Pictures that illustrate a photographic technique. Colour transparencies with impact and strong colour sense. Covers: Colour pictures with good impact; 35mm acceptable.

Text: Illustrated articles on photogtaphic techniques. 2,500 words.

Overall freelance potential: Around 10 per cent of the magazine is contributed by freelances.

Editor's tips: Study the magazine first.

Fees: Negotiable.

Railways

INTERNATIONAL RAILWAY JOURNAL

Simmons-Boardman Publishing Corporation, PO Box 8, Falmouth, Cornwall. Tel: 0326 313945.

Editor: Mike Knutton.

Monthly publication for the principal officers of the railways of the world, outside the USA; ministers and commissioners of transport, railways equipment manufacturers and suppliers.

Illustrations: B&W and a little colour inside the magazine. Pictures of new line construction projects, electrification projects, track or signalling improvements, new locomotives, passenger coaches and freight waggons. Interesting pictures of railway operations from far-flung corners of the world. No steam or nostalgia material. Covers: Colour shots to be in with the theme of a particular issue; 35mm acceptable.

Text: Features on any sizeable contracts for railways equipment; plans for railway developments, i.e. new line construction, track or signalling improvements; almost anything which involves a railway spending money or making improvements. News about developments on underground systems, i.e. plans, construction, new equipment and techniques. No padding or speculation.

Overall freelance potential: Quite good; for the right business-oriented material; 15–20 per cent is bought.

Editor's tips: Accuracy is vital.

Fees: Rising scale according to size of pictures; text, £35 per printed page.

RAILNEWS

British Railways Board, 222 Marylebone Road, London NW1 6JJ. Tel: 01-262 3232 ext. 5480.

Editor: D. K. Horrox.

Monthly newspaper for British Rail staff, giving latest news of technical and industrial developments on the system.

Illustrations: B&W and colour *prints*. Railway news pictures, unusual pictures with good captions. Shots of track working, Sealink shipping, BR engineering activities etc. for stock. Pictures should always contain people and action. Covers: B&W or colour prints of topical railway happenings.

Text: Difficult market for those outside the industry. Diary pieces, 100 words; features 1,000–1,250 words.

Overall freelance potential: A frequent need for freelance pictures in certain areas for specific commissions. Contact the publication for details.

Editor's tips: Approach before submitting.

Fees: By negotiation.

Religion

BRITISH JOURNAL OF RELIGIOUS EDUCATION

Christian Education Movement, 2 Chester House, Pages Lane, Muswell Hill, London N10 1PR. Tel: 01-444 9843.

Editor: Dr. J. M. Hull.

Published three times per year for school teachers, student teachers and clergy interested in religious education.

Illustrations: Only for cover use. B&W pictures of children and pupils at work on religious and related themes.

Text: No freelance market.
Overall freelance potential: Small.
Editor's tips: Financial side should be worked out with business manager, Brian Sharp.
Fees: By agreement with above.

CATHOLIC GAZETTE

Harris Printers, 114 West Heath Road, London NW3 7TX. Tel: 01-458 3316/7.
Editor: Fr. John Walsh.
Monthly publication covering all aspects of the spiritual life for educated Catholics.
Illustrations: B&W only. Pictures of nature or the countryside, plus people with natural or unusual expressions to illustrate points in articles.
Text: Well researched articles on religious topics and human stories from personal experience with a moral. 2,000–3,000 words.
Overall freelance potential: Around 80 per cent is contributed by freelances.
Editor's tips: Articles should not be over written and the human element should be kept to the forefront. Don't preach.
Fees: By agreement.

CATHOLIC HERALD

Lamb's Passage, Bunhill Row, London EC1Y 8TQ. Tel: 01-588 3101.
Editor: Gerard Noel.
Weekly newspaper covering home and foreign news with a Catholic background.
Illustrations: B&W only. News pictures of Catholic interest. Pictures for features.
Text: News stories and news features with a Catholic interest. Up to 1,000 words.
Overall freelance potential: Most of the paper's material is supplied by freelances.
Fees: Good; on a rising scale according to the size of reproduction or length of article.

THE CHRISTIAN HERALD

Herald House Ltd., Grafton Place, Worthing, West Sussex BN11 1QX. Tel: 0903 61456.
Editor: Colin Reeves.
Weekly publication for Christians of all Protestant denominations.
Illustrations: B&W only. Stock pictures of family life, nature, scenic views, novelty and fun items. Covers: B&W pictures of happy people, charming animals and lively historical subjects.
Text: No freelance market.
Overall freelance potential: Several freelance pictures used every week.
Fees: Variable.

FAMILY

Buzz Christian Ministries, 51 Haydons Road, London SW19 1HG. Tel: 01-542 7661.
Editor: Anne Townsend.
Monthly Christian magazine for people who are regular or irregular Church-goers.
Illustrations: B&W and colour. Pictures mainly for use with features; 35mm acceptable.

Text: Articles on Christian living and family problems with a Christian viewpoint. Up to 1,600 words.
Overall freelance potential: Good; many contributed articles used each month.
Fees: Up to £20 for 1,600 words.

THE INQUIRER
Inquirer Publishing Co. Ltd., Essex Hall, 1–6 Essex Street, Strand, London WC2R 3HY. Tel: 01-240 2384.
Editor: Revd. Fred Ryde.
Fortnightly publication aimed at Unitarians and the liberal members in Christianity and other religions.
Illustrations: B&W and only as illustrations to articles.
Text: Features on social problems from a liberal angle. 1,000 words.
Overall freelance potential: Small.
Fees: £10 per 1,000 words.

JEWISH CHRONICLE
Jewish Chronicle Newspapers Ltd., 25 Furnival Street, London EC4A 1JT. Tel: 01-405 9252.
Editor: Geoffrey Paul.
Weekly newspaper publishing news and features about, and of interest to, the Jewish community.
Illustrations: B&W and colour. Any pictures related to the purpose stated above, plus material for its wide range of supplements that deal with subjects such as holidays, fashion, furniture, video, regional development, etc. Pictures also required for colour magazine published twice a year. 35mm acceptable.
Text: Features on topics detailed above. 600–2,500 words.
Overall freelance potential: At least 40 per cent of the content comes from freelance sources.
Fees: By negotiation.

NEWS TODAY
Appleford House, Appleford, Abingdon, Oxford OX14 4PB. Tel: 023-582 319.
Editor: G. E. Duffield.
Monthly Church magazine insert.
Illustrations: B&W only. Few pictures used inside. Covers: Christian and cultural subjects.
Text: Features on Christian and cultural topics that have an impact on society. 600 words.
Overall freelance potential: Most articles are commissioned.
Fees: Variable.

REALITY
Redemptorist Publications, 75 Orwell Road, Rathgar, Dublin 6. Tel: 0001 961688/961488.
Editor: Revd. Kevin Donlon.
Monthly Christian magazine, covering all areas to do with a good quality of life.

Illustrations: B&W only. Pictures connected with subjects detailed below. Covers: B&W pictures of any good human interest subject.
Text: Features on religion, overpopulation, literature, the environment, nature studies, nuclear subjects, politics, poetry and travel. 1,200 words maximum.
Overall freelance potential: Around 90 per cent comes from freelance sources.
Editor's tips: Contributors should be concrete, practical and specific in their approach to a subject. No contributions of a general or philosophic nature.
Fees: £20–£25 (Irish) per 1,000 words.

THE SIGN
A. R. Mowbray and Co. Ltd., Saint Thomas House, Becket Street, Oxford OX1 1SJ. Tel: 0865 42507.
Editor: Canon W. E. Purcell.
Monthly insert for Church of England parish magazines.
Illustrations: Unusual and human interest subjects. Seasonal scenes, family occasions. Christmas and Easter subjects. B&W pictures for stock. Covers: Chosen once a year in December/January for year's magazines. Prefers 6 × 6 cm.
Text: Limited market for features on people and places of unusual interest and with a Christian connection. 300 words maximum.
Overall freelance potential: Good for pictures; poor for text.
Editor's tips: Most copy is commissioned from known writers and space is very limited.
Fees: Variable according to size of picture.

Science and Technology

CHANGE
Science Policy Foundation, Benjamin Franklin House, 36 Craven Street, London WC2N 5NG. Tel: 01-839 4985.
Editor: Maurice Goldsmith.
Bi-monthly publication for educators in developing countries.
Illustrations: B&W only. Pictures showing technology for development, developing countries, etc. Covers: B&W pictures of same.
Text: Features on traditional technology in developing countries. 800–1,000 words.
Overall freelance potential: Variable.
Fees: Negotiable.

CHEMISTRY IN BRITAIN
The Royal Society of Chemistry, Burlington House, Piccadilly, London W1V 0BN. Tel: 01-734 9864.
Editor: Dr. P. J. Farago.
Monthly publication for all members of the Royal Society of Chemistry.

Illustrations: B&W inside. General pictures with a chemical bias. Covers: Colour pictures of same. 35mm acceptable, but 6 × 6 cm preferred.
Text: No freelance market.
Overall freelance potential: Varies.
Fees: By agreement.

CLEAN AIR
National Society for Clean Air, 136 North Street, Brighton BN1 1RG. Tel: 0273 26313.
Editor: Jane Dunmore.
Quarterly publication for professionals in the field of air pollution and environmental control; selected representatives of local authorities, researchers; and anyone generally interested in the subject.
Illustrations: B&W only. Pictures on air pollution, environment and conservations.
Text: Features on air pollution, noise, water pollution control, wastes, open cast mining, conservation and energy issues. 4,000–8,000 words.
Overall freelance potential: Very small.
Fees: Negotiated individually.

EDUCATION IN CHEMISTRY
The Royal Society of Chemistry, Burlington House, Piccadilly, London W1V 0BN. Tel: 01-734 9864.
Editor: Michael Withers.
Bi-monthly publication for teachers, students, lecturers in schools, universities, polytechnics etc.
Illustrations: B&W only. Pictures that deal with classroom laboratories or the chemical industry. Covers: B&W pictures relating to specific articles inside.
Text: Features concerned with chemistry or the teaching of it. Under 3,000 words.
Overall freelance potential: Low.
Fees: By agreement.

ENERGY POLICY
Butterworth Scientific Ltd., PO Box 63, Westbury House, Bury Street, Guildford GU2 5BH. Tel: 0483 31261.
Editor: L. H. Driscoll.
Quarterly publication, dealing with the politics, economics and planning of energy resource production. Aimed at policy researchers, analysts, decision makers in industry and government.
Illustrations: No freelance market.
Text: Articles or reports on an aspect of energy policy, i.e. economic and political issues; not technology or engineering aspects. Book reviews. Conference reports. Features, around 6,000 words; reports, up to 2,000 words.
Overall freelance potential: Small, mostly written by academic specialists. Slight market for reports and book reviews.
Fees: Negotiable.

NEW SCIENTIST
New Science Publications, Commonwealth House, 1–19 New Oxford Street, London WC1A
1NG. Tel: 01-404 0700.
Editor: Michael Kenward.
Weekly magazine about science and technology for people with some scientific or technical
education and also for the intelligent layman.
Illustrations: B&W and colour. Pictures on any topic that can be loosely allied to science
and technology. Covers: B&W and colour pictures, usually connected with a feature inside.
35mm acceptable.
Text: Features on scientific/technical subjects that might appeal to a wide audience.
Overall freelance potential: A lot of freelance work used, but best to consult the magazine
before submitting.
Fees: On a rising scale according to the length of article or size of reproduction.

NEXT
Sightline Publications Ltd., 141/143 Drury Lane, London WC2B 5TE. Tel: 01-379 6342.
Editor: Richard Maybury.
Monthly consumer magazine devoted to all aspects of consumer technology. Attempts to take
the mystery out of technological subjects for an up-market readership.
Illustrations: Some B&W; mostly colour. High quality pictures covering any aspect of
current consumer oriented technology, such as motoring, hi-fi, photography, video, etc. The
application of technology in art and architecture. Also coverage of some high-technology
fields like aerospace or nuclear power.
Text: High quality illustrated articles and features on suitable topics.
Overall freelance potential: Good scope for contributors able to produce suitable material
to a very high standard.
Editor's tips: Due to the broad coverage of the magazine, potential contributors are advised
to contact the editor before sending any submissions.
Fees: By negotiation.

PHYSICS BULLETIN
The Institute of Physics, Techno House, Redcliffe Way, Bristol BS1 6NX. Tel: 0272 297481.
Editor: C. I. Pedersen.
Monthly house journal of the Institute of Physics, aimed at physics graduates generally, but
usually read only by Institute members.
Illustrations: B&W only. Pictures used as illustrations to features. Covers: B&W pictures
of physics-related subjects, usually in connection with an inside feature.
Text: Features on new developments or research in physics. 700–800 words and 1,000–4,000
words.
Overall freelance potential: Short articles always welcome.
Editor's tips: All contributors must have a reasonable knowledge of physics.
Fees: Full-length articles, £30; short items, £15, No payment for pictures.

RESOURCES POLICY
Butterworth Scientific Ltd., PO Box 63, Westbury House, Bury Street, Guildford GU2 5BH.
Tel: 0483 31261.
Editor: L. H. Driscoll.
Quarterly dealing with all aspects of materials production, consumption and conservation.
Aimed at policy makers in industry and government.
Illustrations: No freelance market.
Text: Articles and reports on any aspect of resource policy. Book reviews. Conference reports.
Articles, around 6,000 words; reports, up to 2,000 words.
Overall freelance potential: Small, mostly reports and book reviews.
Fees: Negotiable.

STRAIN
British Society for Strain Measurement, Department of Civil Engineering and Building
Science, University of Edinburgh, King's Buildings, Mayfield Road, Edinburgh EH9 3JL.
Tel: 031-667 1081, Ext. 3387.
Editor: Dr. R. Royles.
Quarterly practical scientific journal, relating to measurements of parameters in the whole
field of engineering.
Illustrations: Pictures are used only as illustrations to articles. They are B&W only and
there is no market for cover pictures.
Text: Features on any topic related to engineering measurement of an original or
educational nature. Usually around 4,000 words.
Overall freelance potential: Contributors are unpaid, but some revenue is obtained from
advertisers who sometimes use photographic work.
Editor's tips: Contact magazine before submitting material.

Sport

ADVENTURE SPORTS
Grosvenor Publications Ltd., 17 South Molton Street, London W1. Tel: 01-408 1790.
Editor: Nigel Gifford.
Bi-monthly publication for interested and active people involved with the wide spectrum of
adventure sports and travel.
Illustrations: B&W and colour. Action shots of every type of adventure sport and unusual
travel pictures. Covers: Colour pictures showing strong action in adventure sports; 35mm
acceptable.
Text: Up to date stories in the risk sports world and remote travel in unusual places.
1,000–1,500 words.
Overall freelance potential: About 65 per cent is bought from freelances.
Fees: By arrangement. Guide: around £150 for colour/B&W spread with 1,000 words.

AIRGUN WORLD
Burlington Publishing Company, 10 Sheet Street, Windsor, Berks. SL4 1BG. Tel: 075-35 56061.
Editor: Paul Dobson.
Monthly magazine for all airgunners.
Illustrations: B&W only inside. Pictures of any form of airgun shooting, e.g. target, field and 'back garden'. Pictures of typical airgun quarry, e.g. rabbits, pigeon, squirrels, crows, etc. Covers: Colour pictures of airgunners in action, 6 × 6 cm minimum.
Text: Articles on all forms of airgunning, including club profiles. Up to six pictures should be submitted with features. Profiles, 300 words, general features, 1,000 words.
Overall freelance potential: Most of the magazine is written and illustrated by freelances.
Fees: Negotiable.

CANOE FOCUS
British Canoe Union, Flexel House, 45–47 High Street, Addlestone, Weybridge, Surrey KT15 1JV. Tel: 0932 41341.
Editor: Dave Lawrence.
Quarterly magazine covering canoe-based sport and recreation.
Illustrations: B&W only inside. Good quality pictures showing the sport in action. Covers: Colour action shots of canoeing. 35mm acceptable.
Text: Features on canoe expeditions and sports events.
Overall freelance potential: The magazine uses an appreciable amount of freelance work each quarter.
Fees: Covers, £15. Being a free magazine, most of the inside material is contributed for credits only.

CLIMBER AND RAMBLER
Holmes McDougall Ltd., Ravenseft House, 302 St. Vincent Street, Glasgow G2 5RG. Tel: 041-221 7000.
Editor: Walt Unsworth.
Monthly magazine on commercial sale but which also acts as the official journal of the British Mountaineering Council. Upmarket publication dealing with world-wide mountain climbing from Lakeland fells to Everest. Highly literate readership. Contributors range from 'unknowns' to top climbers like Chris Bonnington.
Illustrations: B&W and colour. First ascents and newsworthy events but, in the main, used only with text. Occasional feature on a hard rock climb recorded in a sequence of six to eight B&W pictures. Covers: Action shots of climbers or dramatic mountain pictures; 35mm acceptable.
Text: Features on hill walking, trekking, rock climbing, Alpinism, high altitude climbing, cross-country and mountain skiing (*not* downhill racing). 1,500–4,000 words.
Overall freelance potential: Good; 90 per cent of articles and 100 per cent of pictures come from freelances.

JOHN WOODHOUSE

Editor's tips: This is a specialist field and is full of good writer/photographers. There is potential for the freelance to break in, but the magazine is usually well stocked with material.
Fees: Variable and constantly under review.

COMPASS SPORT (THE ORIENTEER)
Compass Sport Publications, 37 Sandycoombe Road, Twickenham, Middlesex TW1 2LR. Tel: 01-892 9429.
Editor: Ned Paul.
Bi-monthly publication for enthusiasts of orienteering, fell running, mountain marathons, challenge walks, etc.
Illustrations: B&W and limited colour. Action pictures of orienteering and fell running etc, with detailed captions of participants. Head and shoulders shots of competitors, organisers, etc. Covers: Colour pictures of people in orienteering, mountain marathons, fell running, etc. 35mm acceptable.
Text: Features on technique, training and fitness; equipment reviews, profiles. 500–1,800 words.
Overall freelance potential: Fairly limited. Biggest scope is for orienteering pictures.
Fees: By negotiation.

THE CRICKETER INTERNATIONAL

The Cricketer Ltd., 29 Cavendish Road, Redhill, Surrey, Tel: 0737 72221.
Editor: Christopher Martin-Jenkins.
Monthly publication for cricket enthusiasts of all ages. Covers all aspects of the sport.
Illustrations: B&W inside. Pictures of less fashionable players needed, plus historical pictures. Covers: Colour pictures of cricketing subjects, usually supplied by staff photographers, but occasionally bought from freelances. 35mm acceptable.
Text: Features taking an original look at the subject. Up to 1,000 words.
Overall freelance potential: A high percentage comes from freelances, but usually by commissions.
Fees: Covers, £65; Inside pictures and text by agreement.

CUE WORLD

B. R. Hubbard (Printers) Ltd., Collywhite Lane, Dionfield, Sheffield S18 6XP.
Editor: John Carty.
Monthly publication for amateur and professional snooker players.
Illustrations: B&W only. Pictures of notable *amateur* players anywhere in the UK. The magazine is in the market for finding photographers in areas all over the country to whom commissions could be given.
Text: No freelance market.
Overall freelance potential: A known photographer in the right area could average as many as ten published pictures per year.
Editor's tips: The photographer must know something about the game. Contact the magazine for a list of local officials or clubs who can assist in finding the right pictures.
Fees: £5–£7.50 per picture, depending on size.

DARTS WORLD

World Magazines Ltd., 2 Park Lane, Croydon, Surrey CR9 1HA. Tel: 01-681 2837.
Editor: A. J. Wood.
Monthly magazine for darts players and organisers.
Illustrations: B&W only inside. Pictures on any darts theme. Covers: Colour pictures of star players, 35mm acceptable.
Text: Features on all darts subjects.
Overall freelance potential: Most of the copy and pictures comes from freelances.
Fees: Good, on a rising scale according to size of reproduction or length of feature.

FIGHTERS' MONTHLY

Peterson Publishing Co. Ltd., Peterson House, Northbank, Berryhill Industrial Estate, Droitwich, Worcestershire WR9 9BL. Tel: 0905 775564.
Editorial Director: B. P. Ayling.
Monthly magazine for martial arts and similar disciplines.
Illustrations: B&W inside the magazine on events, clubs and individuals and any general martial arts interests. Covers: Action shots in colour; 6 × 6 cm minimum.

Text: Features on martial arts events, profiles of clubs and individuals and any other martial arts interests. 500–3,500 words.
Overall freelance potential: Quite good.
Fees: By negotiation.

FOOTLOOSE
Footloose Ltd., 26 Commercial buildings, Dunston, Gateshead NE11 9AA. Tel: 0632 608113.
Editor: Cameron McNeish.
Bi-monthly publication for the self-propelled traveller. Covers walking, canoeing, touring canoes and kayaks, wilderness photography, Nordic Ski-ing, backpacking, etc.
Illustrations: B&W and occasional colour. Pictures for stock, covering items detailed above. Must be well captioned.
Text: Technical features by arrangement only. 850–2,500 words.
Overall freelance potential: Mostly from established contacts.
Editor's tips: Keep watching the magazine. Readers are often reminded of certain items that are needed; from photographs to short stories.
Fees: By negotiation.

GOLF MONTHLY
Munro-Barr Publications Ltd., 256 West George Street, Glasgow G2 4QP. Tel: 041-248 4667.
Editor: Malcolm Campbell.
Monthly international consumer magazine for golfers.
Illustrations: B&W and colour. Mainly for use as illustrations to articles. Small market for one-off pictures from golf tournaments of golf-related events. 35mm acceptable.
Text: Illustrated features on golf instruction, golf-related features and occasional fiction. Also in-depth profiles of leading world players. Around 2,000 words, but not critical.
Overall freelance potential: Most of the magazine is contributed by freelances, but a good deal is commissioned. Room for more material of the right type.
Editor's tips: This is an international magazine and so articles must have a wide appeal. No features of a parochial nature.
Fees: Text, £50 per 1,000 words; pictures by agreement.

GOLF WORLD
Golf World Ltd., 41 Maltby Street, London SE1 3PA. Tel: 01-237 0043-6.
Editor: Peter Haslam.
Monthly publication for golfers.
Illustrations: B&W only. Unusual golfing pictures.
Text: Profiles of golfers and features on the sport. 1,500–2,000 words.
Overall freelance potential: Around 30 per cent of the publication comes from freelance sources.
Fees: By agreement.

GYMNASTICS

Errey's Printers Ltd., 62 High Street, Heathfield, East Sussex. Tel: 04352 4253.
Editor: Peter Ackroyd.
Monthly official journal of the British Amateur Gymnastics Association. Covers all aspects of gymnastics as a sport, and biased towards a fairly young readership.
Illustrations: B&W only. News photographs, mainly concerned with local gymnasts or clubs rather than major national competitions. Pictures of gymnasts in action should depict facial expressions and movement, rather than simple poses. Covers: Colour pictures of top gymnasts in action, probably taken at major competitions worldwide.
Text: Limited scope for short human interest features relating to gymnastics, perhaps filling in the background to a particular achievement in the sport.
Overall freelance potential: Limited, but the sport is growing in popularity.
Editor's tips: Bear in mind that most gymnasts are young, and that children form a large proportion of the readership.
Fees: £5 per black and white reproduction; £25 to £30 for the colour cover. £20 per 1,000 words for text.

HARPERS SPORTS

Harper Trade Journals Ltd., Harling House, 47–51 Great Suffolk Street, London SE1 0BS. Tel: 01-261 1604.
Editor: Stephen Blake.
Fortnightly magazine aimed at the UK sports trade, especially retailers.
Illustrations: B&W only. Pictures used only to illustrate features on news stories.
Text: Illustrated features and news stories on anything to do with the sports industry, including manufacturers, retailer profiles etc.
Overall freelance potential: Quite good.
Fees: Text, £20–£80 per 1,000 words; pictures £2–£8, depending on quality and subject.

MARATHON AND DISTANCE RUNNER

Peterson Publishing Company Ltd., Peterson House, Northbank Berryhill Industrial Estate, Droitwich, Worcester WR9 9BL. Tel: 0905 775564.
Editor: Geoff Harrold.
Alternate-monthly publication dealing with all aspects of long distance running, marathons and road races—distances of over ten miles.
Illustrations: B&W only. Scope for coverage of any form of long distance running. Photographers planning to cover a particular event should approach the editor beforehand. Covers: Colour pictures of distance runners, but these are often commissioned.
Text: In-depth and accurate articles of 1,500–3,000 words. Written for a knowledgeable specialist readership.
Overall freelance potential: Good—almost all published material is supplied by free-lances.
Fees: £5 per black and white photograph; colour covers negotiable. £15 per 1000 words for articles.

MATCH WEEKLY
EMAP National Publications Ltd., Stirling House, Bretton Centre, Bretton, Peterborough PE3 8DJ. Tel: 0733 260333.
Editor: Melvyn Bagnall.
Weekly publication, looking at the whole spectrum of soccer. Aimed at readers in the 10–17 age group.
Illustrations: Action soccer shots. Usually bought only after consultation with the editor. B&W and colour considered. Covers: colour action shots; 35mm acceptable.
Text: Profiles and interviews concerning personalities in the soccer field. Length by prior arrangement.
Overall freelance potential: Fair.
Fees: By agreement.

RACING PIGEON PICTORIAL
The Racing Pigeon Publishing Co. Ltd., 19 Doughty Street, London WC1N 2PT. Tel: 01-242 0565.
Editors: Colin and Grace Osman.
Monthly magazine for pigeon fanciers. Provides in-depth articles on methods, successful fanciers, scientific information, etc.
Illustrations: B&W and colour. Pictures used as illustrations for features, plus some one-off pictures of pigeons. Covers: Colour pictures of pigeons, pigeon fanciers and related subjects. 35mm acceptable.
Text: Features on pigeons, pigeon fanciers and related subjects. 1,500 words.
Overall freelance potential: Around 10–15 per cent of the pictures come from freelance photographers. Articles are mostly by specialist pigeon writers.
Fees: £15 per published page.

RANGERS NEWS
Peebles Publications (Scotland) Ltd., 19 North Claremont Street, Glasgow G3 7NR. Tel: 041-331 1933.
Editor: Ian Peebles.
Weekly newspaper of Rangers Football Club. Aimed at supporters, although the paper also carries a small amount on other Scottish, English and world clubs.
Illustrations: B&W only. General action pictures of Scottish, English or world football. Individual action pictures of leading players are preferred.
Text: No freelance market.
Overall freelance potential: About 25 per cent of the paper is supplied by freelance photographers.
Fees: Good; on a rising scale according to the size of reproduction.

RUGBY POST
Burlington Publishing Company, 10 Sheet Street, Windsor, Berks. SL4 1BG. Tel: 075-35 56061.

Editor: Nigel Starmer-Smith.
Monthly Rugby Union magazine.
Illustrations: B&W only inside. Pictures with brief write-ups from minor rugby clubs and schools. Team photos. Covers: Colour pictures relevant to the sport. 35mm acceptable.
Text: Illustrated articles considered on the sport, but short write-ups preferred. Reports, 300 words; features, 1,000 words.
Overall freelance potential: Reasonable.
Fees: Negotiable.

RUNNING MAGAZINE
BEL Ltd., 5–8 Lower John Street, London W1. Tel: 01-439 9682.
Editor: Andrew Etchells.
Monthly publication for running and jogging enthusiasts.
Illustrations: No freelance market.
Text: Features on running and jogging, only by prior consultation with the editor.
Overall freelance potential: Fair.
Fees: By agreement.

THE SCOTTISH SPORTING GAZETTE
John Ormiston, 22 Market Brae, Inverness. Tel: 0463 32104/222757.
Editor: John Ormiston.
Annual publication to market Scottish shooting, fishing, stalking and allied services. Aimed at the upper income bracket in the UK, Europe and America.
Illustrations: B&W and colour. Pictures of shooting, fishing, stalking; live game animals; subjects relating to whisky distilleries; antique Scottish weapons; tartans, castles and hunting lodges. Covers: Exceptional colour pictures of game animals or action sporting shots; 35mm acceptable.
Text: Features on shooting, fishing and stalking in Scotland or articles on other topics that are particularly Scottish, e.g. whisky, tartans, castles, antiques, etc. Also, Scottish Fashions for women. 600–2,000 words.
Overall freelance potential: Good, but most of the material comes from known freelances.
Editor's tips: Pictures and text must be unusual, not the normal anecdotes associated with this field. Material should have a good Scottish flavour. It does not have to be essentially sporting, but should be allied in some way.
Fees: Open to negotiation.

SHOOTING MAGAZINE
Burlington Publishing Company, 10 Sheet Street, Windsor, Berks. SL4 1BG. Tel: 075-35 56061.
Editor: Paul Dobson.
Monthly magazine for all forms of shotgun shooting, with particular emphasis on clay pigeon shooting.

Illustrations: B&W inside. Pictures of clay pigeon shoots. Covers: Colour pictures of same, 6 × 6 cm minimum.
Text: Articles on any form of shotgun shooting, e.g. clay pigeon, game, rough, wildfowling, etc. 1,000 words.
Overall freelance potential: A substantial amount is bought each month.
Editor's tips: Freelance photographers are welcome to telephone with a view to having their name added to the magazine's list for possible future commissions.
Fees: Negotiable.

SNOOKER SCENE

Everton's News Agency, Cavalier House, 202 Hagley Road, Edgbaston, Birmingham B16 9PQ. Tel: 021-454 2931.
Editor: Clive Everton.
Monthly publication for snooker players and enthusiasts.
Illustrations: B&W only. Snooker action pictures and others related to actual tournaments. Covers: similar themes. B&W only.
Text: Features on snooker and billiards. 250–1,000 words.
Overall freelance potential: Small.
Fees: By arrangement.

SPORTSCOPE

Focal Communications, 72 Boston Place, London NW1 6EX. Tel: 01-262 4405.
Editor: David Kennedy.
Alternate-monthly publication featuring sport as an aid to health and fitness. Distributed free through sports shops.
Illustrations: B&W and colour. Pictures depicting any aspect of keeping fit through sporting activity. Not just pictures of joggers, but any form of non-professional physical sports.
Text: Short articles and features up 1,500 words on any aspect of sport and health aimed at the general public. Personality pieces on particular sporting figures will also be considered.
Overall freelance potential: Fairly limited.
Fees: By negotiation.

SPORT AND LEISURE

Eyre and Spottiswoode, The Sports Council, 16 Upper Woburn Place, London WC1H 0QP. Tel: 01-388 1277.
Editor: John Ingham.
Bi-monthly publication for leisure departments of district and county councils, schools, colleges, libraries, sports centres and leisure centres, as well as sports administrators generally.
Illustrations: B&W only. Pictures showing sports in deprived areas, urban areas, being played on wasteland or in the street. Also unusual sports that might not normally get a lot of publicity.

Text: Features on subjects similar to above. 1,000–2,000 words.
Overall freelance potential: Quite good.
Fees: Good; on a rising scale, according to the size or reproduction or length of feature.

SPORTS TRADER
Benn Publications Ltd., Sovereign Way, Tonbridge, Kent, TN9 1RW. Tel: 0732 364422.
Editor: John Couzens.
Fortnightly publication for retailers, manufacturers, importers and exporters.
Illustrations: B&W only. General sporting pictures, sporting events linked to sponsorship by manufacturers, sponsorship, sports products pictures.
Text: General news stores linked to the sports industry, i.e. manufacturers, retailers, importers and exporters. General features concerning the sports industry. In-depth features on trends, legal articles on legislation. News stores, 250 words; features 750–1,000 words.
Overall freelance potential: Good market for the right type of material.
Editor's tips: Telephone first.
Fees: Text, £35 per 1,000 words; pictures £7.50–£12.50.

TARGET GUN
Peterson Publishing Co. Ltd., Peterson House, Northbank, Berryhill Industrial Estate, Droitwich, Worcestershire WR9 9 BL. Tel: 0905 775564.
Editor: Geoffrey Hoyle.
Monthly publication for target shooters.
Illustrations: B&W only. Pictures of weapons, events, technical/engineering matters and general interest in the sport.
Text: General and technical instructional articles; reports of meetings. 500–3,500 words.
Overall freelance potential: Quite good.
Fees: By negotiation.

WATFORD
Watford Football Club, Vicarage Road Stadium, Watford, Herts. WD1 8ER. Tel: 0923 49747.
Editor: Caroline Gillies.
Published on matchdays during September to May, and read by supporters of Watford Football Club.
Illustrations: B&W and colour. Watford players in action at home or at away matches. Covers: Colour pictures of same. 35mm acceptable.
Text: No freelance market.
Overall freelance potential: This is an outlet only for professional or very good amateur sports photographers.
Fees: By negotiation.

WISDEN CRICKET MONTHLY
Wisden Cricket Magazines Ltd., 313 Kilburn Lane, London W9 3EQ. Tel: 01-969 5333.
Editor: David Frith.

Monthly publication aimed at all cricket-lovers. Concentrates on the game at first class level.
Illustrations: B&W and colour. Pictures of first class cricket. Big demand for topical county cricket matches, especially away from the major grounds such as Lords and The Oval. Covers usually provided by a retained photographer. 35mm acceptable.
Text: Wide scope for features about first class cricket, but check first before submitting. Up to 800 words.
Overall freelance potential: Around 15 per cent comes from freelance sources.
Fees: On a rising scale according to size of pictures or length of article.

Trade

THE BOOKSELLER
J. Whitaker and Sons Ltd., 12 Dyott Street, London WC1A 1DF. Tel: 01-836 8911.
Editor: Louis Baum.
Weekly trade paper aimed at librarians, booksellers, publishers, agents, authors and anyone interested in the book industry. Covers financial news, government affairs, trade trends and events, new titles, etc.
Illustrations: B&W only. Pictures of bookshops and book-related activities outside London. Busy book fairs, busy book shops etc.
Text: Humorous, serious, analytical, descriptive articles connected with the book trade. No author interviews or book reviews.
Overall freelance potential: Only of interest to those freelances who have a good knowledge of the book publishing world.
Fees: Variable.

CHEMIST AND DRUGGIST
Benn Publications Ltd., Benn House, Sovereign Way, Tonbridge, Kent TN9 1RW. Tel: 0732 364422.
Editor: R. E. Salmon.
Weekly publication for retail pharmacists; the pharmaceutical, toiletries and cosmetics industries; pharmaceutical wholesalers etc.
Illustrations: B&W only. News pictures such as chemistrs shops involved in flooding etc.
Text: Only commissioned features.
Overall freelance potential: Small.
Fees: On a rising scale, according to contribution.

DIRECT RESPONSE
Macro Publishing Ltd., 41b High Street, Hoddesdon, Herts EN11 8TA. Tel: 09924 69556.
Editor: Paul Rowney.
Monthly trade magazine for people in direct marketing and direct mail.
Illustrations: No Freelance market.

Text: Features on anything related to the subject. Up to 2,000 words.
Overall freelance potential: Up to 50 per cent is contributed by freelances.
Fees: On a rising scale according to the length of the article.

DOMESTIC HEATING PLUS PLUMBING BATHROOMS
Maclean Hunter Ltd., 76 Oxford Street, London W1N 0HH. Tel: 01-434 2233.
Editor: Neville Davis.
Monthly trade journal for heating installers, plumbers, builders' merchants, specifiers, buyers, etc.
Illustrations: B&W and rare use of colour. Pictures relating to domestic heating, plumbing, bathrooms, air conditioning, insulation, solar power, ventilation, heat pumps, etc.
Text: Only after prior consultation. 1,000 words.
Overall freelance potential: Fairly good for the contributor with a specialist knowledge.
Fees: Good; on a rising scale according to the size of reproduction or length of article.

DRAPERS RECORD
Textile Trade Publications, 20 Soho Square, London W1V 6DT. Tel: 01-734 1255.
Editor: Gerald Saunders.
Weekly publication for clothing and textile retailers.
Illustrations: B&W only. News pictures of retail events considered. Other pictures are commissioned.
Text: Features and news items of relevance to retailers in the fashion and textile fields. 1,000 words.
Overall freelance potential: Writers used occasionally, most pictures are commissioned.
Fees: On a rising scale according to the length of article.

EUROFRUIT MAGAZINE
Market Intelligence Ltd., 440–441 Market Towers, New Covent Garden Market, London SW8 5NQ. Tel: 01-720 8822.
Editor: Heather Slough.
Monthly magazine of the fruit and vegetable trade, published in French, German and English. Aimed at leading producers, importers, merchants and buyers of fruit and vegetables.
Illustrations: B&W only, subjects such as harvesting fruit, loading fruit on to ships or lorries, quality checks on fruit, packing etc. Pictures are usually provided with articles and are not paid for separately.
Text: Features on fruit and vegetables, e.g. Canadian apples in Europe, Iceberg lettuce, Egypt's expanding export range, Norway as an alternative market etc. 1,250–2,000 words.
Overall freelance potential: Quite good. Some regular contributors, but scope for the freelance writer who can also supply pictures.
Editor's tips: It is best to work in close contact with the editorial department to get names of people who would be of interest to the publication.
Fees: £35 per 1,000 words.

FASHION WEEKLY
Fashion Weekly 1981 Ltd., 6–7 Cambridge Gate, Regents Park, London NW1 4JR. Tel: 01-486 0155.
Editor: Rebecca Collings.
Weekly retail trade paper, covering women's and children's fashion.
Illustrations: B&W only. Fashion pictures, always commissioned. Covers: B&W news pictures concerning the fashion trade.
Text: Specialist and therefore commissioned.
Overall freelance potential: Good for the specialist freelance.
Fees: Negotiable.

THE FLORIST TRADE MAGAZINE
Lonsdale Publications Ltd., 120 Lower Ham Road, Kingston On Thames, Surrey KT2 5BD. Tel: 01-546 1535.
Editor: Caroline Marshall-Foster.
Monthly publication for retail florists.
Illustrations: B&W only. Pictures of floristry or retailing.
Text: Features on anything relating to floristry and retailing.
Overall freelance potential: Limited.
Fees: Text, £35 per 1,000 words published; pictures by agreement.

FREE TRADE
Limehouse Publications Ltd., The Mouse Building, South West India Dock, London E4 9SL. Tel: 01-987 3887.
Editor: Billy Walker.
Monthly controlled circulation journal for the independent licensed trade. Distributed free to all free-house pubs, restaurants and wine bars.
Illustrations: B&W only. News pictures connected with free-trade operations.
Text: Limited scope for news features, and for profiles of individual free-houses.
Overall freelance potential: Small.
Editor's tips: There is no requirement for coverage of the large brewery-owned pub sector.
Fees: By negotiation.

FURNISHING RETAILER AND CONTRACTOR
Acorn Publishing Co. Ltd., 105 Ardara Avenue, Raheny, Dublin 13. Tel: 0001 470085.
Editor: David Collins.
Monthly publication for the furnishing, carpet, furniture and lighting trades.
Illustrations: B&W only. Any pictures relating to general furnishing.
Text: No freelance market.
Overall freelance potential: Small.
Fees: By agreement.

THE GARMENT WORKER
National Union of Tailors and Garment Workers, 16 Charles Square, London N1 6HP. Tel: 01-251 9406.
Editor: Alec Smith.
Monthly journal of the above union, 90 per cent of the members of which are women.
Illustrations: B&W only. Pictures of general or specific interest to members of the union. Covers: B&W pictures of same.
Text: Small use for features that might interest this particular readership. 600 words.
Overall freelance potential: Very little.
Fees: On a rising scale, according to size of picture or length of article.

GLASS AGE
Link House Magazines (Croydon) Ltd., Dingwall Avenue, Croydon CR9 2TA. Tel: 01-686 2599.
Editor: Peter Butler.
Monthly magazine for the flat glass and allied industries. Aimed at builders, architects, double glazing producers, shopfitters, glass merchants, stained glass artists and all glass-related workers.
Illustrations: B&W only. Particularly interested in pictures of glass in new buildings. Good captions essential.
Text: Features on glass in construction.
Overall freelance potential: Small.
Editor's tips: Make contact before submitting any material.
Fees: On a rising scale according to the size of reproduction or length of feature.

HAIRFLAIR
Acorn Publishing Co. Ltd., 105 Ardara Avenue, Raheny, Dublin 13. Tel 0001 470085.
Editor: Una O'Hagan.
Quarterly publication for the beauty, hairdressing and associated equipment trades.
Illustrations: B&W only. Pictures of new products, new hair styles, shows, exhibitions, etc.
Text: No freelance market.
Overall freelance potential: Small.
Fees: By agreement.

INDEPENDENT GROCER
Industrial Media Ltd., Blair House, 184–186 High Street, Tonbridge, Kent TN9 1BE. Tel: 0732 359990.
Editor: Alan Toft.
Fortnightly publication for independent grocers and symbol group grocers, i.e. Spar, Mace, VG, Wavy Line etc. Assists them in being more profitable and aware of new products and campaigns.
Illustrations: B&W and colour. News page pictures and picture stories; 6 × 6 cm minimum. No covers.

Text: Articles about successful grocers, stories about grocers fighting off the giants. Stories about unfair trading, warnings of unscrupulous dealings and novelty ideas. Price surveys and comparisons. 650 words minimum.

Overall freelance potential: Obtain 99 per cent of news pictures from freelances and about 20 per cent of stores from either freelance writers or from freelance tip-offs.

Editor's tips: A sample copy of the magazine is available to potential contributors from Assistant Editor, Jenny Campbell. Always ring first with ideas.

Fees: £25 for a commissioned feature; 20p per line for news stories; £20 for commissioned B&W picture; £25 for colour.

INDEPENDENT GROCERY NEWS

William Reed Ltd., 5/7 Southwark Street, London SE1 1RQ. Tel: 01-407 6981.

Editor: Bill Jones.

Fortnightly paper for independent grocers. Aimed at all retailers involved in running small independent grocery outlets, and their wholesale suppliers.

Illustrations: B&W only. Little scope for photographs on their own.

Text: Illustrated features or stories concerning independent local grocery shops. Such material should feature a grocer who is doing something a bit different, or who has been highly successful in some way.

Overall freelance potential: Very limited, but the editor will be pleased to hear from freelances who can produce an interesting illustrated feature in this field.

Fees: By negotiation.

INTERNATIONAL TAX-FREE TRADER

International Trade Publications Ltd., Queensway House, 2 Queensway, Redhill, Surrey RH1 1QS. Tel: 0737 68611.

Editor: Ian Lyon.

Quarterly publication for executives in duty-free trade world-wide on airlines, cruise ships, ferry services etc.; executives running duty-free shops; suppliers of duty-free goods in all fields, e.g. alcohol, tobacco, cosmetics, toiletries, watches, luxury gifts etc.

Illustrations: B&W only inside. Specially interested in pictures which illustrate the location and displays at duty-free shops, both general views and particularly close-ups of customers, individual displays and individual products. Covers: Colour pictures of duty-free shops at airports, on ships and ferries etc.

Text: Features on products, shop and personalities in the international duty-free trade. 2,000–2,500 words.

Overall freelance potential: Around 50 per cent comes from freelances.

Editor's tips: Send an outline of ideas in the first instance.

Fees: £50–£100 per 1,000 words; pictures by agreement.

KITCHEN NEWS

P.F. Publications Ltd., 47 Hale Road, Farnham, Surrey GU9 9QR. Tel: 0252 722957.

Editor: Richard Heritage.

Monthly trade journal aimed at planners, specifiers, specialists, stockists and manufacturers/importers.
Illustrations: No freelance market.
Text: Company profiles, exhibition coverage and special features on the subject in hand. 1,000 words.
Overall freelance potential: Approximately 50 per cent comes from freelances.
Fees: By negotiation.

KITCHENS
Maclean Hunter Ltd., 76 Oxford Street, London W1N 0HH. Tel: 01-434 2233.
Editor: Neville Davis.
Monthly trade journal for kitchen special retailers, builders' merchants, distributors, manufacturers, importers, installers, builders, developers, architects, local authorities, nationalised industries, etc.
Illustrations: B&W and occasional colour. Pictures of kitchen units, built-in appliances, other major appliances, sinks, taps, waste disposers, worktops, laminates, tiles, floor and wall coverings, accessories, ceilings, blinds, etc. 35mm acceptable.
Text: Only after prior consultation. 1,000 words.
Overall freelance potential: Fairly good for the contributor with a specialised knowledge of the subject.
Editor: Good; on a rising scale according to the size of reproduction or length of article.

LEATHERGOODS
Benn Publications, Sovereign Way, Tonbridge, Kent TN9 1RW. Tel: 0732 364422.
Editor: David Dambe.
Monthly trade publication for specialist retailers of leathergoods, i.e. handbags, luggage and accessories like gloves and scarves. Synthetic materials are also covered.
Illustrations: B&W only. Interested in fashion pictures for stock, but by prior negotiation only.
Text: Features on the legal, insurance and cash side of the business. Specialist articles on all aspects of selling to the consumer. Retail trends. Fashion articles. Up to 1,000 words.
Overall freelance potential: Small but regular income possible for outside contributors. About 15 to 20 per cent is contributed.
Editor's tips: No padded copy.
Fees: By negotiation.

LIBRARY ASSOCIATION RECORD
The Library Association, 7 Ridgmount Street, London WC1E 7AE. Tel: 01-636 7543.
Editor: Roger Walter.
Monthly publication dealing with news of libraries and librarianship for professionals.
Illustrations: B&W only. Pictures concerned with library subjects. Covers: B&W pictures within the general subject area.

Text: No freelance market.
Overall freelance potential: Little at present.
Fees: Negotiable.

LICENSEE

National Union of Licensed Victuallers, Boardman House, 2 Downing Street, Farnham, Surrey GU9 7NX. Tel: 0252 714448.
Editor: Garry Edwards.
Fortnightly businessman's journal/newspaper containing news of organisation activities, aims, services and aimed at all self-employed licensees.
Illustrations: B&W only. LVA activities where affiliated to the NULV. General public house activities only in members' houses. The photographer should check this with the licensee first.
Text: Pub stories concerning NULV members.
Overall freelance potential: Slight.
Editor's tips: Check ideas with the news editor before proceeding.
Fees: Good; on a rising scale according to the size of reproduction or length of feature.

MEAT

Northwood Publications Ltd., 93–99 Goswell Road, London EC1V 7QA. Tel: 01-253 9355.
Editor: Graham Large.
Monthly trade journal for the slaughtering, processing and retail sectors of the meat industry.
Illustrations: B&W only. Pictures to illustrate articles on specific stories regarding meat plants.
Text: Technical features on meat plants. Profiles on individuals or companies in the trade. 1,000 words.
Overall freelance potential: About 10 per cent bought each month.
Fees: £50 per 1,000 words; pictures by agreement.

MEAT TRADER

National Federation of Meat Traders, 1 Belgrove, Tunbridge Wells, Kent TN1 1YW. Tel: 0892 44046/7.
Editor: Vincent Champion.
Monthly publication for the independent meat trader.
Illustrations: B&W only. Pictures related to the meat trade.
Text: Features on meat and livestock. Up to 2,000 words.
Overall freelance potential: Small since most material is written by the editor.
Editor's tips: Any material that is considered must be exclusive.
Fees: By negotiation.

MEN'S WEAR

Thomson Magazines Ltd., Knightway House, 20 Soho Square, London W1V 6DT. Tel: 01-734 1255.

Editor: Linda Laderman.
Weekly publication for retailers and buyers in men's and boy's wear.
Illustrations: B&W mostly. Fashion and news pictures.
Text: Illustrated news and features on the trade.
Overall freelance potential: Small, but more market for pictures than for text.
Text: On a rising scale according to size of reproduction or length of article.

MODERN CHEMIST
Accolade Publications Ltd., 100 Great Portland Street, London W1N 5PD. Tel: 01-636 6943.
Editor: Stewart Farr.
Monthly publication for all concerned with the marketing and retailing of cosmetics, toiletries, propriety medicines and allied products. Aimed at retail chemist shops.
Illustrations: No freelance market.
Text: Articles of direct relevance to the retail chemist trade. 500–1,000 words.
Overall freelance potential: Approximately 75 per cent of the text is written by freelances, but they are all specialists.
Fees: By arrangement.

NEWSAGENT
Haymarket Publishing Ltd., 38–42 Hampton Road, Teddington, Middlesex. Tel: 01-977 8787.
Editor: Ms Lesley Delaney.
Weekly publication aimed at retail newsagents as well as publishers, distributors and wholesalers.
Illustrations: B&W only. Pictures of any item directly related to the newstrade.
Text: Profiles of retail newsagents or news stories about the trade. 1,000–2,000 words.
Overall freelance potential: Small.
Fees: By agreement.

PROPERTY GAZETTE
Barradown Ltd., 69 Fleet Street, London EC4. Tel: 01-353 5787.
Editor: Mike Goodman.
Monthly publication concerned with commercial and industrial property. Aimed at estate agents, property developers, pension funds, banks, local councils, development corporations and leading UK companies.
Illustrations: Potential freelance market. Contact Editor for details.
Text: Features on industrial and commercial property.
Overall freelance potential: Relevant articles are always welcome.
Fees: Negotiable.

RETAIL FRUIT TRADE REVIEW
Retail Fruit Trade Federation Ltd., 108–110 Market Towers, 1 Nine Elms Lane, London SW8 5NS. Tel: 01-720 9168.

Editor: Mrs. Elizabeth Pretty.
Monthly house journal of the Federation. Read by all fresh produce marketing organisations in the UK and abroad.
Illustrations: No freelance market.
Text: Features on shopfitting, self-employed legislation, insurance for the self-employed, staff training, marketing and promotion of fresh produce, re-investment for profit and coping with staff problems. 1,000–1,500 words.
Overall freelance potential: Low due to specialist subject.
Fees: £25–£30 per 1,000 words.

SHOE AND LEATHER NEWS

New Century Publishing Co., 84–88 Great Eastern Street, London EC2A 3ED. Tel: 01-739 2071.
Editor: K. Longworth.
Weekly trade publication for specialist footwear retailers plus repairers, shoemakers and suppliers to footwear trade and leather industry.
Illustrations: B&W only. Pictures of news items relating to the market and items of interest to the trade in general. No portraits of trade personalities.
Text: Features on all aspects of the trade, especially on footwear retailing and repairing. Manufacturing of footwear or allied products of less interest. 500–1,500 words.
Overall freelance potential: Variable, but wider than currently obtained from freelances.
Editor's tips: The market requires succinct writing in an even tone with plenty of relevant details and figures, e.g., turnover, stockturn, styles carried, floorspace of shops etc.
Fees: By agreement.

TACKLE AND GUNS

East Midland Allied Press, Bretton Court, Bretton, Peterborough PE3 8DZ. Tel: 0733 264666.
Editor: Cyril Holbrook.
Monthly magazine, sold on subscription only to members of the tackle industry and gun trade.
Illustrations: Pictures concerning personnel, products and firms in the above trades.
Text: Features on personnel, products and firms, plus general retail matters, 1,000 words maximum.
Overall freelance potential: Difficult to break into, unless the writer/photographer has a specialist knowledge of the appropriate trades.
Editor's tips: Telephone first to discuss ideas before submitting.
Fees: Negotiable.

TILES AND TILING

Giddings Business Journals Ltd., AFI House, 283–289 Cricklewood Broadway, London NW2 6NZ. Tel: 01-450 0466.

Editor: George Mills.
Monthly publication aimed at retail end of the ceramic tile industry.
Illustrations: No freelance market.
Text: Features on the historical production of tiles; business advice to small retailers.
1,500–2,000 words.
Overall freelance potential: Small market for the freelance who knows the subject.
Fees: £35 per 1,000 words.

TOBACCO

International Trade Publications Ltd., Queensway House, 2 Queensway, Redhill, Surrey.
Tel: 0737 68611.
Managing Editor: Bill Heard.
Monthly trade journal covering the marketing of tobacco products through wholesale and
retail outlets, as well as the licensed and leisure trade. Also accessories, such as lighters, pipes,
etc.
Illustrations: B&W only. Pictures of shop interiors and exteriors connected with trade,
poster sites and sponsored events. All pictures by prior arrangement.
Text: Illustrated interviews with retailers. 800–1,500 words.
Overall freelance potential: Growing.
Editor's tips: Copies of the journal will be sent to potential freelances on request.
Fees: £58 per 1,000 words; £10–£15 per pictures plus expenses.

TYRES AND ACCESSORIES

Tyre Industry Publications Ltd., 136 Valley Road, Clacton-on-Sea, Essex CO15 6LX. Tel:
0255 421295.
Editor: G. Marshall.
Monthly journal for the tyre industry.
Illustrations: B&W only. Pictures of unusual uses for tyres or damage to tyres.
Text: Features on tyres. Up to 1,000 words.
Overall freelance potential: Small.
Fees: By negotiation.

VIDEO BUSINESS

Record Business Publications Ltd., Hyde House, 13 Langley Street, London WC2H 9JG.
Tel: 01-836 9311.
Editor: Tim Smith.
Bi-monthly publication aimed at the video business and its associated retail trades.
Illustrations: Only by prior consultation.
Text: No freelance market.
Overall freelance potential: Excellent.
Fees: By arrangement.

Transport

BUSES

Ian Allan Ltd., Terminal House, Shepperton, Middlesex TW17 8AS. Tel: 093-22 28950.
Editor: Stephen Morris.
Monthly magazine for bus enthusiasts, bus operators (traffic and engineering) and the bus manufacturing industry.
Illustrations: B&W only. Pictures of buses and coaches, especially those that are newsworthy, topical or historical. Covers: General B&W pictures of buses.
Text: Features on present-day bus service departments, mainly UK, some overseas; new vehicles, historical surveys, nostalgia. 1,500–2,000 words.
Overall freelance potential: Limited.
Fees: £7.50 per 1,000 words; £1.50 per picture.

COACHING JOURNAL AND BUS REVIEW

Travel and Transport Ltd., 122 Newgate Street, London EC1A 7AD. Tel: 01-606 8465.
Editor: John Taylor.
Monthly publication, covering the road passenger transport industry with the accent on luxury touring and express coaches.
Illustrations: B&W only. Pictures with captions for use on news pages.
Text: Operating articles on bus and coach companies with specific reference to a point of particular interest, as opposed to general history. 1,000–1,500 words.
Overall freelance potential: Small; the magazine usually works with its own contacts on a regular or occasional basis.
Fees: By negotiation.

COACHMART

Coachmart Ltd., 33 Humber Street, Hull HU1 1TF. Tel: 0482 224935.
Editor: Houston Ramm.
Weekly magazine covering coaching operations. Aimed at independent licensed coach and tour operators.
Illustrations: B&W only. Pictures as illustrations to features mentioned below. Places of interest to coach parties. Covers: No freelance market.
Text: Features on coach operators, hotels, ferry operations, resorts and venues, anything that would be of interest to a coach party or its operator, articles on subjects that an operator might find useful in his day to day business. Up to 3,000 words.
Overall freelance potential: Little at present, but always interested in seeing work from freelances.
Fees: £30 per 1,000 words; £7.50 per picture.

TRUCK

F.F. Publishing Ltd., 64 West Smithfield, London EC1A 9EE. Tel: 01-606 7836.
Editor: Paul Barden.

Monthly magazine for drivers and directors of truck companies. Features tests and industrial news.
Illustrations: B&W and colour. Pictures on commission only from professional freelances. Covers: Colour pictures tied in with inside article. 35mm acceptable.
Text: Features on any aspect of commercial vehicles. 250–3,000 words.
Overall freelance potential: All pictures and 40 per cent of copy comes from freelance sources.
Fees: By agreement.

Travel

BUSINESS TRAVELLER
Travel Editions Ltd., 60–61 Fleet Street, London EC4Y 1LA. Tel: 01-583 0967.
Editor: Nick Parsons.
Monthly (except February and August) consumer journal aimed at the frequently travelling business executive in Britain and abroad.
Illustrations: B&W and colour. Pictures to illustrate destination report articles on a wide variety of cities around the world. No photo features.
Text: Only by consultation with the Editor.
Overall freelance potential: Around 75 per cent of the magazine is contributed by freelances.
Fees: Text, £80 per 1,000 words; pictures on a similar scale to London photo agencies.

HOLIDAY HAUNTS IN GREAT BRITAIN
Haymarket Publishing Ltd., 38–42 Hampton Road, Teddington, Middlesex TW11 0JE. Tel: 01-977 8787.
Editor: Colin Pringle.
Annual gazetteer of popular holiday towns, villages and resorts.
Illustrations: B&W only inside. Scenic views, castles, houses, steam railways, etc. Pictures from coast and countryside. Covers: Colour post card type views of resorts, countryside or castles. 35mm acceptable.
Text: Illustrated articles on regions of England, Scotland, Wales, the Channel Islands or Isle of Man. 2,500 words.
Overall freelance potential: Around 25 per cent of the material is contributed by freelances.
Fees: Subject to negotiation.

HOLIDAY TIME-SHARING
Domus Publications Ltd., 52 South Molton Street, London W1Y 1HP. Tel: 01-629 6039.
Editor: Judith Rose.
Bi-monthly middle to up-market magazine for people interested in taking holidays at home or abroad on a time-sharing basis.

Illustrations: B&W and colour. Travel and holidays with a time-sharing bias. Covers: Colour pictures on a similar theme, but rarely bought from freelances. 35mm acceptable.
Text: Travel-orientated articles, e.g. overseas property, time-sharing, finance, etc. 1,000–2,000 words.
Overall freelance potential: Fairly high.
Fees: £50 per 1,000 words; pictures by agreement.

HOLIDAY USA AND CANADA
Hanover Publications, 80 Highgate Road, London NW5 1PB. Tel: 01-267 9521.
Editor: Mary Moore Mason.
European magazine aimed specifically at the holidaymaker going to North America. Published three times a year.
Illustrations: B&W and colour. Pictures used mostly as illustrations to features detailed below. Covers: Colour pictures of typically American girls, looking as though they would entice you to visit the country; 35mm acceptable.
Text: Illustrated features that present a new aspect on the USA and Canada. Regular destinations such as New York, Miami and Los Angeles are only of interest if the storyline is unique. 1,000–1,500 words.
Overall freelance potential: Over 50 per cent of the magazine comes from outside contributors.
Fees: Inside pictures, £25–£30; covers negotiable; features, £60–£65 per 1,000 words.

HOMES AND TRAVEL ABROAD
Domus Publications Ltd., 52 South Molton Street, London W1Y 1HF. Tel: 01-499 8311.
Editor: Judith Rose.
Bi-monthly magazine for all those interested in international property and travel.
Illustrations: B&W and colour. Travel and pictures of homes outside the UK. Covers: Colour pictures of the same. 35mm acceptable.
Text: Features on travel and overseas property. 1,000–2,000 words.
Overall freelance potential: Fairly high.
Fees: Text, £50 per 1,000 words; pictures by arrangement.

MIDDLE EAST TRAVEL
I.C. Magazines Ltd., PO Box 261, 69 Great Queen St, London WC2B 5BZ. Tel: 01-404 4333.
Editor: Terence Mirabelli.
Publication for senior personnel in the Middle East travel industry. Published 10 times per year.
Illustrations: B&W only inside. General travel shots, places of interest, airlines, hotels. Covers: colour pictures connected with current contents; 35mm acceptable.
Text: Trade-related stories. 800–1,000 words.
Overall freelance potential: Around 75 per cent contributed from outside sources.
Editor's tips: Do not get in touch unless you have a specific idea in mind.
Fees: £40 for covers; £10 for mono.

DEREK FURLONG

RAMS NEWS

Welbeck Public Relations Ltd., 84 Baker Street, London W1M 1DL. Tel: 01-486 8561.
Editor: Julien Speed.
Bi-monthly publication for senior management, directors and owners of travel agencies
throughout the UK and Republic of Ireland.
Illustrations: Pictures relate to articles. They are B&W only and there is no market for
cover pictures.
Text: Illustrated features on subjects such as advertising, media, shop design, direct mail etc.
Anything that will help a travel agent market his business better.
Overall freelance potential: A good percentage of the publication comes from outside
contributors, both photographers and writers, though the pictures *must* be tied in with text.
Fees: By negotiation.

THE TRAVELLER

WEXAS International Ltd., 45 Brompton Road, London SW3 1DE. Tel: 01-581 4130.
Editor: Rita Perry.
Quarterly publication containing informative and entertaining articles on travel and tourism
in the developing countries of the world. Aimed at the independent traveller who prefers to
travel off the beaten track and with minimal cultural impact.
Illustrations: B&W and colour. Travel pictures, especially close-ups of local people, shot
in developing countries, not Europe or North America unless there is an adventure travel
angle. No landscapes or tourist 'brochure' shots. Covers: colour pictures in close-up of local
people with space at the top and one side for logo and coverlines.
Text: Travel articles with the angles detailed above. Contact editor for specification sheet.
Features up to 2,000 words.
Overall freelance potential: The magazine uses a lot of freelance contributions, but the
excellence of the transparencies is what sells the feature.
Editor's tips: Seasonality is important.
Fees: Text, £35 per 1,000 words; £10 per colour illustration; £8 for B&W

TRAVELLING

Moorgate Publications Ltd., 382–6 Edgware Road, London W2 1EP. Tel: 01-723 1142/3022.
Editor: Roy Johnstone.
Bi-monthly magazine aimed at travellers, either for pleasure or for business.
Illustrations: B&W and colour showing travel destinations world-wide. Plenty of blue skies.
Covers: colour on travel-related topics; 35mm acceptable.
Text: Always on the lookout for suggestions for articles on travel-related topics. 1,000 words.
Overall freelance potential: About 75 per cent bought from outside contributors, but
most are already established with the magazine.
Editor's tips: The magazine does not require photographs or articles to be submitted direct.
They prefer a list of pictures held by the photographer and/or suggestions only for articles.
Contributors will then be contacted when necessary.
Fees: Negotiable.

Women's Interest

BLUE JEANS
D.C. Thompson & Co. Ltd., Albert Square, Dundee DD1 9QJ. Tel: 0382 23131.
Editor: Kathy Troup.
Weekly publishing romantic stories and aimed at young girls between the ages of 12 and 15.
Illustrations: B&W and Colour boy/girl romantic situation pictures to illustrate stories. Current pop stars. 35mm acceptable.
Text: Romantic stories appealing to a teenage readership.
Overall freelance potential: Fair.
Editor's tips: Submit only professional quality material. Study the magazine first.
Fees: Negotiable.

HARPERS AND QUEEN
National Magazine Company Ltd., 72 Broadwick Street, London W1V 2BP. Tel: 01-439 7144.
Editor: Willie Landels.
Monthly magazine featuring fashion, fiction, design, travel, beauty and health.
Illustrations: B&W and colour. Only by commission.
Text: Any general interest features. 1,500–3,000 words.
Overall freelance potential: Very good.
Fees: Good; on a rising scale according to length of feature.

HERS
IPC Magazines Ltd., King's Reach Tower, Stamford Street, London SE1 9LS. Tel: 01-261 5000.
Editor: Hamish Dawson.
Monthly magazine publishing first-person stories and practical features for women.
Illustrations: B&W and Colour situation pictures to illustrate stories. Imaginative B&W pictures involving single girls or couples; such shots should ideally evoke a strong emotional response in the viewer either by use of lighting, location or model composition and expression. Covers: 6 × 6 cm colour transparencies preferred.
Test: First-person romantic stories. Practical features aimed at women.
Overall freelance potential: Good.
Fees: Good; on a rising scale according to size of reproduction or length of story/article.

HOME AND COUNTRY
NFWI, 39 Eccleston Street, London SW1W 9NT. Tel: 01-730 0307.
Editor: Gill Hudson.
Monthly publication for Women's Institute members.

Illustrations: Pictures are considered from freelance photographers, but they are advised to check with the editor before submitting.
Text: Only features commissioned in advance. 800–1,200 words.
Overall freelance potential: A small, but regular amount bought each month.
Editor's tips: Send cuttings in first instance before attempting to sell to this market.
Fees: By agreement.

HOME AND FREEZER DIGEST
British European Associated Publishers Ltd., Digest House, 84 North End Road, London W14 9EZ. Tel: 01-602 6331.
Editor: Jill Churchill.
Monthly 'service' magazine aimed at all women. Contains material on cookery, home, health, parenthood, etc.
Illustrations: Most pictures are commissioned. There is a market, however, for colour pictures of food, especially fresh fruit and vegetables. 35mm acceptable.
Text: Personal experience features relating to women's interests. 1,000 words.
Overall freelance potential: Around 5 per cent comes from freelance sources.
Editor's tips: Especially interested in female humour.
Fees: By negotiation.

LOOK NOW
IPC Magazines Ltd., King's Reach Tower, Stamford Street, London SE1 9LS. Tel: 01-261 5000.
Editor: Josephine Fairley.
Monthly magazine for 18–22 year old girls, concerning all issues of interest to that readership.
Illustrations: B&W only. Pictures of personalities, fashion etc.
Text: Features of interest to teenage and early twenties girls. 600–2,000 words.
Overall freelance potential: Small, but always welcome.
Editor's tips: Read the magazine.
Fees: By agreement.

MOTHER
IPC Magazines Ltd., King's Reach Tower, Stamford Street, London SE1 9LS. Tel: 01-261 5000. Editorial Department: Commonwealth House, 1–19 New Oxford Street, London WC1A 1NG. Tel: 01-404 0700.
Editor: Margaret Carter.
Monthly magazine aimed at young mothers, covering all aspects of child care.
Illustrations: B&W and Colour. Requires top quality, situation pictures of children under 7 years of age. Does not normally use posed shots; pictures should show children engrossed in some activity.
Overall freelance potential: Fair.
Fees: Good; on a rising scale, according to size of reproduction or length of article.

MOTHER AND BABY
Illustrated Publications Co. Ltd., 12–18 Paul Street, London EC2A 4JS. Tel: 01-247 8233.
Editor: Mrs. Else Powell.
Monthly aimed at pregnant women and mothers of young children.
Illustrations: B&W situation pictures of mothers and babies and mothers and toddlers.
Shots of young mothers in various situations—walking, eating, sitting, moody pictures, etc.
Babies, toddlers and young children in various situations such as sleeping, feeding, crying,
laughing, etc. Situation pictures of young couples. Covers: Colour mother-and-baby shots.
6 × 6 cm transparancies.
Text: Articles on all subjects related to the care of babies and children.
Overall freelance potential: Good.
Editor's tips: Mothers pictured must by young (under 30) and attractive. Only top quality
pictures will be considered.
Fees: £10 and upwards for a single B&W picture.

MS LONDON WEEKLY
Employment Publications Ltd., 6–7 Cambridge Gate, Regent's Park, London NW1 4JR.
Tel: 01-486 0155.
Editor: Alison Rice.
Weekly magazine for young, independent, working Londoners.
Illustrations: B&W and colour. Mostly fashion and portraits, some still life and reportage
work. 35mm Kodachrome acceptable inside. Covers: Colour fashion and general interest
subjects. 6 × 6 cm preferred.
Text: Off-beat, sharply-written features of interest to young, aware, working Londoners.
500–1,000 words.
Overall freelance potential: Around 90 per cent of the magazine comes from freelances.
Editor's tips: Best to send copies of recently-published work plus list of ideas before actual
submission.
Fees: Approximately £50 per 1,000 words; pictures by agreement.

OPTIONS
IPC Magazines Ltd., King's Reach Tower, Stamford Street, London SE1 9LS. Tel: 01-261
5159.
Editor: Penny Radford.
Monthly magazine for women in the 25–45 age group, those who have grown out of the
younger magazines and who want a magazine relevant to their lifestyle now.
Illustrations: B&W and colour. Small B&W shots for 'Briefing', 'Lifeline' and 'Leisure'
features. Travel shots, personalities etc. Covers: Good quality headshots; 35mm acceptable.
Text: Features of interest to a readership, most of whom are married, 50 per cent of whom
work full- or part-time. Fashion, health, cookery, entertaining articles, plus strong individual
general features, e.g. personality profiles, investigative, sociological, money and legal
subjects.

Overall freelance potential: Very good. A lot of outside contributors are used.

Editor's tips: Read the magazine carefully and try to work out the requirements for yourself.

Fees: Around £80 per 1,000 words.

SHE

National Magazine Company Ltd., National Magazine House, 72 Broadwick Street, London W1V 2BP. Tel: 01-439 7144.

Editor: Eric Bailey.

Monthly magazine for wide-minded, lively people of any age. Although primarily aimed at women, it has a lot of interest to men as well.

Illustrations: A terrific range of subjects is covered, but most one-off pictures are a little off-beat. All pictures should be supplied with good captions or information sheets. Inside, the magazine uses mostly B&W and colour occasionally. Covers: Bright, jolly, interesting girls. Colour; minimum size 6 × 6 cm.

Text: Anything except traditional romance, beauty and cooking from 1,000 words upwards.

Overall freelance potential: A lot of 'on spec' submissions are used, but many of the pictures come from agencies.

Editor's tips: Don't forget that stamped addressed envelope if you want your work back!

Fees: From £35 per 1,000 words. Pictures by negotiation.

SLIMMING

SM Publications Ltd., 4 Clareville Grove, London SW7 5AR. Tel: 01-370 4411.

Editor: Patience Bulkeley.

Bi-monthly magazine for slimmers.

Illustrations: B&W pictures of celebrities for stock, but usually supplied by Press Association. Covers shot in-house.

Text: Mostly written by staff.

Overall freelance potential: Because of specialist subject matter, the magazine has a team of regular consultants and therefore has little use for general freelance contributions.

Fees: By agreement.

SUPERSTORE

Home and Law Magazines Ltd., 2–16 Goodge Street, London W1P 1FF. Tel: 01-631 4092.

Editor: Ann Scutcher.

Quarterly magazine for shoppers in Co-op superstores. Aimed at young families.

Illustrations: Colour only. Pictures of interest generally to women, e.g. holidays, gardening etc. Covers: Colour family pictures, e.g. mothers and children.

Text: Features on general women's interests, including humour. 1,000 words.

Overall freelance potential: Most of the written material comes from freelances.

Fees: Negotiable.

THE TOWNSWOMAN
The National Union of Townswomen's Guilds, 2 Cromwell Place, South Kensington, London SW7 2LG. Tel: 01-581 5581.
Editor: Hazel Thompson.
Monthly magazine for those who belong to the Townswomen's Guild in Britain. Contains general interest subjects, opinions and business of interest to women.
Illustrations: B&W and colour. Pictures connected with features and subjects detailed below. Covers: Colour pictures on subjects mentioned below, usually food, home-interest and people. Must show a lot of colour. 35mm acceptable.
Text: Features on handicrafts, answers to health problems, gardening and indoor plants, cooking, dinner parties, wines, knitting, sewing, books and book reviews, fashion for middle-age women, beauty for the same age range, slimming, yoga, exercises, sex, car maintenance, pensions, investments, insurance, antiques, houses, furniture, personalities, pets, children, education . . . everything and anything of interest to women.
Overall freelance potential: Good.
Editor's tips: Features should be bright and chatty, *not* cosy.
Fees: £3 per 100 words. Pictures by agreement.

VOGUE PATTERNS
Butterick Fashion Marketing Co. (UK) Ltd., New Lane, Havant, Hants. PO9 2ND. Tel: 0705 486221.
Editor: Wendy Rawlins.
Bi-monthly magazine for home dress-makers, particularly the fashion conscious. The magazine is an informative dress-making, fashion guide, giving hints and tips on sewing techniques, fabrics, accessories etc. It shows colour shots of made-up *Vogue* patterns.
Illustrations: B&W only of any subject of interest to a fashion-conscious woman, e.g. hair care, accessories, fabrics etc.
Text: Features on anything apertaining to the fashion-conscious woman. One page maximum.
Fees: To be negotiated on submission.

WOMAN
IPC Magazines Ltd., King's Reach Tower, Stamford Street, London SE1 9LS. Tel. 01-261 5000.
Editor: Jo Foley.
Weekly magazine devoted to all women's interests.
Illustrations: B&W and Colour. Most pictures specifically illustrate features in the magazine and are commissioned. Some scope for human interest shots which are dramatic, offbeat or unusual.
Text: Features on beauty, fashion, cookery, knitting, home, etc., but these tend to be commissioned or staff-produced. Submit a synopsis in the first instance. Fiction stories (both serials and short stories) will be considered on a speculative basis.
Overall freelance potential: Small.
Fees: Good; on a rising scale according to size of reproduction or length or article.

TONY BOXALL

WOMAN AND HOME

IPC Magazines Ltd., King's Reach Tower, Stamford Street, London SE1 9LS. Tel: 01–261 6102.

Editor: Sue Dobson.

Monthly magazine for all women concerned with running a home. Its aim is to provide sensible advice, good value for money and entertainment. Subjects covered include cookery, dressmaking, knitting, fashion, home features, special offers, gardening, travel, financial advice, good romantic fiction and personality articles.

Illustrations: Much of the magazine's content is provided by staff photographers. The freelance market includes travel, beauty and Royalty, each of which can be colour or B&W; gardening, usually in B&W only; and personalities, colour and B&W but only to accompany a relevant feature. There is no freelance market for covers.

Text: Articles on personalities, either well-known or who lead interesting lives. 1,500–4,000 words. Romantic fiction, 3,000–6,000 words.

Overall freelance potential: Including regular contributors, about 50 per cent of the magazine is contributed by freelances.

Fees: £45 per 1,000 words. Pictures by negotiation.

WOMAN'S JOURNAL

IPC Magazines Ltd., King's Reach Tower, Stamford Street, London SE1 9LS. Tel: 01-261 6448.

Editor: Laurie Purden.

Monthly glossy magazine for women.

Illustrations: B&W and colour. Pictures on home, beauty, cookery, fashion and general features. 35mm acceptable. No cover market.

Text: Features of general interest and on subjects detailed above. 2,000 words maximum.

Overall freelance potential: Nearly all work from outside is commissioned.

Fees: Negotiable.

WOMAN'S OWN

IPC Magazines Ltd., King's Reach Tower, Stamford Street, London SE1 9LS. Tel: 01-261 5000.

Editor: Iris Burton.

Weekly publishing articles and practical features of interest to women.

Illustrations: B&W and Colour pictures, mostly illustrating commissioned articles and features. Not a great deal of scope for single pictures, although the occasional unusual or offbeat shot may be used.

Text: Features on beauty, fashion, cookery and other women's interests are used, but tend to be commissioned or staff-produced. Send a brief outline of any proposed feature in the first instance. Short stories (fiction) also published, and these may be submitted speculatively.

Overall freelance potential: Small, as far as speculative submissions are concerned.

Fees: Good; on a rising scale according to size of reproduction or length or article.

PUTTING WORDS TO YOUR PICTURES

There are undoubtedly a lot of markets crying out for your pictures. But even a cursory glance through the pages of this book will tell you that there are also a lot of markets looking for illustrated articles—features that use pictures only to illustrate the words.

Any editor will tell you that the freelance who can both write and take half-way decent pictures is a rarity, and one to be cultivated. Anyone who can do it stands the chance of doubling his freelance sales overnight. It is therefore in your interests to learn something about the craft of writing. Because make no mistake about it, writing *is* a craft and one that can be learnt in much the same way as you learnt to use a camera. All it needs is the ability to learn and apply a few simple rules.

Find your Market

Your first objective is to find a market and, in this, you should already have a certain amount of experience. As a freelance photographer, you know the importance of supplying exactly the type of picture required by an editor. It's no different for writers. There is little point in writing an article, then looking round for a place to sell it. Instead, you must first find your market, analyse it, then write a feature that complies with the correct style.

Magazines are the biggest market for illustrated articles. So first buy a magazine that attracts you and take a good, in-depth look at it. Check it against its entry in the *Handbook* and decide the following:

1. What type of articles do they use?

2. Which are written by staff or regular contributors and what fields are therefore open to you?

3. How many words and pictures do they require per article?

4. Is the style directed at the layman or the professional, consumer or trade?

Finding ideas

Next you have to find an idea for a feature. This can actually be influenced by features already in the magazine, looking at them and finding an extension to an idea already covered. Ideas can come from just being nosey, keeping an ear and eye open for unusual subjects. They can also come from other people.

Wherever the idea comes from, it must be of interest to a majority of people in a certain market. So don't be led astray by the enthusiasm of the person giving you certain information. That person might be over-enthusiastic about his own minority interest. Ignore the enthusiasm and examine the facts. Are they of real interest?

By the same token, don't ignore an idea just because it doesn't interest you personally. You, for instance, might be totally uninterested in football, but you would be foolish to ignore the fact that millions of people are avid followers of everything connected with the sport.

Article ideas very often revolve around people—those who lead interesting or different lives, who have done something special, who are unique or unusual in some way. They can come too from interesting places or objects. Anything which is of interest and, preferably, of which little is known can make the basis for an illustrated article.

Gathering facts

At the start, it is a good idea to write primarily about what you know. The busy freelance, however, is soon likely to run out of subjects that way and that is the time to start learning how to research other subjects. Before you begin to write, then, you must learn how to gather facts . . . and how to make sure the facts you gather are the relevant ones. There are several ways of doing that.

Interviews with people who know their subject better than you are one way of gathering facts, but the experience can be a daunting one. The first time you set out to interview someone, you are bound to be a little nervous; the trick is not to show it. Be confident.

Don't be afraid to show your ignorance on the subject you are tackling. After all, if you knew as much as the person you were interviewing there would be little point in an interview in the first place.

Some writers make a list of the questions they want to ask before the interview starts. It's a good idea and it gives you something to fall back on if you begin to dry up. But don't be afraid to deviate from your list. Most successful interviews are conducted in a casual, conversation-like way. If you notice that your subject seems nervous (and it's very likely that he or she will be), try to put them at their ease with a little general conversation at the start, leading yourself naturally into the pertinent questions you need answering.

Six basic words

Most interviews can be conducted around six basic words which will guide you towards the sort of questions you will need answering. The six words are these: *Who, what, where, when, how and why.* Learn them and remember them and, as your interview draws to a close, check to see that they have each been basically answered in some way.

Always ask direct questions. Don't waffle. Don't ask negative questions like, *I don't suppose you could tell me when all this started?* Instead, say something more like, *Tell me when all this started.* Always give your subjects plenty of time to answer and to finish what they have to say before you ask your next question. Make sure you get all the details. Don't be afraid of appearing stupid. If you don't understand an answer, ask your subject to explain more fully. Ask for spellings of words you are not familiar with. Write them down and, when you come to write the article, make sure you get them right.

Research for an article can also come from books. It is against the copyright laws to reproduce part of any book word for word, but there is nothing against you taking facts from books and then writing them up in your own way. But make sure they *are* facts, and not the author's opinions. Where possible, try to obtain more than one book on your subject and check facts against each other before committing them to paper.

Using PR people

Certain types of article can be researched from public relations people, many of whom will have fact sheets already prepared on your chosen subject. Again, don't re-write the PR handout word for word, put new words together in your own style.

Most large companies have a PR office or someone who deals with PR enquiries. It is best to telephone such people, rather than writing to them. When dealing with them, remember they get a lot of time-wasters on the phone so don't give them any reason to believe you are another. State exactly who you are, what you are doing and how you hope they can help. Be cool and confident. Treat the person at the other end of the phone in much the same way as you would treat someone you might be interviewing.

However you gather your facts, you will need some way of recording the information. The traditional way is in a small notebook and, despite the convenience of modern miniature tape recorders, the old way is still often the best. You don't have to know shorthand but as you become more adept at interviews, you will inevitably develop a style of fast writing, abbreviating certain words and missing out others as you write.

A notebook is also useful for those moments when you dry up. You can pretend to be busy writing something down, while thinking of what next to say. At the writing stage it is more useful too. With a tape recorder your interview is reconstructed in exactly the order you conducted it; with a notebook, you can flip backwards and forwards through the pages, writing the feature in an order different to the way the interview originally ran.

The salient points

Having gathered your facts, you now have to get them down on paper. Before you begin, it is a good idea to make a list of the salient points you wish to cover. It doesn't have to be in the order in which the article will be written, it doesn't have to be intelligible to anyone but yourself, it doesn't even have to be followed religiously. But it will keep you on the right track and prevent you from forgetting the key points while you are actually writing.

Every article has a beginning, a middle and an end. The beginning is the intro. This is a short, sharp paragraph, usually of no more than about thirty words, designed to serve two purposes. It tells the reader what the article is about and it whets his appetite to make sure he reads on.

Here is the intro from an article about a lady fakir:

Geraldine Williams is England's Queen of Fakirs. She earns her living lying on a bed of nails while her husband drives a three-ton lorry over her.

That's the ideal intro. It is short enough to be read practically at a glance, it sums up the subject of the whole article ahead, but it leaves a lot of questions needing to be answered and so encourages the reader to read on.

After the intro we come to the main part of the article, the middle, where you start to present the facts in the most entertaining way possible.

In the Queen of Fakirs article whose intro you have just read, for instance, we learnt that Geraldine was known professionally as The Amazing Miranda, we were told some of the other feats she performs, that she was a twenty-five-year-old mother of two, that her husband was also a magician and fakir . . . all the facts that were gathered at a face to face interview. In short, the main body of the article showed proof of what had been said in the intro, giving examples and evidence to back it up while, at the same time, keeping the reader entertained.

When you come to the end you need some sort of conclusion. Leave them with a bang, a punchline, even a laugh; something that emphatically says, *this is the end of the article*, while also wrapping up all the details that have gone before.

Here is how that particular feature on The Amazing Miranda ended:

'I'm into stunts now,' she says. 'My husband is going to teach me how to escape from a straightjacket while hanging upside down from a helicopter. Oh yes—and I aim to break the record for riding a motorbike through the world's longest tunnel of fire.'

Amazing!

Putting the words down

Now we come to the real nitty-gritty of article writing. Having gathered your facts and planned the shape of the article, you now have to put the words on paper. Anyone can write words down to make sentences but, if you want to make a name for yourself as a decent article writer, you must acquire a style of your own. Writing style is something that comes with practice and experience; it's something for which you gradually get a 'feel'.

That is something that is impossible to teach. What *can* be taught is a few basic rules that, if followed, will hopefully get you accepted and which will gradually lead you to a style of your own. Here is an eight-point guide to writing the acceptable article:

1. Keep it simple. Write the facts down in short, easy-to-understand, easy to read sentences. Write it down the way you imagine you might be telling a story to a friend. Never use a long and complicated sentence, however clever and correct it might be gramatically, when two or three might make things clearer. If you want an example of this style of writing, look no further than the chapter you are presently reading. That's the way it has been written.

2. Scan your sentences. Written words should have a pleasant flow to them, the sort of sentences that trip easily off the tongue. Very often, the alteration of an odd word here or there can give the stress to different syllables in the words and so to different sections within a sentence. If in doubt, read your work aloud. If you find yourself stumbling over certain parts, then re-write them. Your concern should be to entertain your reader while, at the same time, educating him to the subject of your article. If he has difficulty reading it, he will stop and pass on to something else.

3. Make a mess. Don't be afraid to produce an untidy manuscript. Every good writer thinks of points he should have written into sections a few paragraphs or a few pages before. In those circumstances, always go back and insert the extra words, scribbled in margins or anywhere else on the sheet that is convenient. It doesn't have to be neat. It doesn't even have to be intelligible to anyone else. All you need is a record of the way your article should look, ready for the final typing. That one, the manuscript that goes to the editor, should of course be as neat as possible.

4. Write and re-write. Never be afraid to tear something up and start again. Don't be ashamed of having to re-write whole sections at a time. Keep writing and re-writing until you have polished your article to what you consider to be perfection. Then, if time permits, put it away and come back to it fresh a few days later. It's amazing how many changes you might want to make.

5. Read everything in sight. The more you read, the better you will write. Don't be afraid to copy the style of others. You'll never actually acquire another writer's style but, in attempting to copy it, and that of others, you will gradually evolve a style of your own.

6. Contrast the length of sentences. Very often, an extremely effective way of putting ideas across is to write one long sentence followed by a short one. Like those in this very paragraph.

7. Forget your grammar. Well, not entirely. But there are certain rules you learnt at school which, in journalism, you are at liberty to break. Like starting a sentence with 'but' the way the one above started. Or writing a sentence with no real subject-verb-object construction. Like the one you've just read. And starting a sentence with 'and'. Gramatically, it's wrong; journalistically, and if the end justifies the means, it's okay.

8. Learn the correct meaning of words. The English language is rich in words that appear to mean one thing but which, on closer examination, actually mean something else. Work with two books constantly at your side: a good dictionary and a thesaurus. Whenever you are not entirely certain of a word's meaning, check it in the dictionary; whenever you need a different word for a particular meaning, check it in the thesaurus.

The finishing touch

When you have finished your article, you will need to give it a title. Titles should be slick, brief and to the point. They should sum up the subject of the article, but should not be too clever or obscure.

There is much that could be written about the art of titling but, strange as it might at first seem, it need not concern the freelance writer too much. The person who needs to be well versed in this particular art is the sub-editor of the magazine for which you are writing. Titling is one of his jobs and he will probably change yours to match the overall style of the magazine.

Features will fail to sell through bad writing, but they will never be rejected for bad titling. The best advice then is to write a simple, straightforward title and not be disappointed if it is changed.

Follow these points and there is no reason why you shouldn't soon be seeing your words in print alongside your pictures. If you have read everything in this chapter and still have doubts about your abilities, there is one further piece of advice that is worth following.

Don't worry about writing. Just start.

Any regular writer will tell you that the most difficult part is persuading yourself to make that initial start. Once you are over that hurdle, it's amazing how easily the words begin to flow.

And that's something you won't experience until you have tried it.

This chapter has been freely adapted from the lesson on article writing in the BFP Postal Course in Freelance Photography.

CARDS & CALENDARS

This section lists publishers of postcards, greetings cards and calendars, along with their requirements. Additionally, companies producing allied material, such as posters and prints have been included for convenience. With the exception of postcard producers, who have traditionally offered rather meagre fees for freelance material, fees in this area are generally quite good. However, only those who can produce precisely what is required as far as subject matter, quality and format are concerned, are likely to succeed.

Traditionally, greetings card and calendar publishers have required large format transparencies of the highest quality. While they still demand optimum quality material, the requirement for the really large format has eased up in recent years. Just as a decade ago the $10'' \times 8''$ transparency gave way to the $5'' \times 4''$, so the $5'' \times 4''$ has now yielded to the 6×6 cm. Well, almost. The majority of the companies listed here will consider 6×6 cm, and there are half-a-dozen firms that will even consider 35mm.

The need for material of the highest quality cannot be too strongly emphasised. The greetings card market, in particular, is highly specialised with very specific requirements. If you aim to break into this market, you must be very sure of your photographic technique. You must be able to produce professional quality material which is pin sharp and has excellent colour saturation. You must also know *exactly* what the market requires. The listing will help you (particularly the Wilson Brothers' listings which includes very detailed information about the requirements of a greetings card publisher), but you should also carry out your own field study, by examining the photographic greetings cards on general sale. Unfortunately, there are fewer of them on sale than was once the case, many publishers employing only art or graphics nowadays. This means that there is greater competition than ever to supply material for those photographic cards that are produced.

None of this is to suggest that the calendar market is necessarily easier to supply. It is equally demanding, though fortunately there are still large numbers of calendars using photographs being produced every year. Once again, though, you must be sure of your photographic technique and be able to produce top quality work. Before submitting material, make sure you know *exactly* what the market requires. Read carefully *all* of the listings that follow; they all contain information likely to help you. And again, make a point of studying the calendars that you see on general sale and hanging up in offices and in other places you visit. Don't rely solely on what *you* think would make a good calendar picture; familiarise yourself with the type of pictures actually being used by calendar publishers.

Rights and fees

Where given to us by the company concerned, fees have been quoted. Some companies prefer to negotiate fees individually, depending upon the type of material on offer. If you are new to this field, the best plan is to submit your transparencies (preferably after making an initial enquiry, outlining the material you have available), and let the company concerned make you an offer. Generally speaking, you should not accept less than about £30 for Greetings Card or Calendar Rights. Remember, you are not selling your copyright in the transparency for this fee; you are free to submit the same transparency to any *non-competitive* market (for example, a magazine), at a later date. But you should not attempt to sell a transparency to another greetings card publisher once you have sold Greetings Card Rights to a competing firm.

JOSEPH ARNOLD & CO. LTD.
Church Bridge Works, Accrington, Lancs. Tel: 0254 382121.
Contact: J. M. Hill, Art Director.
Action subjects suitable for children's or male greetings cards acceptable in 6 × 6 cm square format, but scenic subjects must be 5″ × 4″ minimum. Subjects: cottages, boats, autumn scenes, scenes featuring water.
Fees: £45.00–£65.00.
Joseph Arnold buys exclusively for Webb Ivory Ltd., Raphael Tuck & Sons, Studio Cards Ltd., Delgado Ltd., Arnold Barton Cards Ltd. and Image Arts.

ATHENA INTERNATIONAL
PO Box 13, Bishops Stortford, Herts. Tel: 0279 56627/8.
Contact: B. M. Everitt, Head of Publishing.
Requires material for posters. All types of subjects considered, especially humour. Prefers 6 × 6 cm or larger formats, but will consider 35mm if it is of the highest quality.

BEAUCARDS LTD. (incorporating RIDGEWAY CARDS)
Unit 2, Southfield Road Trading Estate, Nailsea, Avon BS19 1JB. Tel: 0272 855013.
Contact: E. J. Golding, Design Manager.
Publishers of greetings cards. Interested in floral arrangements, landscape and scenic views (not postcard type), rural subjects, children (not studio poses), gardens, Christmas arrangements, old inns and pubs, sports (including professional football), cars, ships, sailing, general male interest, nostalgia. All outdoor subjects must be sunny and bright. Minimum transparency size: 6 × 6 cm (except for pro. football material where 35mm is acceptable).
Fees: £60.00 upwards for World Greetings Card Rights.

CASTLE PUBLISHING CO. LTD.
Great George Street, Preston, Lancs PR1 1TJ. Tel: 0772 59267.
Contact: Irene A. Nicholas, Design Manager.
Publishes greetings cards and calendars. A variety of subjects considered, including sports, hobbies, vehicles, animals, etc. Minimum transparency: 5″ × 4″.
Fees: approximately £60.00–£80.00 for Worldwide Repro Rights for five years.

CAVENDISH CARDS LTD.
Wildeck House, Reform Road, Maidenhead, Berkshire SL6 8BX. Tel: 0628 36123.
Contact: S. Williamson, Director.
'Occasionally' buys transparencies from freelances for its range of greetings cards. Subjects: landscapes, animals, vehicles, floral, Christmas, etc. Minimum transparency size: 6 × 6 cm, prefers 5″ × 4″.
Fees: £50.00 for World Greetings Card Rights.

E. T. W. DENNIS & SONS LTD.
Printing House Sq., Melrose Street, Scarborough, Yorks. Tel: 0723 61317.
Contact: C. G. Rhodes, Managing Director.
Postcards and calendars. Requires views of seaside and inland towns, countryside showing

well known places of interest, floral, animals, steam locomotives, diesel locomotives, interesting cars, traction engines, etc. Prefers 35mm or $2\frac{1}{4} \times 3\frac{1}{4}''$ although any size acceptable if it will mask to postcard proportions.

J. ARTHUR DIXON (DRG UK) LTD.
Forest Side, Newport, Isle of Wight PO30 5QW. Tel: 0983 523381.
Contacts: Miss J. Warder (greetings cards); Mr. C. Johnson (postcards).
Greetings cards and postcards. Prefers to work from 5″ × 4″ Ektachromes. "We are always willing to consider interesting work from freelances".
Fees: from £10.00 (presumably for postcards) to £90.00.

SIMON ELVIN LTD.
Wooburn Industrial Park, Wooburn Green, Bucks HP10 0PE. Tel: 06285 26711.
Contact: Simon Elvin, Managing Director.
Greetings cards. Subjects: florals and landscapes. No minimum or preferred transparency size specified.

GIESEN & WOLFF LTD.
Kaygee House, Dallington, Northampton NN5 7QW. Tel: 0604 55411.
Contact: Gordon W. Good, Director.
Greetings cards, calendars and jigsaw puzzles. Requires floral, landscapes, cottages, sports and subjects suitable for teenage birthday cards. Minimum transparency size is normally 5″ × 4″, but will consider 35mm in exceptional circumstances.
Fees: negotiable. Worldwide rights required.

KARDONIA LTD.
Farrier Street, Worcester. Tel: 0905 611294.
Contact: P. Everden, Art Editor.
Greetings cards. Requires British landscapes, cottages and floral subjects (mainly single and multiple rose themes). Prefers 5″ × 4″ but will consider 6 × 6 cm. Will consider material at any time of the year, but the critical periods are March/April and October/November.
Fees: negotiable.

LOWE ASTON CALENDARS LTD.
Saltash, Cornwall PL12 4HL. Tel: 075 55 2233.
5″ × 4″ transparencies only of scenes, animals, children and pin-ups.
Fees: negotiable.

THE MEDICI SOCIETY LTD.
34–42 Pentonville Road, London N1 9HG. Tel: 01-837 7099.
Greetings cards. Interested in flowers, animals and birds in their natural surroundings, snowscenes and woodland scenes, but not views of the picture postcard type. 35mm transparencies can be accepted if of a high professional quality, but larger formats are preferred.
Fees: from £60.00.

PHOTO PRODUCTION LTD.
Featherby Road, Gillingham, Kent ME8 6PJ. Tel: 0634 33241.
Contact: I. A. Surita, Publishing Manager.
Greetings cards. Subjects: views, cottages, public houses, veteran and vintage cars, boats and flowers. Minimum transparency size: 5″ × 4″. All transparencies must be of the upright format, be bright and colourful and have clear uncluttered space at the top to overprint the greeting.
Fees: negotiable.

PILLANS & WILSON LTD.
20 Bernard Terrace, Edinburgh EH8 9NY. Tel: 031-667 2036.
Contact: Ian Wilson, Chairman.
Calendars. 5″ × 4″ transparencies of Scottish and North of England scenes, all seasons. Transparencies normally retained for several weeks before a decision can be given. Submissions in November only.
Fees: negotiable.

ROYLE PUBLICATIONS LTD.
Royle House, Wenlock Road, London N1 7ST. Tel: 01-253 7654.
Contact: Anthony Hilder, Art Director.
Calendars. Scenic subjects only suitable for 'Moods of Nature' and 'Gardens of Britain' calendars. Best time to submit: September. Minimum transparency size: 5″ × 4″.
Fees: negotiable.

RUST CRAFT GREETINGS CARDS (UK) LTD.
Mill Street East, Dewsbury, West Yorkshire WF12 9AW. Tel: 0924 465200.
Contact: Mrs Jeanette Middleton, Editorial and Creative Administration.
Greetings cards. Will consider any subject suitable for greetings card publication. Minimum transparency size: 6 × 6 cm but prefers 5″ × 4″ or 10″ × 8″.
Fees: £60.00–£120.00 for World Greetings Card Rights for five years.

J. SALMON LTD.
100 London Road, Sevenoaks, Kent TN13 1BB. Tel: 0732 452381.
Calendars, postcards and Christmas cards. Requires flower arrangement studies, cat and dog studies, horse studies, rose studies, countryside and farmyard scenes, natural history and garden subjects. 5″ × 4″ preferred; occasionally buys 6 × 6 cm, and will consider 35mm in the natural history field (only).
Fees: 'depend upon the type of material offered, and would be quoted on sight of the transparencies'.

W. N. SHARP LTD.
Bingley Road, Bradford BD9 6SD. Tel: 0274 41365.
Contact: R. Hutchings, Publishing Director.
Greetings cards. Subjects: all motorsport; action shots of sporting subjects; vintage vehicles; vintage aircraft; scenes with middleground or foreground interest (but not human); shots of

paintings out of copyright especially winter scenes and views of London. Minimum transparency size: 6 × 6 cm.
Fees: 'negotiable for World Greetings Card Rights for all time'.

UNIVERSAL GREETINGS LTD.
Dowgate Works, Douglas Road, Tonbridge, Kent TN9 2TS. Tel: 0732 351216.
Contact: Mrs E. Mays, Publishing Director.
Greetings cards. Subjects: floral, scenic, sporting, animals, veteran cars, etc. Minimum transparency size: 35mm.
Fees: £50.00–£80.00 for World Greetings Card Rights.

ANDREW VALENTINE LTD.
Arrol Road, Wester, Gourdie Industrial Estate, Dundee DD2 4UJ. Tel: 0382 644111.
Greetings cards. Requires floral, animals, wedding subjects, juvenile designs suitable for children's birthday cards and pictorial scenes. Prefers 5″ × 4″ but will consider top quality 6 × 6 cm transparencies of subjects not readily available on the larger format.
Fees: negotiable.

VALENTINES OF DUNDEE LTD.
PO Box 74, Kinnoull Road, Dundee DD1 9NQ.
Contact: Director, Product Management.
Greetings cards. Requires floral, animal and scenic subjects. Minimum transparency: 5″ × 4″.

WHITETHORN PRESS LTD.
PO Box 237, Thomson House, Withy Grove, Manchester. Tel: 061-834 1234.
Contact: Editor-in-Chief.
Calendars. Interested in good transparencies for range of scenic calendars covering the counties of Cheshire, Lancashire, Yorkshire, Warwickshire and Worcestershire, Gloucestershire and Avon. Vertical format preferred. Minimum transparency size: 6 × 6 cm. Pictures must be identifiable—a woodland scene which could have been taken anywhere in Britain, for example, would not be acceptable.
Fees: negotiable.

WILSON BROS. GREETING CARDS LTD.
Academy House, 45 Uxbridge Road, Hayes, Mddx. Tel: 01-573 3877.
Contact: E. W. Stewart, Creative Manager.
Greetings cards. The Creative Manager writes: 'We find that it is technically better to use transparencies either 5″ × 4″ or 10″ × 8″ in size, but good 6 × 6 cm square shots are acceptable. But definitely nothing smaller than that. In all cases, a vertical format is preferred, although some landscape shapes could be considered.

   'The floral market is the largest and most competitive. To succeed in this is to make the conventional (in the main, rose subjects) different by means of clever lighting effects, background treatment and presentation. You will not sell a straight floral subject with plain background and flat lighting however perfect the flowers or technical aspect may be. Unusual props also help to give a hackneyed subject a sales lift.

'Exposure must be accurate as good colour saturation is essential. All greetings cards are sold to a very large extent on colour appeal. Underexposed or sombre pictures are out.

'Roses are still the most popular flowers for greetings cards, but in recent times the odd different bloom is included in a range. On a roughly one in three basis, chrysanths, daisies and anemonies are used, but it is still the rose that leads the field.

'Landscapes are mostly used in the male bracket and so should obviously be taken with this in mind. Unfortunately for the photographer, these again have to be vertical in format. Subjects range from boats (sea and river), cars in country settings, veteran cars, fishing (sea and river), cottages and general rustic views. Only a limited number of views are used for the female section and these usually take the form of flower gardens and cottages.

'Again, colour saturation is vital; subjects must be taken in bright sunshine at small aperture for large depth of field. Skies should be bright blue with preferably the odd white cloud or two. It is extremely unlikely that a shot taken on a day without sunshine would ever sell to a greetings card publisher.

'There is not such a large demand for animal studies; they are, of course, used, but in far less quantity than florals or landscapes. There are, in fact, certain areas in the North where an animal design is difficult to sell. However, those that are used require all the colour aspects already mentioned and again fall into two categories: For male designs: Alsations, Great Danes, Boxers, etc., and for female designs: poodles, puppies and almost any fluffy appealing cat or dog. Horses are not widely used these days but a small percentage do find their way into the male bracket.

'Child shots are always in short supply, although not used in vast quantities. These need to feature children aged between three and fourteen engaged in some form of activity; definitely not posed portraits. Action shots, although not widely used, are also difficult to obtain.

'In the majority of cases, space at the top for a greeting is required. However, more and more companies are dropping photographic designs into panels or creating subsidiary art to go with these to produce different overall effects. Because of this, a good picture, even one excluding the space for a greeting, is purchasable.'
Fees: negotiable.

AGENCIES

Picture agents are in the business of selling pictures. They are not in the business of teaching photography or advising photographers how to produce saleable work—although they can sometimes prove remarkably helpful in the latter respect to those who show promise. Their purpose is strictly a business one: to meet the demand for stock pictures from such markets as magazine and book publishers, advertising agencies, tour operators, greetings card and calendar publishers, and many more. Their markets also include audio visual firms and television companies looking for stills of particular subjects for particular programmes. A typical agency has many thousands of pictures in its files, each one of which is carefully categorised and filed so that it can be easily located when an editor or picture buyer wants to see a selection of pictures of a particular subject.

If you hope to interest an agency in your work, you must be able to produce pictures which the agent feels are likely to sell to one of his markets. For, although the acceptance of your work by an agent is no guarantee that it will sell, an agent will not clutter up his files with pictures which do not stand a reasonably good chance of finding a market. Many amateurs look upon an agent as a 'last resort'; they have been unable to sell their photographs themselves, so they think they might as well try unloading them on an agent. This is the wrong attitude. No agent will succeed in placing pictures which are quite simply unmarketable. In any event, it's better for the photographer to gain some experience in marketing his work himself before he approaches an agent. The photographer who has had at least some success in selling his pictures is in a far better position to approach an agent.

Even if you eventually decide that you want to place all your potentially saleable material with an agent, you cannot expect to leave every aspect of the business to him. You must continue to study the market, watching for trends; you must continue to study published pictures. For example, if your speciality is travel material, you must use every opportunity to study the type of pictures published in tour brochures and other markets using such material. Only by doing this—by being aware of the market—can you hope to continue to provide your agent with marketable pictures.

The subjects required

Agents handle pictures of virtually every subject under the sun. Some specialise in particular subjects—such as sport, natural history, etc.—while others act as general agents, covering the whole spectrum of subject matter. Any picture that could be published in one form or another is a suitable picture for an agency.

Commission and copyright

Agents generally work on a commission basis, 50 per cent being the most usual rate—if they receive £30 for reproduction rights in a particular picture, the photographer will get £15 of this.

A 50 per cent commission rate may seem high, but it should be remembered that a picture agency, like any other business, has substantial overheads to cover. Apart from office rent, rates and staff salaries, the agent has to cover the costs involved in making prospective buyers aware of the pictures he has available. Many agencies produce colour catalogues featuring selections of the pictures they have available. Nevertheless, agencies are sometimes willing to negotiate a lower rate of commission with their more prized contributors.

Agents do not normally sell pictures outright; indeed, they should never do so without the permission of the photographer concerned, who would normally still retain copyright in all pictures placed with the agent. They merely sell 'reproduction rights', the transparency normally being loaned to the buyer for a specified period of time while printing plates are produced.

Agents will sometimes offer to buy pictures outright from a photographer, instead of working on the normal commission basis. The price in these cases will be a matter for negotiation between photographer and agent, but it should be remembered that, once a picture is sold outright, the photographer has effectively disposed of his copyright and has no further rights in the picture.

A long-term investment

When dealing with a photographer for the first time, most agents require a minimum initial submission—which can consist of anything from 100–500 pictures. Most also stipulate that you leave your material with them for a minimum period of anything from one to five years.

When an agent takes on the work of a new photographer, he is involved in a lot of work—categorising, filing, cross-indexing, and in most cases, re-mounting the transparencies in the agency's mounts (or, at least, adding the agency's name to the existing mounts). His next step will often be to make it known to picture buyers that these new pictures are available, sometimes including reproductions of them in any new catalogues or publicity material currently being prepared. Having involved himself in all this work and expense, it is not unreasonable for him to want to be given a fair chance to market the pictures. If the photographer is able to demand the return of his work after only a few months, the agent will have been involved in a lot of work and expense for nothing.

Dealing with an agent must therefore be considered a long-term investment. Having initially placed, say, a few hundred pictures with an agent, it could be several months before any are selected by a picture buyer, and even longer before any monies are seen by the photographer. Normally, the photographer will also be expected to regularly submit new material to the library. Indeed, only when you have several hundred pictures lodged with the library, can you hope for regular sales, and a reasonable return on your investment.

Making an approach

Many agents prefer to meet new photographers personally to see and discuss their work. It is not a good idea, however, to turn up on an agent's doorstep without an appointment. The best plan is to write or telephone the agency of your choice, outlining the material you have available, and possibly, details of any sales you have made yourself. If the agency is interested, they may suggest a mutually convenient appointment when you can bring your material along—or they may suggest that you initially post some samples to them.

But remember that there is little point in approaching an agency until you have a sizeable collection of potentially saleable material. Most agents will not feel it worth their while dealing with a photographer who has only a dozen or so pictures which he thinks are marketable; it just wouldn't be worth all the work and expense involved. And the chances of the photographer seeing a worthwhile return on just a dozen pictures placed with an agent are remote indeed—he'll be lucky to see more than one cheque in ten years!

In the listings that follow, you'll find full information on more than forty agencies: the subjects they handle, the markets they supply, their terms of business including any minimum initial submission and retention period, commission charged on sales effected, etc. Prefacing the listings you'll find an Agency Subject Index; this can be used to find the names of agents handling subjects you can supply.

Remember: simply placing material with an agent doesn't guarantee sales—and no agent can sell material for which there is no market. On the other hand, if you are able to produce good quality, marketable work, and can team up with the right agent, you could see a very worthwhile return from the sale of your pictures.

Agency Subject Index

Abstracts
ACE Photo Agency
Vision International

Aerial
Aerofilms Ltd

Architecture & Archaeology
Ancient Art & Architecture Photo Library
Bruce Coleman Ltd
Middle East Photographic Archive
Vision International

Art & Antiques
Ancient Art & Architecture Photo Library
The Bridgeman Art Library

Botany
A–Z Botanical Collection Ltd
Natural Science Photos

Business & Industry
ACE Photo Agency
Art Directors Photo Library
Colorific Photo Library Ltd
Daily Telegraph Colour Library

Fashion & Beauty
BIPS—Bernsen's International Press Service Ltd
Camera Press Ltd

General (all subjects)
ACE Photo Agency
Adams Picture Library
Art Directors Photo Library
Barnabys Picture Library
J. Allan Cash Ltd
Colorific Photo Library Ltd
Daily Telegraph Colour Library
Elisabeth Photo Library London Ltd
Susan Griggs Agency Ltd
The Robert Harding Picture Library
Alan Hutchison Library
The Northern Picture Library
Photo Library International
Pictor International Ltd
Picturepoint Ltd
Paul Popper Ltd
Spectrum Colour Library
Tony Stone Associates Ltd
John Topham Picture Library
Vision International
Woodmansterne Publications Ltd
ZEFA (UK) Ltd

Geography & World Environment
J. Allan Cash Ltd
Bruce Coleman Ltd
Geoslides
Interfoto Archives Ltd
Natural Science Photos
Picturepoint Ltd

Glamour
Barnabys Picture Library
Pictorial Press Ltd
Rex Features Ltd
Spectrum Colour Library

Historical
Ancient Art & Architecture Photo
  Library
The Bridgeman Art Library
Pictorial Press Ltd
John Topham Picture Library

Landscapes
Art Directors Photo Library
Scene International Colour Picture Library
Vision International

Natural History
Aquila Photographics
Bruce Coleman Ltd
Frank Lane Agency
Natural Science Photos
Seaphot/Natural Earth Pictures

News & Current Affairs
Black Star Publishing Co. Ltd
Camera Press Ltd
Keystone Press Agency Ltd
Rex Features Ltd
United Press International (UK) Ltd

People/Human Behaviour
ACE Photo Agency
Art Directors Photo Library
Daily Telegraph Colour Library
Susan Griggs Agency Ltd
Interfoto Archives Ltd

Personalities
Black Star Publishing Co. Ltd
Camera Press Ltd
Monitor International
Pictorial Press Ltd
Rex Features Ltd

Photo-journalism
BIPS—Bernsen's International Press Service
  Ltd
Camera Press Ltd
United Press International (UK) Ltd

Science & Technology
BIPS—Bernsen's International Press Service
Ltd

Sport
All-Sport Photographic Ltd
Daily Telegraph Colour Library

Transport
Art Directors Photo Library
Pictorial Press Ltd

Travel/Tourist
Feature-Pix Colour Library

Tony Stone Associates Ltd
Travel Trade Photography

Underwater
Natural Science Photos
Seaphot/Planet Earth Pictures

ACE PHOTO AGENCY*
22 Maddox Street, Mayfair, London W1R 9PG. Tel: 01-629 0303.
Principal: John Panton.
Specialist subjects/requirements: Humour and human behaviour; industry, technology and alternative energy; nature and the environment; world travel; music and the performing arts; abstracts and textures.
Markets supplied: Audio visual; design consultants; advertising; publishing—books and magazines.
Stock: B&W and colour. 35mm to 10″ × 8″ colour transparencies. 10″ × 8″ reference print plus negative in the case of black and white.
Usual terms of business: Minimum 3 years retention of material. Minimum initial submission: 100 accepted pictures.
Commission: 50 per cent.
Additional information and/or advice for intending contributors: 'We look for high quality work with good composition and precise captions.'

ADAMS PICTURE LIBRARY*
17/18 Rathbone Place, London W1. Tel: 01-636 1468.
Principal: John Adams.
Specialist subjects/requirements: All subjects except hot news.
Markets supplied: All markets including advertising and publishing.
Stock: Colour only. 35mm and 6 × 6 cm transparencies.
Usual terms of business: No minimum submission. No minimum retention period, although 'written notice is required'.
Commission: 50 per cent.

AEROFILMS LTD.
Gate Studios, Station Road, Boreham Wood, Herts WD6 1EJ. Tel: 01-207 0666.
Principal: W. H. Brooker.
Specialist subjects/requirements: Air to ground and air to air only. 'We are prepared to consider for inclusion in our library, any aerial photography that may be submitted if not already included from the work of our own photographers'.
Stock: B&W and colour. Minimum 6 × 6 cm colour transparencies.
Usual terms of business: Negotiable: 'Our prime business is not that of an agency'.
Commission: Negotiable.

Additional information: 'The exact location of every photograph must be specified. We will not look at 35mm transparencies nor any photograph that has been taken through the windows of an aircraft'.

ALL-SPORT PHOTOGRAPHIC LTD.
All-Sport House, 55/57 Martin Way, Morden, Surrey SM4 4AH. Tel: 01-543 0988.
Principals: Tony Duffy, Steve Powell.
Specialist subjects/requirements: All sports. Most material is supplied by All-Sport staff photographers, but will consider top quality generic colour shots of an unusual or spectacular nature.
Markets supplied: Prestige publications at home and abroad; advertising, commercial, etc.
Stock: Colour only. 35mm transparencies.
Usual terms of business: Negotiable.
Commission: By negotiation, but usually 50 per cent.
Additional information: 'We do not accept much work from outside contributors unless the work is exceptionally good in an area that our own photographers would not normally cover.'

ANCIENT ART & ARCHITECTURE PHOTO LIBRARY*
6 Kenton Road, Harrow, Middx. Tel: 01-422 1214.
Principal: Ronald Sheridan.
Specialist subjects/requirements: All historical material, including buildings of every period from archaeological pre-history up to 19th century. Historical art and artefacts mainly from pre-history up to the Middle Ages; everything which can illustrate the civilisations of the ancient world, its cultures and technologies, religion, ideas, beliefs and development. Also, warfare, weapons, fortifications and military historical movements. Statues, portraits and contemporary illustrations of historically important people—kings and other rulers.
Markets supplied: Mainly book publishers, but including magazines and TV.
Stock: Colour 6 × 6 cm preferred. 'Only the rarest items accepted in 35mm and then only if most critical standards are met.'
Usual terms of business: 3 years minimum retention of material; 24 months notice of return.
Commission: 50 per cent.
Additional information: 'All submissions must be accompanied by return s.a.e. Only material of the highest quality can be considered. Verticals must be vertical always. Historical buildings or sites must not include cars or brightly clothed tourists whose presence would destroy the illusion of the period which the author works hard to create. Normally no people should be visible but occasionally one person (not obviously posed) where necessary to show scale and never brightly dressed unless in local costume (e.g. an Arab). All material must be fully and historically accurately captioned with names, dates, places, etc.'

ART DIRECTORS PHOTO LIBRARY*
Image House, 86 Haverstock Hill, London NW3. Tel: 01-485 9325/6.
Principal: Jack Stanley.
Specialist subjects/requirements: Landscapes, industry, skies and seas, people, geographical, tourist interest, transport, animals, glamour, architecture, interiors, food, vintage cars and planes, business, etc.
Markets supplied: Advertising agencies, design groups, magazines, audio visual producers, record companies, book publishers, calendar and poster printers.
Stock: Colour only. All formats including 35mm.
Usual terms of business: No minimum contribution. 36 months minimum retention.
Commission: 50 per cent.

AQUILA PHOTOGRAPHICS
PO Box 1, Studley, Warwickshire B80 7JG. Tel: 052 785 2357.
Principals: Alan J. Richards, Jennifer M. Richards.
Specialist subjects/requirements: All natural history. Birds a speciality.
Markets supplied: Book and magazine publishers, calendars, greetings cards, TV, video, etc.
Stock: B&W and colour. 6 × 6 cm transparencies preferred but 35mm acceptable.
Usual terms of business: Minimum initial submission of 100 transparencies and/or 100 B&W prints.
Commission: 40 per cent.

A–Z BOTANICAL COLLECTION LTD.*
Holmwood House, Mid Holmwood, Dorking, Surrey RH5 4HE. Tel: 0306 6130.
Principals: M. H. MacAndrew, J. Finlay.
Specialist subjects/requirements: All aspects of botany (not just flowers).
Markets supplied: Publishers and advertising agencies.
Stock: Colour only. Minimum 6 × 6 cm transparencies.
Usual terms of business: No minimum initial submission, but contributors expected to 'continually supply' pictures. Minimum retention period: 3 years.
Commission: 50 per cent.
Additional information: 'We do not want UK subject matter except outstanding garden scenes. We are always prepared to consider overseas material, but it must be captioned with Latin botanic name.'

BARNABY'S PICTURE LIBRARY*
19 Rathbone Street, London W1P 1AF. Tel: 01-636 6128.
Principals: Ken Lambert, Gill Stewart.
Specialist subjects/requirements: All subjects, excluding 'hot' news.
Markets supplied: Books, magazines, television, advertising, audio visual.
Stock: B&W and colour. All formats colour.

Usual terms of business: Minimum submission: 200 pictures. Minimum retention period: 4 years.
Commission: 50 per cent.

BIPS—BERNSEN'S INTERNATIONAL PRESS SERVICE LTD.

2 Barbon Close, Great Ormond Street, London WC1N 3JS. Tel: 01-405 2723.
Principals: Theo C. Bernsen (Managing Director), M. E. de Vries.
Specialist subjects/requirements: General interest feature material; popular science; technology; medicine; education; inventions; animal situations; material suitable for women's magazines, etc.
Markets supplied: Magazines at home and abroad.
Stock: B&W and colour. 35mm and 6 × 6 cm transparencies.
Usual terms of business: Negotiable.
Commission: 'Depends upon material. We also buy rights.'
Additional information: Specialises primarily in photo features and general feature material. 'We prefer to get story ideas which we can assign.' Leaflet containing guidelines for photographers available. Only deals with professional photo-journalists.

BLACK STAR PUBLISHING CO. LTD.*

Cliffords Inn, Fetter Lane, London EC4Y 1DA. Tel: 01-636 1317.
Principals: R. H. Seedorff, G. A. Boreham.
Specialist subjects/requirements: Personalities and events.
Markets supplied: All markets worldwide.
Stock: B&W and colour. 35mm transparencies.
Usual terms of business: Negotiable.
Commission: 50 per cent.

THE BRIDGEMAN ART LIBRARY*

19 Chepstow Road, London W2 5BP. Tel: 01-727 4065 and 01-229 7420.
Principal: Mrs. Harriet Bridgeman.
Specialist subjects/requirements: European and Oriental paintings and prints, antiques, antiquities, arms and armour, botanical subjects, ethnography, general historical subjects and personalities, maps and manuscripts, natural history, topography and transport.
Markets supplied: Publishing, advertising, television, greetings cards, calendars.
Stock: Mainly colour but some B&W. Minimum 5″ × 4″ transparencies.
Commission: 50 per cent.

CAMERA PRESS LTD.*

Russell Court, Coram Street, London WC1. Tel: 01-837 4488/1300/9393/0606.
Principals: Tom Blau (Managing Director), D. A. Donald.
Specialist subjects/requirements: Mainly photo reportage. Also portraits of newsworthy personalities. Material suitable for women's magazines: beauty, interior decoration, do-it-yourself, child care, exercises.

Stock: B&W and colour. All formats.
Usual terms of business: 'By mutual agreement.'
Commission: 50 per cent.
Additional information: 'Please submit only material that is excellent artistically, technically and, ideally, also journalistically.'

J. ALLAN CASH LTD.
74 South Ealing Road, London W5 4QB. Tel: 01-840 4141.
Principal: Alan Greeley.
Specialist subjects/requirements: 'All types of technically good and interesting subjects reflecting the world and its people.'
Markets supplied: General and educational publishing, travel, advertising, design.
Stock: B&W and colour. 35mm transparencies accepted if of top quality. Prefers roll-film and 5″ × 4″.
Usual terms of business: Minimum initial submission: 100 pictures. Minimum period of retention: 2 years; 3 months notice of withdrawal.
Commission: 50 per cent.
Additional information: 'Please write in for further details first.'

BRUCE COLEMAN LTD.*
17 Windsor Street, Uxbridge, Middx UB8 1AB. Tel: Uxbridge 57094.
Principals: B. Coleman, G. Coleman, P. D. James.
Specialist subjects/requirements: Natural history; geographical; travel; scenics; archaeology; medical; science; anthropology; geological.
Markets supplied: Book publishers, advertising agencies, calendar publishers.
Stock: Colour only. 35mm, 6 × 6 cm and 5″ × 4″.
Usual terms of business: Minimum submission: 500 transparencies. Minimum period of retention: 5 years.
Commission: 50 per cent.
Additional information: Contributors are asked to write for literature first.

COLORIFIC PHOTO LIBRARY LTD.*
Garden Offices, Gilray House—Rear, Gloucester Terrace, London W2. Tel: 01-723 5031; 01-402 9595.
Principals: Terence and Shirley Le Goubin.
Specialist subjects/requirements: General top quality, mainly photojournalistic material. Also, industry; agriculture; beaches; couples; sunsets.
Markets supplied: Advertising, books, brochures, calendars.
Stock: Mainly colour. 35mm.
Usual terms of business: Minimum initial submission: 500 transparencies. Minimum retention period: 3 years.
Commission: 50 per cent.
Additional information: 'Material must be fully captioned and carry photographer's name.'

DAILY TELEGRAPH COLOUR LIBRARY*

Gordon House, 75–79 Farringdon Street, London EC4A 4BL. Tel: 01-353 4242 ext. 3686/7/8.

Specialist subjects/requirements: Agriculture, animals, architecture, catering, commerce, ecology, education, entertainment, fashion, health, horticulture, industry, landscape, military, occupations, people, personalities, religion, technology, transport, sport.

Markets supplied: Advertising and publishing.

Stock: Colour only: 35mm, 6 × 6 cm and 5″ × 4″.

Usual terms of business: Minimum initial submission: 100 'followed up with regular additional submissions'. Minimum retention period: one year. Prefers exclusive representation.

Commission: 50 per cent.

Additional information: 'We're always seeking new top quality material on a variety of subjects, particularly action, animals and sports, natural and man-made disasters, bad weather (including electrical storms), people (especially crowds, children and families), industry and technology.'

ELISABETH PHOTO LIBRARY LONDON LTD.*

51 Cleveland Street, London W1A 4ER. Tel: 01-580 7285/6.

Principal: Ms. Elisabeth Templeton.

Specialist subjects/requirements: Geography; pop music; travel; space; sport; animals; art; commerce; agriculture; religion; etc.

Markets supplied: Educational and general publishers, advertising.

Stock: Mainly colour. 6 × 6 cm preferred.

Usual terms of business: Minimum initial submission: 500. Minimum retention period: 60 months.

Commission: 40 per cent.

FEATURE-PIX COLOUR LIBRARY*

21 Great Chapel Street, London W1V 3AQ. Tel: 01-437 2121.

Principals: Gerry Brenes and Ken Hackett.

Specialist subjects/requirements: Travel material: cities, resorts, hotels worldwide plus girls, couples and families on holiday suitable for travel brochure use.

Markets supplied: Tour operators, airlines, design houses, advertising agencies.

Stock: Colour only. 6 × 6 cm preferred, otherwise 6 × 7 cm and 5″ × 4″. No 35mm.

Usual terms of business: No minimum submission but usually likes the chance of placing material for minimum period of 2 years.

Commission: 50 per cent.

FOTOBANK INTERNATIONAL COLOUR LIBRARY*

30 Kingly Court, London W1R 5LE. Tel: 01-734 4764/2915.

Principal: Ray Daffurn.

Specialist subjects/requirements: English subjects and landscapes; natural history; food and drink; growing section of international subjects.
Markets supplied: Travel and leisure markets.
Stock: Colour only. 35mm, 6 × 6 cm and 6 × 7 cm.
Usual terms of business: Minimum initial submission: 200 transparencies on two or three subjects. Minimum retention period: 5 years.
Commission: 50 per cent.

GEOSLIDES (PHOTOGRAPHY)
4 Christian Fields, London SW16 3JZ. Tel: 01-764 6292.
Principal: John Douglas.
Specialist subjects/requirements: Africa (S. of Sahara); Asia; Antarctic; Arctic; sub-Arctic (including Scandinavia, N. Canada, Alaska). Subjects of general and educational interest.
Markets supplied: Books and magazines, advertising and television.
Stock: Mainly colour. 35mm.
Usual terms of business: Normal initial submission: 500 pictures.
Commission: 50 per cent (UK sales); 60 per cent (overseas sales).
Additional information: Send s.a.e. for leaflet before making any other inquiry.

SUSAN GRIGGS AGENCY LTD.*
17 Victoria Grove, London W8 5RW. Tel: 01-584 6738.
Principal: Susan Griggs.
Specialist subjects/requirements: Travel, people, nudes, decorating.
Markets supplied: Books and magazines, advertising, design houses.
Stock: Colour. 35mm.
Usual terms of business: Minimum retention period: 3 years.
Commission: 50 per cent.
Additional information: 'We are now only taking in new material if it is of a subject or place we do not have in our files. Photographers should therefore write in first, indicating the subjects they have available. We need to be the exclusive agent in the UK for the photographers we represent. Transparencies must be technically good and visually interesting. They must also be fully and accurately captioned.'

THE ROBERT HARDING PICTURE LIBRARY*
5 Botts Mews, Chepstow Road, London W2 5AG. Tel: 01-229 2234/5.
Principal: Robert Harding.
Specialist subjects/requirements: People, places and objects worldwide.
Markets supplied: Publishers, advertising agencies, design groups, calendar publishers, etc.
Stock: B&W and colour. 35mm transparencies.
Usual terms of business: An initial sample of 100 transparencies 'to enable us to judge quality and saleability'. Minimum retention period: 3 years; 12 months notice of withdrawal.
Commission: 50 per cent.

ALAN HUTCHISON LIBRARY

31 Kildare Terrace, London W2.Tel: 01-229 7386.

Principals: Alan Hutchison, Sarah Hawkins, Vanessa Fletcher.

Specialist subjects/requirements: World-wide coverage of agriculture, industry, landscapes, festivals and ceremonies, decoration, religion, urban and village life, tourism, flora and fauna, medicine and education, architecture, art, craft, etc. etc.

Markets supplied: Publishing, company reports, calendars, advertising, audio visual.

Stock: Mostly colour (35mm and 6 × 6 cm), 'but we do take B&W if it complements a colour collection'.

Usual terms of business: Minimum initial submission: 500. No minimum retention period.

Commission: 50 per cent.

Additional information: 'We are always interested in seeing new pictures. They should be of a good illustrative style. We try to embrace all aspects of any country we cover.'

INTERFOTO ARCHIVES LTD.

110 Kennington Road, London SE11 6RE. Tel: 01-582 3060.

Principals: Kenneth A. Shirley, James Hone Walker.

Specialist subjects/requirements: Countries and their landmarks and places of interest; People, family life at work and play. A separate department is dedicated to archival photographs.

Markets supplied: Publishers, advertising agencies, etc.

Stock: Mainly colour; 6 × 7 cm preferred, but will consider 35mm.

Usual terms of business: Negotiable.

Commission: 'Minimum of 50 per cent.'

KEYSTONE PRESS AGENCY LTD.*

Bath House, 52/62 Holborn Viaduct, London EC1A 2FE. Tel: 01-236 3331.

Principal: David Bassil (Photographic Manager).

Specialist subjects/requirements: World news and timeless feature pictures.

Markets supplied: National newspapers in UK and abroad; leading periodicals and publishers.

Stock: B&W and colour. All formats.

Usual terms of business: 'Submissions usually after initial introduction by letter or personal meeting.'

Commission: Negotiable.

FRANK LANE AGENCY*

Drummoyne, Southill Lane, Pinner, Middlesex HA5 2EQ. Tel: 01-866 2336.

Principals: Frank E. Lane, Jean Lane.

Specialist subjects/requirements: Natural History and Weather Phenomena: Birds, clouds, fish, fungi, insects, marine, mammals, pollution, rainbows, sea reptiles, sea, snow,

seasons, trees, underwater, hurricanes, earthquakes, lighting, volcanoes, dew, frost, rain, fog, etc. Ecology, Nature and its environment.
Markets supplied: Publishers, audio visual organisations, advertising agencies.
Stock: B&W and Colour. 35mm and 6 × 6 cm transparencies. Kodachrome preferred for 35mm.
Usual terms of business: Minimum initial submission: 100 transparencies; no minimum retention period.
Commission: 50 per cent.
Additional information: 'The competition in the natural history field is fierce, so only really sharp, well composed pictures stand a chance. Sales are slow to start with, and a really keen photographer must be prepared to invest money in building up his stock to the 1000 mark.'

MIDDLE EAST PHOTOGRAPHIC ARCHIVE*
MEED House, 21 John Street, London WC1N 2BP. Tel: 01-404 5513.
Principal: Jonathan Wallace (Managing Director).
Specialist subjects/requirements: Specialists on the Middle East. Also covers Indian sub-continent, Africa and South-East Asia.
Markets supplied: Books, magazines, newspapers, brochures, calendars, greetings cards, exhibition displays, etc.
Stock: B&W and colour. 35mm and other formats.
Usual terms of business: Minimum initial submission: usually 500 but will consider smaller submissions. Minimum retention period: 18 months.
Commission: 50 per cent.

MONITOR INTERNATIONAL
17 Old Street, London EC1V 9HL. Tel: 01-253 7071/2 and 01-253 6281/2.
Principal: S. R. White (Managing Director).
Specialist subjects/requirements: Portraits of personalities from sport, commerce, politics, showbusiness. Travel. General.
Markets supplied: National and international press, television, advertising, publishers, etc.
Stock: Colour only for travel and general subjects (6 × 6 cm or larger). B&W and colour (35mm) for portraits.
Usual terms of business: No minimum submission or minimum retention period.
Commission: 50 per cent.

NATURAL SCIENCE PHOTOS*
33 Woodland Drive, Watford, Herts WD1 3BY. Tel: Watford 45265.
Principals: P. H. Ward, S. L. Ward.
Specialist subjects/requirements: Natural science in all its aspects: animals, birds, reptiles, fish, amphibia, insects, plants, habitats, geography, climate, prehistoric animal reconstructs, plant pests and diseases. Subjects from various parts of the world, strong in British, African and Australasian material.

Markets supplied: Books and magazines, audio visual and television, some advertising: UK and overseas. Some inter-agency deals.

Stock: Colour, mainly 35mm, but larger formats accepted.

Usual terms of business: No minimum submission. Standard contract allows for 3 years retention, but carries blank clause for mutually agreed variances, e.g. photographer can retain right to sell direct or through other agencies.

Commission: 33 per cent.

Additional information: 'All material to be well documented—English and scientific names (clearly written), country of origin and photographer; also any useful binomic information.'

THE NORTHERN PICTURE LIBRARY*

Unit 2, Bentinck Street Industrial Estate, Ellesmere Street, Manchester M15 4LN. Tel: 061-834 1255.

Principals: Roy Conchie, Janet Conchie.

Specialist subjects/requirements: UK and world views, industrial archaeology, glamour, sport, industrial scenery, tourist views, natural history, people at work.

Markets supplied: Advertising, packaging, calendars, greetings cards.

Stock: Mainly colour. Minimum 35mm, prefers 6×7 cm or $5'' \times 4''$.

Usual terms of business: Minimum retention period: 'normally 3 years but not obligatory'. No minimum submission: 'we want quality rather than quantity'.

Commission: 50 per cent.

PHOTO LIBRARY INTERNATIONAL*

St Michaels Hall, Bennett Road, Leeds LS6 3HN. Tel: 0532 789321.

Principal: Kevin Horgan (Managing Director).

Specialist subjects/requirements: General worldwide subjects including agriculture, animals, beach scenes, botany, children, fairs, fishing, girls, sunsets, etc.

Markets supplied: Advertising, travel brochures, greetings cards, publishers, etc.

Stock: Colour only. From 35mm up.

Usual terms of business: Minimum first submission: 200. Minimum retention period: 3 years with 12 months notice of withdrawal.

Commission: 50 per cent—or picture purchased outright.

PICTOR INTERNATIONAL LTD.

Lynwood House, 24/32 Kilburn High Road, London NW6 5XW. Tel: 01-328 9221.

Principal: A. Sciama (Managing Director).

Specialist subjects/requirements: General library handling all subjects.

Markets supplied: Advertising, calendars, posters, greetings cards, holiday brochures, books, encyclopedias, company reports, box tops, etc.

Stock: Colour. Minimum 6×6 cm colour transparencies.

Usual terms of business: Minimum initial submission: 200 transparencies.

Commission: 50 per cent.

PICTORIAL PRESS LTD.
30 Aylesbury Street, London EC1R 0BL. Tel: 01-253 4023.
Principal: Anthony F. Gale.
Specialist subjects/requirements: Feature stories; glamour sets (as seen in *Mayfair*, etc.); girl portraits; historical war pictures; vintage transport (cars, bikes, buses); natural history; pop stars; Royalty.
Markets supplied: Publishing, etc.
Stock: Mostly colour.
Usual terms of business: By individual arrangement. No minimum submission.
Commission: By individual arrangement.
Additional information: Suitable s.a.e. must be sent or material will not be returned. 'Ask yourself: is it sharp, is the colour balance good, does it tell a story, would I buy it if I was the editor?'

PICTUREPOINT LTD.
Hurst House, 157/169 Walton Road, East Molesey, Surrey KT8 0DX. Tel: 01-948 4520.
Principals: G. W. Constantine, K. Gibson.
Specialist subjects/requirements: World economic geography; sports; pastimes; industry; agriculture; travel.
Markets supplied: Books, travel, advertising, etc.
Stock: Colour only. 6 × 6 cm or larger preferred, but top quality 35mm acceptable.
Usual terms of business: Minimum initial submission must produce at least 100 retained transparencies. Minimum retention period: 3 years.
Commission: 50 per cent.
Additional information: 'We only handle work of the highest quality.'

PAUL POPPER LTD.*
24 Bride Lane, Fleet Street, London EC4Y 8DR. Tel: 01-353 9665.
Principal: W. R. Blackmore (Managing Director).
Specialist subjects/requirements: General library handling all subjects.
Markets supplied: Book and periodical publishers.
Stock: B&W and colour. 6 × 6 cm and 5″ × 4″ transparencies preferred; 35mm accepted. B&W 10″ × 8″ prints.
Usual terms of business: Minimum retention period: 3 years.
Commission: 50 per cent.

REX FEATURES LTD.*
18 Vine Hill, London EC1R 5DX. Tel: 01-278 7294.
Principals: F. Selby, E. Selby, A. G. Day.
Specialist subjects/requirements: Human interest and general interest features; personalities; animals (singles and series); humour; high class glamour; current affairs; topographical; general library stock material.
Markets supplied: UK national newspapers and magazines, book publishers, audio visual, television, etc., and international press.

Usual terms of business: No minimum submission, 'though not really interested in the one off'. Preferred minimum retention period: 2 years.
Commission: 50 per cent.

SEAPHOT LTD./PLANET EARTH PICTURES*

23 Burlington Road, Bristol BS6 6TJ. Tel: 0272 741206.
Principal: Gillian Lythgoe (Managing Director).
Specialist subjects/requirements: Natural history—marine and land; wildlife; marine photography—surface and underwater; watersports; landscape/ecology photography.
Markets supplied: Books, magazines, advertising.
Stock: Colour only. Minimum 35mm; prefers 6 × 6 cm, 6 × 7 cm or 5″ × 4″.
Usual terms of business: No minimum submission, but 'the more photographs that a photographer can leave in the library, the more chance he has of a reasonable return'. Terms of business in more detail available on request.
Commission: 50 per cent.
Additional information: 'We like to have close working relationships with all our photographers.'

SPECTRUM COLOUR LIBRARY*

146 Oxford Street, London W1. Tel: 01-637 3681.
Principals: Keith Jones, Ann Jones.
Specialist subjects/requirements: Travel; natural history; people; general.
Markets supplied: Advertising, publishing, travel brochures, etc.
Stock: B&W and colour. Minimum 35mm transparencies, but prefers larger formats.
Usual terms of business: Minimum initial submission: 300 transparencies. Minimum retention period: 5 years.
Commission: 50 per cent.
Additional information: 'We require only top quality material—the buying market is so competitive at present that only the best will do! We can only view photographers' work *by prior appointment.*'

TONY STONE ASSOCIATES LTD*

28 Finchley Road, St. John's Wood, London Nw8 6ES. Tel: 01-586 3322.
Principal: Tony Stone (Managing Director).
Specialist subjects/requirements: Subjects commonly used in advertising.
Markets supplied: Advertising agencies; travel industry worldwide.
Stock: Colour; all formats.
Usual terms of business: On application. Send three outstanding pictures in first instance.
Commission: 50 per cent.
Additional information: Only truly outstanding material considered.

JOHN TOPHAM PICTURE LIBRARY*
Edells, Markbeech, Edenbridge, Kent TN8 5PB. Tel: 034 286 313.
Principals: Alan and Joanna Smith.
Specialist subjects/requirements: Personalities; history; warfare; world news; royalty; travel; topography and geography; France and French life; natural history; agriculture; Australiana; Middle Eastern affairs; etc.
Markets supplied: Publishers.
Stock: B&W and colour. All formats.
Usual terms of business: Sample selection initially followed by a minimum submission of 500 pictures. Minimum retention period: 3 years.
Commission: 50 per cent.

TRAVEL TRADE PHOTOGRAPHY
18 Princedale Road, London W11 4NJ. Tel: 01-727 5471.
Principal: Teddy Schwarz.
Specialist subjects/requirements: Holiday destinations worldwide and activities of tourists (games on beaches, shopping, markets, excursions to places of historic interest, displays of fruit and food, national dances, surfing, boating, eating in the open and in restaurants, etc.). Ethnographical, archaeological, ancient monuments, folkloristic.
Markets supplied: Travel brochures, guidebooks, etc.
Stock: Colour only. 6 × 6 cm only. No 35mm.
Usual terms of business: No minimum submission. Minimum retention period: 1 year.
Commission: 50 per cent.
Additional information: 'Please stress that we only handle 6 × 6 cm transparencies—no 35mm. Ideally, it would be best if would-be contributors phone for an appointment to show what they have to offer. Unsolicited material will not be returned. Postal inquiries will only be answered if s.a.e. is provided. As for the actual pictures—shots must have been taken under sunny conditions, be of excellent quality and have deep saturated colour.'

UNITED PRESS INTERNATIONAL (UK) LTD.
8 Bouverie Street, London EC4Y 8BB. Tel: 01-353 2282.
Principal: Eugene H. Blabey.
Specialist subjects/requirements: World news pictures and feature material.
Markets supplied: World press.
Stock: B&W and colour.
Usual terms of business: Direct purchase of material only.

VISION INTERNATIONAL*
30 Museum Street, London WC1A 1LH. Tel: 01-636 9516.
Principals: Sue Pinkus, David Alexander.
Specialist subjects/requirements: Landscapes; natural history; children; pregnancy; birth; gardens; girls; medicine and health; fine art; architecture; travel.

Markets supplied: Books, magazines, advertising, calendars, greetings cards, audio visual, etc.

Stock: Principally colour. 35mm, 6 × 6 cm and 5″ × 4″ transparencies.

Usual terms of business: Minimum initial submission: usually 500. 3 year contracts, usually exclusive.

Commission: 50 per cent.

Additional information: Vision International also has on its premises a retail gallery, which exhibits and markets mostly colour prints.

WOODMANSTERNE PUBLICATIONS LTD.*

Greenhill Crescent, Holywell Industrial Estate, Watford, Herts WD1 8RD. Tel: Watford 28236/45788.

Principals: G. Woodmansterne, J. W. Woodmansterne.

Specialist subjects/requirements: Air transport; animals; archaeology; architecture; arms and armour; ballet; biography; birds; carving; cathedrals; ceramics; churches; coastal scenes; costume; countryside; flowers; furniture; geological features; mountain scenes; parks and gardens; seasonal scenes; water transport; etc.

Markets supplied: Publishing, souvenir/novelties, tourism, travel.

Stock: Colour only. 35mm, 6 × 7 cm, 5″ × 4″.

Usual terms of business: Requires 'good selection of one subject' to be retained 'on semi-permanent basis'.

Commission: 50 per cent.

Additional information: 'Only top quality pictures per subject, ranging from the record shot to the unusual.'

ZEFA (UK) LTD.*

PO Box 210, 20 Conduit Place, London W2 1HZ. Tel: 01-262 0101.

Principal: Harold Harris.

Specialist subjects/requirements: Generally library handling most subjects.

Markets supplied: Advertising, publishing.

Stock: Colour and historic B&W. 6 × 6 cm transparencies.

Usual terms of business: Minimum initial submission: 200–500: Minimum retention period: 3–5 years.

Additional information: 'Please write for photographers guide first.'

Member of the British Association of Picture Libraries and Agencies.

PHOTOGRAPHIC SERVICES & SUPPLIES

Accessories & Specialised Equipment

R. R. BEARD LTD.
10 Trafalgar Avenue, Old Kent Road, London SE15 6NR. Tel: 01-703 3136/9638.
Manufacturers and distributors of masking frames, vacuum easels, quartz studio lighting, light boxes, etc.

BOWENS OF LONDON LTD.
Royalty House, 72 Dean Street, London W1V 6DQ. Tel: 01-439 1781.
Design and manufacture of studio and location flash, control equipment, etc.

CAMERA BELLOWS LTD.
Runcorn Works, 2 Runcorn Road, Birmingham B12 8RQ. Tel: 021-440 1695.
Bellows for all photographic purposes in leather and other materials. Replacements for antique cameras.

CAMERA CARE SYSTEMS CO.
30 Alexandra Road, Clevedon, Avon BS21 7QH. Tel: 0272 871791.
Manufacturers of padded camera bags and pouches. Approved by the Design Centre.

COURTENAY PHOTONICS LTD.
2–6 Boswell Court, London WC1N 3PS. Tel: 01-405 2065.
Courtenay electronic flash systems.

H. W. ENGLISH
469 Rayleigh Road, Hutton, Brentwood, Essex CM13 1SU. Tel: 0277 221685.
Optical components, adaptors, rings, converters, etc. Ex-government and second-hand optical equipment.

JESSOP OF LEICESTER LTD.
Photo Centre, Hinckley Road, Leicester LE3 0TE. Tel: 0533 20641.
Powerflash Portable Studio flash systems.

KEITH JOHNSON PHOTOGRAPHIC LTD.
11 Great Marlborough Street, London W1. Tel: 01-439 8811.
Distributors of Arca, BEE, Norman, Multiblitz, etc.

KENNETT ENGINEERING CO. LTD.
The Lodge Works, Drayton Parslow, Bucks. Tel: 029-672 605.
Makers of dry-mounting and heat-sealing equipment and materials.

S. W. KENYON
6 Fore Street, Wellington, Somerset TA21 8AQ. Tel: 082-347 4151.
K-Line sprays and heater pads.

MALHAM PHOTOGRAPHIC EQUIPMENT LTD.
65–67 Malham Road, London SE23. Tel: 01-699 0917.
Makers of lighting and background control systems. Sole English agent for Gitzo equipment.

MELICO
Medical & Electrical Instrumentation Co. Ltd., Unit 5, 7 Chalcot Road, London NW1 8LH. Tel: 01-586 5144.
Makers of densitometers, colour analysers, photometers, camera test equipment, etc.

POLLOCK AUDIO-VISUAL
Netherwood, Stones Lane, Westcott, Dorking, Surrey RH4 3QH. Tel: 0306 881641.
Manufacturers and suppliers of audio-visual equipment.

B. J. POWER ELECTRONICS LTD.
84 Hilltop Court, Downs Road, Luton, Beds. Tel: 0582 410394. 24 hour Answerphone.
Manufacture and mail-order sales of studio lighting equipment and accessories.

THE PROCESS CONTROL COMPANY
Griffin Lane, Aylesbury, Buckinghamshire HP19 3BP. Tel: 0296 84877.
Makers of processing equipment: racks, spirals, hangers, dryers, cabinets, sinks, etc.

REMART INTERNATIONAL LTD.
8–10 Ingate Place, London SW8. Tel: 01-720 6871.
Manufacture and distribution of silver recovery units.

JAMIE WOOD PRODUCTS LTD.
Cross Street, Polegate, Sussex. Tel: 032-12 3813.
Makers of photographic hides.

Art Services

BERRY'S MODEL AGENCY & STUDIO
107 Burnham Road, Great Barr, Birmingham B44 8HX. Tel: 021-360 3913.
Design and printing services for mailers, leaflets, etc.

COLOUR PROCESSING LABORATORIES LTD.
Head Office: Fircroft Way, Edenbridge, Kent TN8 6ET. Tel: 0732 862555.
Laboratories also in London, Birmingham, Bristol, Eastleigh and Nottingham.
Exhibition design facility, retouching, etc.

LONGACRE COLOUR LABORATORIES
Gate House, 1 St John's Square, London EC1. Tel: 01-253 2336.
Photo-composition and retouching.

MALLARD
Graphic House, Noel Street, Kimberley, Nottingham NG16 2NE. Tel: 0602 382670.
Retouching, litho printing, typesetting and graphic arts department.

MINISTIK COLOUR
North West Road, Leeds LS6 2PY. Tel: 0532 449241.
Producer of self-adhesive photographic prints.

OBSCURA LTD.
34a Bryanston Street, Marble Arch, London W1H 7AH. Tel: 01-723 1487.
Photocomposition, retouching, etc.

PHOTOLEAFLETS (LEEDS) LTD.
Leodis House, Woodhouse Street, Leeds LS6 2PY. Tel: 0532 449241.
Single-sided photo leaflets, combining lettering and photographic colour printing.

STEEPLEPRINT LTD.
5 Mallard Close, Earls Barton, Northampton NN6 0LS. Tel: 0604 810781.
ABLE-LABELS—printed self-adhesive labels.

TRENCH ENTERPRISES LTD.
Three Cow Green, Bacton, Stowmarket, Suffolk IP14 4HJ. Tel: 0449 672734.
Manufacture of hand cut wooden jig-saws from photographic and other prints.

UNDERWOOD PHOTO-ENTERPRISES LTD.
39 Northfield Avenue, West Ealing, London W13 9QP. Tel: 01-579 3740.
'In-camera' special effects, overlay negatives, montage, multi-image, vignettes, etc.

WALKERPRINT
46 Newman Street, London W1P 3PA. Tel: 01-580 7031.
Design and publicity printers. Photographers' index cards, posters, catalogues, etc. Publishers and distributors of The Photographers Black Box.

Equipment—Hire

ANGLIA CAMERAS
15–15a St Matthew's Street, Ipswich IP1 3EL. Tel: 0473 58185.
A–V hire, 16mm and overhead projector, screen hire etc. Some still equipment hire.

EDRIC AUDIO VISUAL LTD.
Oak End Way, Gerrards Cross, Bucks SL9 8BR. Tel: 02813 84646.
Also at: Manchester, tel: 061773 7711 and Bristol, tel: 0272 555119.
Hire of A–V equipment, film production and photographic equipment.

GEORGE ELLIOTT & SONS LTD.
Ajax House, Hertford Road, Barking, Essex IG11 8BA. Tel: 01-591 5599.
A–V and professional equipment hire.

LEOPOLD CAMERAS LTD.
17 Hunter Street, London WC1N 1BN. Tel: 01-837 6501 or 6382.
Comprehensive equipment hire service.

NOTTINGHAM PHOTO CENTRE
28–30 Pelham Street, Nottingham. Tel: 0602 55503-4.
Professional equipment hire.

PELLING AND CROSS LTD.
104 Baker Street, London W1M 2AR. Tel: 01-487 5411.
Branches also in Birmingham, Bristol and Manchester.
Comprehensive equipment hire service.

PICCADILLY PHOTO CENTRE LTD.
16–18 Piccadilly Arcade, London SW1Y 6NH. Tel: 01-499 4617-8.
Amateur and professional equipment hire.

UNISON FILMS LTD.
The White House, 41 Carshalton Road, Sutton, Surrey. Tel: 01-643 7277/8.
Hire of professional still and cine equipment.

WOODSTOCK PHOTOSOUND LTD.
The White House, 41 Carshalton Road, Sutton, Surrey. Tel: 01-643 7277/8.
Hire of Video equipment and electronics.

Equipment—Repair

BOURNEMOUTH PHOTOGRAPHIC REPAIR SERVICE LTD.
237 Capstone Road, Bournemouth BH8 8SA. Tel: 0202 513586.
Factory appointed Service Station for Zeiss-Ikon/Voigtlander equipment—Contarex, Contaflex etc.

COUSINS & WRIGHT (TROWBRIDGE)
5 The Halve, Trowbridge, Wiltshire BA14 8SB. Tel: 022-14 4242.
Camera and photographic equipment servicing and repair.

EXPRESS CAMERA REPAIR SERVICE
12–13 Greville Street, Hatton Garden, London EC1. Tel: 01-405 0231.
Servicing and repairs to all types of photographic equipment.

LESLIE H. FRANKHAM
166 Westcotes Drive, Leicester LE3 0SP. Tel: 0533 857771.
Equipment repairs and testing services. Optical instrumentation testing.

H. A. GARRETT & CO. LTD.
300 High Street, Sutton, Surrey SM1 1PQ. Tel: 01-643 5376.
Camera equipment repairs and sales.

INSTRUMENT SERVICES CO. (LONDON) LTD.
208 Maybank Road, London E18. Tel: 01-504 8885.
Sole accredited service centre for Weston meters.

A. J. JOHNSTONE & CO.
395 Central Chambers, 93 Hope Street, Glasgow G2 6LD. Tel: 041-221 2106.
All equipment repairs, including A–V equipment. Bell & Howell service. Appointed Olympus Service Centre.

LEICESTER CAMERA REPAIR SERVICE
166 Westcotes Drive, Leicester LE3 0SP. Tel: 0533 857771.
Mechanical repairs, specialising in older quality equipment—Contax, Zeiss, etc.

LENCOL
177b Moulsham Street, Chelmsford, Essex. Tel: 0254 63806.
All equipment repairs.

PELLING AND CROSS LTD.
104 Baker Street, London W1M 2AR. Tel: 01-487 5411.
Branches also in Birmingham, Bristol and Manchester.
All equipment repairs.

PICCADILLY PHOTO CENTRE LTD.
16–18 Piccadilly Arcade, London SW1Y 6NH. Tel: 01-499 4617-8.
Amateur and professional equipment repair.

SENDEAN LTD.
Formerly Bowens. 6 D'Arblay Street, London W1V 3FD. Tel: 01-439 8418.
All photographic equipment repairs.

UNISON FILMS LTD.
The White House, 41 Carshalton Road, Sutton, Surrey. Tel: 01-643 7277/8.
Repair of professional still and cine equipment.

VANGUARD PHOTOGRAPHIC SERVICES
156 Boston Road, Hanwell, London W7 2HJ. Tel: 01-840 2177.
All photographic equipment repairs.

WOODSTOCK PHOTOSOUND LTD.
The White House, 41 Carshalton Road, Sutton, Surrey. Tel: 01-643 7277/8.
Repair of Video equipment and electronics.

Framing & Picture Finishing

AVONCOLOUR LTD.
131 Duckmoor Road, Ashton Gate, Bristol. Tel: 0272 633456.
Mounting & laminating.

CHATFIELD'S
4 Chaucer Street, Northampton NN2 7HN. Tel: 0604 710013.
Picture frame mouldings. Custom made frames.

DELTA COLOUR LTD.
Wheatfield House, Church Road, Paddock Wood, Tonbridge TN12 6EX. Tel: 089-283
3321.Also at 7–9 Earlham Street, London WC2H 9LL and 129–135 Fulwell Road,
Teddington, Middlesex TW11 0RJ.
Sole agents for Polyboard and Polyframe.

KAY MOUNTING SERVICE
351 Caledonian Road, London N1. Tel: 01-607 7241-2.
Mounting, canvas-bonding, heat-sealing and laminating.

KIMBERS
24 Queens Road, Brighton, East Sussex BN1 3XA. Tel: 0273 36907.
Mail order wholesale and retail of frames, mounts and albums.

GRAEME LAWTON LTD.
Station Industrial Estate, Fleet, Hampshire GU13 8QY. Tel: 025-14 6727.
Wholesale photograph frame manufacturers.

RUSSELL COLOUR LABORATORIES
17 Elm Grove, Wimbledon, London SW19 4HE. Tel: 01-947 6172/3.
Mounting and framing.

WEMBLEY STUDIO SUPPLIES LTD.
788–790 Finchley Road, London NW11 7UR. Tel: 01-458 9020.
Suppliers of albums, mounts, frames, etc.

Insurance

ALLIANCE ASSOCIATES
1 Imperial Square, Cheltenham, Gloucestershire GL50 1QB. Tel: 0242 45127.
Semi-professional and amateur photographers' equipment insurance.

Laboratories—Black & White

ATLAS PHOTOGRAPHY LTD.
4 New Burlington Street, London W1X 1FE. Tel: 01-734 8746 and 01-434 3171.
Comprehensive black and white processing services.

BRADBURY'S PHOTOGRAPHIC PROCESSING LTD.
Raymond Street, Shelton, Stoke on Trent. Tel: 0782 22316/7.
Comprehensive black and white processing services.

CHANDOS PHOTOGRAPHIC SERVICES LTD.
5 Torrens Street, London EC1V 1NQ. Tel: 01-837 1822/7632.
Comprehensive black and white processing services.

CHILTERN PHOTOGRAPHIC ARTS
139 High Street South, Dunstable, Bedfordshire LU6 3SQ. Tel: 0582 63535.
Comprehensive black and white processing services. B&W printing by hand.

CITY COLOUR LTD.
426–432 Essex Road, London N1. Tel: 01-359 0033.
Comprehensive professional black and white processing services.

THE DARKROOM
124 Aldersgate Street, London EC1 4JQ. Tel: 01-251 4147.
Black and white processing and printing, and laboratory hire.

MICHAEL DRAPER
2nd Floor, 23–27 Hatton Wall, London EC1N 8JJ. Tel: 01-242 8346.
Black and white processing and hand printing.

DUNNS PHOTOGRAPHIC SERVICE LTD.
Chester Road, Cradley Heath, Warley, West Midlands B64 6AA. Tel: 0384 69500.
Comprehensive black and white processing services.

FARROWS
Aldwych House, Bethel Street, Norwich NR2 1NR. Tel: 0603 613333.
Comprehensive black and white processing services.

GIANT PHOTOGRAPHIC ENLARGEMENTS LTD.
18 Queen Street, Maidenhead, Berkshire. Tel: 0628 25381.
Black and white processing and giant enlargements from artwork or negatives.

MALLARD
Graphic House, Noel Street, Kimberley, Nottingham NG16 2NE. Tel: 0602 382670.
Commercial studio with full black and white laboratory services.

PHOTOMATIC 80
Dellsome Lane, North Mymms, Hatfield AL9 7DZ. Tel: 070-72 62506.
Black and white processing. Runs of postcards, etc., from customers' own material.

PROPIX LTD.
Rockingham House, Broad Lane, Sheffield S1 3PP. Tel: 0742 739137.
Comprehensive black and white professional processing services.

QUICKSILVER PHOTOGRAPHIC SERVICES
5 North Deven Road, Fishponds, Bristol BS16 2EX. Tel: 0272 651633.
Comprehensive black and white processing and printing services. 35mm to 5″ × 4″.

RUSSELL COLOUR LABORATORIES
17 Elm Grove, Wimbledon, London SW19 4HE. Tel: 01-947 6172/3.
Comprehensive black and white processing services.

VOSPER PHOTOGRAPHY
129 Sidwell Street, Exeter, Devon. Tel: 0392 72364.
Comprehensive black and white processing services.

Laboratories—Colour

ATLAS PHOTOGRAPHY LTD.
4 New Burlington Street, London W1X 1FE. Tel: 01-734 8746 and 01-434 3171.
Comprehensive colour processing services. Audio-visual services.

AVONCOLOUR LTD.
131 Duckmoor Road, Ashton Gate, Bristol. Tel: 0272 633456.
Comprehensive colour processing services, including duping and copying, mounting and laminating, hand printing to 30″ × 60″, etc.

B.C.P.
Formerly Birmingham Ektaprocessing
PO Box 582, Erdington, Birmingham B23 6LX. Tel: 021-350 2193.
E6 processing and mounting. Uprating.

BRADBURY'S PHOTOGRAPHIC PROCESSING LTD.
Raymond Street, Shelton, Stoke on Trent. Tel: 0782 22316/7.
Comprehensive colour processing services, wedding packages, E6, etc.

CC PROCESSING
2 Burley Road, Leeds LS3 1NJ. Tel: 0532 443441.
Comprehensive colour processing services. Agfachrome—$2\frac{1}{2}$ hours; E6—$1\frac{1}{2}$ hours.

CHANDOS PHOTOGRAPHIC SERVICES LTD.
5 Torrens Street, London EV1V 1NQ. Tel: 01-837 1822/7632.
Comprehensive colour processing services.

CHESHIRE COLOUR LABORATORIES LTD.
Dale Street, Broadheath, Altrincham, Cheshire WA14 5EH. Tel: 061-928 6794/4145.
Comprehensive colour processing services. Machine prints up to 30″ × 40″.

CHILTERN PHOTOGRAPHIC ARTS
139 High Street South, Dunstable, Bedfordshire LU6 3SQ. Tel: 0582 63535.
Comprehensive colour processing services.

CITY COLOR LTD.
426–432 Essex Road, London N1. Tel: 01-359 0033.
Comprehensive professional colour processing services.

COLAB LTD.
Herald Way, Binley, Coventry CV3 1BB. Tel: 0203 440404.
Comprehensive colour processing services.

COLORLABS INTERNATIONAL LTD.
The Maltings, Fordham Road, Newmarket, Suffolk CB8 7AG. Tel: 0638 664444.
Comprehensive professional colour processing services.

COLOUR CENTRE LIMITED
41a North End Road, Kensington, London W14 8SZ. Tel: 01-602 0167.
Comprehensive colour processing services.

COLOUR PROCESSING LABORATORIES LTD.
Head Office: Fircroft Way, Edenbridge, Kent TN8 6ET. Tel: 0732 862555.
Laboratories also in London, Birmingham, Bristol, Eastleigh and Nottingham.
E6 and C41 processing. All forms of photographic printing including giant photo-murals, leaflets, etc. Cibachrome and Duratrans.

DEAN COLOUR LABORATORIES
13–14 Dean Street, London W1V 5AH. Tel: 01-437 1863.
Comprehensive colour processing services. 2 hour service for C41.

DELTA COLOUR LTD.
Wheatfield House, Church Road, Paddock Wood, Tonbridge TN12 6EX. Tel: 089-283 3321. Also at 7–9 Earlham Street, London WC2H 9LL and 129–135 Fulwell Road, Teddington, Middlesex TW11 0RJ.
Comprehensive colour processing services.

DUNNS PHOTOGRAPHIC SERVICE LTD.
Chester Road, Cradley Heath, Warley, West Midlands B64 6AA. Tel: 0384 69500.
Comprehensive black and white processing services.

FARROWS
Aldwych House, Bethel Street, Norwich NR2 1NR. Tel: 0603 613333.
Reproduction quality copy transparencies up to 10″ × 8″ from slide, print or negative.
Retouching of transparencies and hand printing.

GWENTCOLOUR LABORATORIES LTD.
North Road, Abersychan, Pontypool, Gwent. Tel: 0495 772355.
Trade processing—C41-type films.

HAMILTON TAIT LTD.
Eastfield Drive, Penicuick, Midlothian EH26 8BD. Tel: 0968 72201.
Comprehensive colour services, canvas bonding, Cibachrome up to 30″ × 40″.

HEART OF ENGLAND
Unit 2, Ashburton Industrial Estate, Ross-on-Wye, Herefordshire HR9 7AQ. Tel: 0989 63941.
Comprehensive colour processing services.

HILLS COLOUR SERVICES
City House, 72–80 Leather Lane, London EC1N 7TR. Tel: 01-405 9965.
Duplicate and enlarged transparencies to 11″ × 14″. Transprints to 20″ × 16″.

HOME COUNTIES COLOUR SERVICES LTD.
12 Leagrave Road, Luton, Beds. Tel: 0582 31899.
Comprehensive colour processing services.

P. & P. F. JAMES LTD.
496 Great West Road, Hounslow, Middlesex. Tel: 01-570 3974/8951.
Comprehensive colour processing services.

THOS LITSTER
PO Box 7, March Street Industrial Estate, Peebles, Scotland EH45 8DE. Tel: 0721 20685.
Comprehensive colour processing services.

LONGACRE COLOUR LABORATORIES
Gate House, 1 St John's Square, London EC1. Tel: 01-253 2336.
Ektachrome processing, 'R' types, dupes, etc. Photo-composition and retouching.

MALLARD
Graphic House, Noel Street, Kimberley, Nottingham NG16 2NE. Tel: 0602 382670.
Commercial studio with full colour processing services.

MINISTIK COLOUR
North West Road, Leeds LS6 2PY. Tel: 0532 449241.
Producer of self-adhesive photographic prints. Specialists in long print runs.

NESS PHOTOGRAPHIC LABORATORIES
Kershaw Street, Widnes, Cheshire WA8 7JH. Tel: 051-424 0514.
Comprehensive professional colour processing services. Schools facilities.

NOTTINGHAM PHOTO CENTRE
28–30 Pelham Street, Nottingham. Tel: 0602 55503-4.
Comprehensive colour processing service.

OBSCURA LTD.
34a Bryanston Street, Marble Arch, London W1H 7AH. Tel: 01-723 1487.
C-type colour prints, dupes, photocomposition, retouching, etc.

PHOTOWORLD
Queens Road, Llandudno, Gwynned LL30 1AZ. Tel: 0492 76406.
Movie film processing services, striping, copying, editing, etc.

JOHN PIERCY LTD.
34a Bryanston Street, Marble Arch, London W1H 7AH. Tel: 01-723 1487.
E6 & C-41 processing. No charge for push/pull. Messenger service available.

P.R. PRESS PHOTOS LTD.
100 St Martins Lane, Covent Garden, London WC2N 4AZ. Tel: 01-836 2676/8.
Comprehensive colour processing services.

PROPIX LTD.
Rockingham House, Broad Lane, Sheffield S1 3PP. Tel: 0742 739137.
Comprehensive professional colour processing services.

RUSSELL COLOUR LABORATORIES
17 Elm Grove, Wimbledon, London SW19 4HE. Tel: 01-947 6172/3.
Comprehensive colour processing services. Colour up to 4 ft × 9 ft. Dupes, Duratrans, graphics, mounting and framing.

SCL
50 Church Street, Edmonton, London N9 9PA. Tel: 01-807 0725.
Comprehensive colour processing services. Handprints up to 30″ × 40″.

TAYLER COLOUR LABORATORY LTD.
33 Lordsworth Road, Harborne, Birmingham B17 9RP. Tel: 021-427 4122.
Comprehensive colour services. Rush E6.

WEYCOLOUR LTD.
Moss Lane, Godalming, Surrey. Tel: 04868 7670/1.
Comprehensive colour processing service.

WRIGHT COLOR LTD.
Millers Road, Warwick CV34 5AN. Tel: 0926 494345.
Comprehensive colour processing services.

Material Suppliers

JARED EDWARDS PHOTOGRAPHIC LTD.
Unit 30/30a Lee Way, Newport Industrial Estate, Newport, Gwent. Tel: 0633 279440.
Wholesale and retail photographic supplies.

ERIC FISHWICK LTD.
Grange Valley, Haydock, St Helens, Merseyside WA11 0XE. Tel: 0744 27384/5/6. 24 hour Answerphone.
Range of over 10,000 products and materials. Mail order. Catalogue on request.

GOLDFINGER LTD.
329–333 Muswell Hill Broadway, London N10. Tel: 01-883 6282/5502.
Mail order and retail. Importers of FB Agfa paper, Agfapan professional films and Kodak developers & toners otherwise unavailable in UK. Phone for catalogue.

KENNETT ENGINEERING CO. LTD.
The Lodge Works, Drayton Parslow, Bucks. Tel: 029-672 605.
Ademco wholesalers.

KENTMERE LTD.
Staveley, Kendal, Cumbria LA8 9PB. Tel: 0539 821365.
Makers of Kentmere, Kenthene and Kentona photographic paper, document paper, polyester film and tinted black and white paper.

THOS LITSTER
PO Box 7 March Street Industrial Estate, Peebles, Scotland EH45 8DE. Tel: 0721 20685.
Wholesale material supplier.

MID-COUNTIES PHOTOGRAPHIC SUPPLIES
Water Buildings, Baldock Road, Letchworth, Herts. Tel: 046-26 79388-9.
Comprehensive wholesale supplies of equipment, chemicals, etc.

PHOTOGRAPHIC & TECHNICAL SERVICES
226 Westbourne Grove, London W11 2RU. Tel: 01-221 0162.
Suppliers of Argenta Photo-linen and photographic paper.

POLLOCK AUDIO-VISUAL
Netherwood, Stones Lane, Westcott, Dorking, Surrey RH4 3QH. Tel: 0306 881641.
Suppliers of audio-visual materials.

POLYSALES PHOTOGRAPHIC LTD..
The Wharf, Godalming, Surrey GU7 1JX. Tel: Godalming 4171.
Full range of equipment and materials by mail order. Catalogue on request.

WEYCOLOUR LTD.
Moss Lane, Godalming, Surrey. Tel: 04868 7670/1.
Suppliers of materials, sprays, slide mounts etc.

WIGGINS TEAPE PAPER LTD.
Keays House, Granby Avenue, Birmingham B33 0SX. Tel: 021-783 9931.
Producers and suppliers of Colorama background paper.

Model Agencies

BERRY'S MODEL AGENCY & STUDIO
107 Burnham Road, Great Barr, Birmingham B44 8HX. Tel: 021-360 3913.
General model agency.

CASTLE STUDIOS
44 Castle Road, Bedford. Tel: 0234 214577.
Large selection of models.

COLORSCOPE STUDIO
Unit 4, Swains Mill, Crane Mead, Ware, Herts. Tel: 0920 61950.
General model agency.

DEREK & CO. LTD.
57 Poland Street, London W1. Tel: 01-734 9261.
General model agency specialising in advertising and fashion.

LEEDS MODEL AGENCY
11a Hyde Park Crescent, Leeds LS6 2NW. Tel: 0532 789869 or 742954.
General model agency with over 100 models.

MANCHESTER MODEL AGENCY
57–63 Princess Street, Manchester M2 4EQ. Tel: 061-236 1335/6.
Fashion and commercial models for photography and advertising. House make-up artist and hair stylist.

STUDIO LONDON
18 Baldwins Gardens, London EC1. Tel: 01-831 9319.
General model agency.

WILLOW PHOTOGRAPHIC
45 Bridge Street, Godalming, Surrey. Tel: 048-68 5441/2.
General model agency.

Storage & Presentation

ALLSLEEVES LTD.
2 Worple Way, Richmond, Surrey TW10 6DF. Tel: 01-948 5488.
Transparency sleeves.

AUDIO VISUAL MATERIAL LTD.
AVM House, 1 Alexandra Road, Farnborough, Hampshire GU14 6BU. Tel: 0252 540721.
Optia and Multiplex slide storage systems.

NICHOLAS HUNTER LTD.
PO Box 22, Oxford OX1 2JT. Tel: 0865 52678.
PVC wallets, etc for presentation and storage of prints, slides and negatives.

JUON PLASTICS LTD.
1 Burfield Road, Old Windsor, Berkshire SL4 2RB. Tel: 075-35 53217.
Protective photofile system for negatives and prints in ringbinder and filing cabinet ranges.

KENRO PHOTOGRAPHIC PRODUCTS
High Street, Kempsford, nr Cirencester, Glos GL7 4EQ. Tel: 028-581 426/7.
Black card transparency masks, slide storage systems, library systems and other presentation materials.

S. W. KENYON
6 Fore Street, Wellington, Somerset TA21 8AQ. Tel: 082-347 4151.
Slide storage systems.

MID-COUNTIES PHOTOGRAPHIC SUPPLIES
Water Buildings, Baldock Road, Letchworth, Herts. Tel: 046-26 79388-9.
Wholesale of filing, storage & presentation materials, etc.

PHOTO-SCIENCE LTD.
Charfleets Road, Canvey Island, Essex SS8 0PH. Tel: 0268 682122.
Slide and negative care and storage systems.

WEMBLEY STUDIO SUPPLIES LTD.
788–790 Finchley Road, London NW11 7UR. Tel: 01-458 9020.
Suppliers of albums, mounts, frames, neg-bags, envelopes, etc.

Studio Hire

BEAR STUDIOS LTD.
124 Aldersgate Street, London EC1 4JQ. Tel: 01-251 4147.
Two large studios, Bowens Quad, two darkrooms, equipped kitchen etc.

BEEHIVE CENTRE OF PHOTOGRAPHY
136 Gloucester Avenue, London NW1. Tel: 01-586 4916.
Two hire studios with electronic flash. Darkroom for up to 5″ × 4″.

BERRY'S MODEL AGENCY & STUDIO
107 Burnham Road, Great Barr, Birmingham B44 8HZ. Tel: 021-360 3913.
Hire studio with in-house model agency.

CASTLE STUDIOS
44 Castle Road, Bedford. Tel: 0234 214577.
Large hire studio with high ceiling. Bowens flash, tungsten and cine lighting. Large wardrobe. In-house model agency.

COLORSCOPE STUDIO
Unit 4, Swains Mill, Crane Mead, Ware, Herts. Tel: 0920 61950.
Hire studio with Courtenay Sola and tungsten lighting. Colorama and backgrounds. Outdoor locations with horses, speedboats etc. In-house model agency.

ISO STUDIOS
21 Little Portland Street, London W1N 5AF. Tel: 01-580 4720/01-636 5308.
Photographic and video studio hire including all facilities.

LEEDS MODEL AGENCY
11a Hyde Park Crescent, Leeds LS6 2NW. Tel: 0532 789869/742954.
Studio hire with 3200K tungsten or Bowens flash, Colorama, props, etc. In-house model agency.

STRINGS PHOTOGRAPHIC
261 Fulham Road, London SW3 6HY. Tel: 01-352 1446/3537.
Studio hire. Bowens Quad, Broncolour front projection. B&W darkroom.

ALAN STRUTT PHOTOGRAPHY
18 Hewett Street, London EC2A 3NN. Tel: 01-247 4945.
Studio hire. Dressing room, kitchen, lighting, etc. Also available: U-matic video equipment and editing suite.

STUDIO LONDON
18 Baldwins Gardens, London EC1. Tel: 01-831 9319.
Four hire studios up to 1000 sq. ft. Bowens flash and tungsten lighting. Backdrops, props and sets. Models available.

WILLOW PHOTOGRAPHIC
45 Bridge Street, Godalming, Surrey. Tel: 048-68 5441/2.
Two hire studios. In-house model agency.

Studio Services

ALLISTER BOWTELL & ASSOCIATES
59 Rotherwood Road, London SW15. Tel: 01-788 0114.
Design and construction of models and all kinds of special effects for film and stills.

FILMCRAFT SERVICES LTD.
43 High Street, New Malden, Surrey KT3 4BY. Tel: 01-942 6533.
Location finders. Props hire, especially vehicles and aircraft old and new. Concorde interiors, agents for 'Flambards Village'.

CHARLES H. FOX LTD.
22 Tavistock Street, London WC2E 7PY. Tel: 01-240 3111.
Suppliers of theatrical and photographic make-up, etc.

KENNETT ENGINEERING CO. LTD.
The Lodge Works, Drayton Parslow, Bucks. Tel: 029-672 605.
Suppliers of hand painted backgrounds and material, posing aids, 'baby sitters', Lastolite reflectors, etc.

LEWIS & KAYE (HIRE) LTD.
50 Eversholt Street, London NW1 1DA. Tel: 01-388 0419.
Large collection of silver, glass, china & objets d'art for hire as studio props.

MESSAGE MINDERS INTERNATIONAL LTD.
42–45 New Bond Street, London EC2M 1QY. Tel: 01-628 0898.
Accommodation address, telephone message and mail forwarding services.

MORELAND TARPAULINS LTD.
25 St Pancras Way, London NW1 0QB. Tel: 01-387 5210.
Textured canvas covers for studio background use.

ROBERT WHITE & SONS
22 Tavistock Street, Covent Garden, London WC2E 7PY. Tel: 01-240 3111.
Period costume hire, armour, costume jewellery, swords, crown jewel replicas, etc.

USEFUL ADDRESSES

ARTLAW
Old Loom House, Backchurch Lane, London E1 1LS. Tel: 01-240 0610.

ARTS COUNCIL OF GREAT BRITAIN
105 Piccadilly, London W1V 0AU. Tel: 01-629 9495.

ASSOCIATION OF BRITISH MANUFACTURERS OF PHOTOGRAPHIC, CINE & AUDIO-VISUAL EQUIPMENT
1 West Ruislip Station, Ruislip, Middlesex HA4 7DW. Tel: 08956 34515.

ASSOCIATION OF CINEMATOGRAPH, TELEVISION AND ALLIED TECHNICIANS
2 Soho Square, London W1V 6DD. Tel: 01-437 9418.

ASSOCIATION OF FASHION, ADVERTISING AND EDITORIAL PHOTOGRAPHERS
10a Dryden Street, Covent Garden, London WC2. Tel: 01-240 1171.

ASSOCIATION OF PHOTOGRAPHIC LABORATORIES
9 Warwick Court, Gray's Inn, London WC1R 5DJ. Tel: 01-405 2762/4253.

ASSOCIATION OF PHOTOGRAPHIC TECHNICIANS
25 Preston Waye, Harrow, Middlesex.

BRITISH ASSOCIATION OF PICTURE LIBRARIES AND AGENCIES
27 Orchard Way, Bubbenhall, Warwickshire. Tel: 0203 306348.

BRITISH FILM INSTITUTE
81 Dean Street, London W1V 6AA. Tel: 01-437 4355.

BRITISH INDUSTRIAL AND SCIENTIFIC FILM ASSOCIATION
15 New Bridge Street, Blackfriars, London EC4 6AU. Tel: 01-353 2805.

BRITISH KINEMATOGRAPH, SOUND AND TELEVISION SOCIETY
110–112 Victoria House, Vernon Place, London WC1B 4DJ. Tel: 01-242 8400.

BRITISH PHOTOGRAPHIC IMPORTERS ASSOCIATION
8 St Bride Street, London EC4. Tel: 01-353 3020.

BRITISH PHOTOGRAPHIC ASSOCIATION
8 St Bride Street, London EC4. Tel: 01-353 3020.

BUREAU OF FREELANCE PHOTOGRAPHERS
Focus House, 497 Green Lanes, London N13 4BP. Tel: 01-882 3315/6.

CITY & GUILDS OF LONDON INSTITUTE
76 Portland Place, London W1N 4AA. Tel: 01-580 3050.

EUROPHOT
Postbus 366, B-2000 Antwerpen, Belgium.

FEDERATION INTERNATIONALE DE L'ART PHOTOGRAPHIQUE
Spiserwis 9, CH-9030 Abtwil SG, Switzerland.

FILM PRODUCERS GUILD LTD.
Guild House, Upper St Martin's Lane, London WC2. Tel: 01-836 5420.

INSTITUTE OF AMATEUR CINEMATOGRAPHERS
63 Woodfield lane, Ashstead, Surrey KT21 2BT. Tel: 03722 76358.

INSTITUTE OF INCORPORATED PHOTOGRAPHERS
Amwell End, Ware, Hertfordshire. Tel: 0920 4011/2.

INSTITUTE OF JOURNALISTS
1 Whitehall Place, London SW1A 2HE. Tel: 01-930 7441.

INSTITUTE OF PHOTOGRAPHIC APPARATUS REPAIR TECHNICIANS
233 High Street, Brentford, Middlesex TW8 0JQ. Tel: 01-560 0415.

INSTITUTE OF REPROGRAPHIC TECHNOLOGY
PO Box 101, Witham, Essex CM8 1QS. Tel: 0376 516297.

IRISH PROFESSIONAL PHOTOGRAPHERS ASSOCIATION
12 Ludford Street, Dublin 14, Eire.

MASTER PHOTOGRAPHERS ASSOCIATION
1 West Ruislip Station, Ruislip, Middlesex HA4 7DW. Tel: 08956 34515.

NATIONAL ASSOCIATION OF INDUSTRIAL PHOTOPRINTERS
c/o Brook-Tella, 2 Exmoor Street, London W10. Tel: 01-969 1121.

NATIONAL UNION OF JOURNALISTS
Acorn House, 314 Gray's Inn Road, London WC1. Tel: 01-278 7916.

PHOTOGRAPHERS GALLERY
5 & 8 Great Newport Street, London WC2. Tel: 01-240 1969.

PHOTOGRAPHIC INSTRUMENT REPAIRING AUTHORITY
166 Westcoates Drive, Leicester LE3 0SP. Tel: 0533 857771.

PHOTOGRAPHIC SOCIETY OF IRELAND
11 Hume Street, Dublin 2, Eire.

THE PRESS ASSOCIATION
85 Fleet Street, London EC4. Tel: 01-353 7440.

**PROFESSIONAL PHOTOGRAPHERS ASSOCIATION OF
NORTHERN IRELAND**
16 Mill Street, Comber, Newtownards, Co. Down, Northern Ireland. Tel: 0247 872578.

PROFESSIONAL PHOTOGRAPHERS OF AMERICA INC
1090 Executive Way, Oak Leaf Common, Des Plaines, Illinois 60018.

PROFESSIONAL PHOTOGRAPHIC LABORATORIES ASSOCIATION
1 West Ruislip Station, Ruislip, Middlesex HA4 7DW. Tel: 08956 30718.

PROFESSIONAL SPORTS PHOTOGRAPHERS' ASSOCIATION
5 Norwich Way, Croxley Green, Rickmansworth, Hertfordshire.

ROYAL PHOTOGRAPHIC SOCIETY
The Octagon, Milsom Street, Bath BA1 1DN. Tel: 0225 62841.

ROYAL SOCIETY OF ARTS
John Adam Street, London WC2N 6EZ. Tel: 01-839 2366.

SCIENTIFIC FILM ASSOCIATION
48 Austen Paths, Stevenage, Hertfordshire SG2 0NR. Tel: 01-427 4380 Ext. 163.

SCOTTISH FILM COUNCIL
16–17 Woodside Terrace, Glasgow G3 7XN. Tel: 041-332 5413.

SIRA INSTITUTE—THE LENS USERS ASSOCIATION
South Hill, Chislehurst, Kent BR7 5EH. Tel: 01-467 2636.

SOCIETY FOR PHOTOGRAPHIC EDUCATION
24a Shaftesbury Road, Earlsdon, Coventry CV5 6FN. Tel: 0203 77524.

SOCIETY OF INDUSTRIAL ARTISTS AND DESIGNERS
12 Carlton House Terrace, London SW1Y 5AH. Tel: 01-930 1911.

SOCIETY OF LITHOGRAPHIC ARTISTS, DESIGNERS, ENGRAVERS AND PROCESS-WORKERS
Slade House, 55 Clapham Common South Side, London SW4 9DF. Tel: 01-720 7551.

SOCIETY OF PHOTOGRAPHIC PRINTERS
67 Albert Road, London E18.

SOCIETY OF PHOTO-TECHNOLOGISTS
PO Box 33, Aldridge, Staffordshire WS9 9BH.

THE WIDESCREEN ASSOCIATION
14 North Approach, Northwood, Middlesex.

INDEX